Praise for Public Relations and Journalism in Times of Crisis

"It's no secret we're living in a time in which we're seeking out more information—and expecting it more instantly—than ever before. Crisis events put both journalists and public relations pros to the test, and the authors present rich examples to depict how the work of reporters and spokespeople combine—or collide—when people want reliable information during fast-changing situations. They offer practical lessons from the people who were at the center of some of the biggest news events and crises in recent years. An essential guide for students and practitioners alike."

Elise Hu, NPR Correspondent

"*Public Relations and Journalism in Times of Crisis* is a must-read for journalists, practitioners and students—and a fascinating exploration for anyone with interest in a peek behind the curtain at some of our culture's most pivotal moments. The authors break new ground in bringing together the convergent perspectives of crises from those who experience them, those who manage them, those who report on them and the social media that engage and sometimes exacerbate them. While crisis prevention, management and mitigation have been the central part of my career and the focus of my writing, presenting and teaching, after just the introduction I came away with a better understanding of crisis and how to best understand and manage them. Far more than just cataloguing elements of a crisis or contrasting the differences among these various interests and perspectives, Miller and Broussard chart a course for a better future for management and coverage of crises. There is no richer text for a unique, thorough, thoughtful study of crisis through differing perspectives and so many recent examples and case studies."

John Deveney, APR, ABC, PRSA Fellow;
President and CEO, Deveney Communications

Public Relations
and Journalism
in Times of Crisis

This book is part of the Peter Lang Media and Communication list.
Every volume is peer reviewed and meets
the highest quality standards for content and production.

PETER LANG
New York • Bern • Berlin
Brussels • Vienna • Oxford • Warsaw

Andrea Miller and
Jinx Coleman Broussard

Public Relations
and Journalism
in Times of Crisis

A Symbiotic Partnership

PETER LANG
New York • Bern • Berlin
Brussels • Vienna • Oxford • Warsaw

Library of Congress Cataloging-in-Publication Data
Names: Miller, Andrea, author. | Broussard, Jinx Coleman, author.
Title: Public relations and journalism in times of crisis: a symbiotic partnership /
Andrea Miller and Jinx Coleman Broussard.
Description: New York: Peter Lang, 2019.
Includes bibliographical references and index.
Identifiers: LCCN 2018052793 | ISBN 978-1-4331-6323-4 (hardback: alk. paper)
ISBN 978-1-4331-6352-4 (paperback: alk. paper) | ISBN 978-1-4331-6336-4 (ebook pdf)
ISBN 978-1-4331-6401-9 (epub) | ISBN 978-1-4331-6402-6 (mobi)
Subjects: LCSH: Journalism and public relations—United States.
Public relations—United States—History.
Classification: LCC HD59.6.U6 M545 2019 | DDC 659.2—dc 23
LC record available at https://lccn.loc.gov/2018052793
DOI 10.3726/b14943

Bibliographic information published by **Die Deutsche Nationalbibliothek**.
Die Deutsche Nationalbibliothek lists this publication in the "Deutsche
Nationalbibliografie"; detailed bibliographic data are available
on the Internet at http://dnb.d-nb.de/.

For Doug, Zach and Gracie

—Andrea Miller

For Robert Broussard Sr.

—Jinx Coleman Broussard

TABLE OF CONTENTS

ACKNOWLEDGMENTS

The authors of this book together have worked more than four decades in journalism and public relations and on top of that, more than four decades in higher education. In that time period, crisis communication and coverage have become mainstays to the professions. Both authors recognized the need for both sides of crisis communication to be evaluated all in one place, in one comprehensive text. Therefore, a goal of this book is to allow scholars, professors, students and professionals a view of crisis from all different angles, from all stakeholders—thinking critically about the roles and perspectives of the victims, press, media audiences, and PR organizations. We hope this book accomplishes this in order to help serve communities in crisis, to make sure all have the information they need to protect lives, livelihoods and reputations.

We would like to thank the Manship School of Mass Communication for its support and professorship donors Huie-Dellmon and Bart R. Swanson whose contributions made the expensive travels to conduct in-depth interviews possible. Thanks to Dr. Shaniece Bickham, assistant professor at Nicholls State University, for co-authoring the Mizzou chapter. We would also like to acknowledge our graduate research assistants Elizabeth Macke and Sirdaria Williams for locating primary and secondary sources and transcribing many hours of interviews.

We set out to explore these perspectives from within, so access to journalists and public relations professionals was crucial. We are indebted to the nearly 60 journalists, public relations professionals and scholars who gave their time and knowledge to this important project. Journalists and public relations professionals are often the first responders to crises and we would like to thank them for giving their best to ethical, transparent communication when times are at their worst.

Finally, we would like to thank our families for their support and encouragement.

INTRODUCTION

Andrea Miller and Jinx Coleman Broussard

"A trusted source of information is the most important resilience asset that any individual or group can have in times of surprise" (Longstaff, 2005, p. 59). The public has an insatiable appetite for information when a crisis strikes a community, an individual or a business. Driven by a theory called anxiety reduction (Gudykunst, 1993) or the need to seek out information in order to ease fear and anxiety, people flock by the millions to social media, websites and television networks to find out the facts of a crisis. Mass communication professionals have a duty to provide what happened and what will happen next to people who are looking for ways to respond, cope and recover. Why is information in a crisis so important? Why does crisis create such a drive to know more? And why is it important that people come together in crisis?

In just ten weeks, the One Fund Boston organization raised almost $61 million for the April 15, 2013 Boston bombing victims. Americans came together after the terror attacks of 9/11 in a surge of patriotism (Abel, 2013). Crises do not play favorites. Journalists, law enforcement and city officials formed a common bond after Hurricane Katrina because there was a sense that they were all in this together. The storm destroyed the houses of journalists and public relations professionals as well as police officers. When people feel connected to others, the walls come down, and differences seem trivial.

And while crises can bring people together, they can also pull them apart. This book will argue that the two information entities that need to work together during crises are the journalists and the public relations professionals. These groups are the providers of the information that allow citizens to make solid, informed decisions in times of crisis. When should I evacuate and along what route? Do I need to throw away all of the contaminated ice cream in my freezer? What has my school done to ensure my child's safety? As we address these and other questions, such as exactly what a crisis is, we will hear from communicators on the front lines of crisis.

There is no question crises bring people together and can tear organizations and people apart. Almost all crises "immediately trigger a deluge of questions from an organization's many different publics. Reporters, employees, stockholders, government officials, and local residents all want—need—to know, What happened? Who did it happen to? When? Where? How? Why?" (Marra, 1998, p. 461). Given this state of affairs, PR professionals and journalists need to work together, despite the often-divergent values, in order to be effective in answering these questions via crisis communication. According to the Society of Professional Journalists (SPJ) Code of Ethics, journalists operate according to the principles of seeking the truth, minimizing harm, acting independently and being accountable and transparent. News organizations must consider what information their audience values and needs as part of an informed electorate. News audiences traditionally value stories that are timely and relevant. But audiences are also attentive to stories with an element of conflict, which are often textbook crisis stories.

According to the Public Relations Society of America's Member Statement of Professional Values (PRSA), important values include loyally advocating on behalf of one's organization, operating with honesty and fairness, and exercising the independence to determine what's in the public's interest. In the intersection of these different sets of values lies the public's need for information. In a time of crisis, both PR practitioners and journalists strive to adhere to their professional, ethical values while serving the public's need for information. Sometimes the two sides work together well in meeting this need. Other times these values cause conflict. It is important to note that public relations practitioners in the private sector enact a different role from colleagues who work for governmental and other public entities. The latter "must provide information to citizens about the work of their respective state agencies at the request of citizens and the media, while private sector practitioners have the latitude to selectively provide information to the public in representing their clients or organizations" (McCollough, 2012, p. 1). This book looks at how public and private sector practitioners function during crises as well as their relationships and interactions with journalists.

Journalists and PR professionals define crisis somewhat differently. Ask PR professionals and they may say a crisis is "a significant threat to operations or reputations that can have negative consequences if not handled properly" (Coombs, 2007). Ask a journalist what a crisis is and he or she might say a non-routine event (either unexpected or expected) that interrupts the daily routine and demands additional time, attention and resources to gather information and cover the story (Berkowitz, 1992). These highly unexpected events of major proportions are often deemed what-a-stories and all-out, large-scale journalistic efforts are put in place to saturate, process and cover the story in often the most challenging of situations (Berkowitz, 1992; Tuchman, 1978).

The two definitions have similarities, yet the end goals are slightly different. In journalism, the end goal is ethical and successful transmission of information to the public to enable citizens to make enlightened decisions. PR practitioners are also interested in disseminating information their publics want and need to know as quickly and correctly as circumstances allow. Excellent PR demands that the practitioners act with both the organization and its publics in mind (Grunig, 1992; Grunig & Hunt, 1984; Ledingham & Bruning, 1998). In other words, PR should go beyond self-interest to mutual benefit. Coombs points out that "To be ethical, crisis managers must begin their efforts by using communication to address the physical and psychological concerns of the victims" (p. 165). Another PR goal is to offer information to help "manage" the crisis in order to preserve an organization's economics and reputation, which "is an aggregate evaluation stakeholders make about how well and organization is meeting stakeholder expectations based on its past behaviors" (Coombs, 2007, p. 164). Often, crisis response for the organization is predicated on mandating that PR practitioners protect its image and reputation. Responses can range from defensive to accommodation and include attacking the accuser, denial, excuse, justification, ingratiation, corrective action and full apology (Benoit, 1995).

This is often where the conflict lies between the two entities. Journalists often believe PR people are more interested in managing reputation, rather than providing solid information. PR practitioners often believe journalists lack sufficient knowledge of what they are covering and are unreasonable in their quest—even demands—for information when practitioners do not have the information. Denise Bentele, who owns the PR firm that initially managed crisis communication in the days and weeks following the shooting of Michael Brown in Ferguson, Missouri, said her staff received thousands of requests, one right after the other, from reporters who wanted answers immediately (personal communication, June, 2016). This conflict between journalists and PR professionals plays out after every crisis event.

This book takes a case study approach to look at various crises, one at a time, through the lens of *both* journalists and public relations professionals. Because a vast body of scholarship explores both journalism and public relations as well as the manner in which both fields cover crises, we take a different approach that looks at the two together and places the cases within the context of established crisis literature relative to PR and journalism. We introduce the crisis, and then walk through how it was handled from a PR perspective, relying on information from the very people who managed the crisis and created and disseminated the crisis communication. We next use the voices of the journalists to analyze their experiences and interactions during the crisis, and we dissect their coverage of the crisis.

We conducted in-depth interviews with almost 60 journalists and public relations practitioners. Then, we read through hundreds of press accounts and press releases for each event. Much formal and informal scholarship and research exist that undergird the development of these practical case studies. As we delve in to each case study, we include theoretical literature in order to better contextualize and explain the case. However, a major goal of this book is to provide practical strategies for working journalists and public relations practitioners to enhance the flow of information in a crisis so that audiences and stakeholders can make educated, rational decisions to protect their families and livelihoods. Another goal of our book is to acquaint professors and students of PR and journalism with the realities of covering and managing crises, including what works and why, as well as mistakes that occur that could damage their organizations. We want all who are involved in crisis communication and coverage to be prepared.

Journalists and Crisis

The importance of the press in the United States is constitutional—an integral part of what the founding fathers believed was necessary to serve the new, democratic electorate. Journalism was considered a noble profession whose goals and duties were to fulfill the surveillance function and recount events for those who could not be there to witness them. From the beginning and through the days of the penny press' sensationalism and the muckrakers' riveting and revealing investigations, it became clear coverage of unique and tragic events sparked much public interest.

Crisis events cause a shift in how the press covers stories. Communication scholars call crises non-routine news because journalists break from the daily, normal routine in order to cover these breaking stories. All time, efforts and resources are used to report and present the story that is unfolding. Journalists also cover "lesser" crises than the obvious natural or public health disasters that have widespread effects. Public relations also differentiates between types of crisis that we address in this book. Additionally, crisis is perceptual—what is a crisis to one individual or group, may not be considered such to the next. But in what journalists call the monumental, unprecedented "holy shit" moments (Berkowitz, 2000) when mortality is salient, journalism becomes the lifeline and the first draft of history. "News is never as important as when we are afraid" (Stephens, 2007, p. 11). In turn, audiences seek out more and more information from the media. In the day that the levees broke after Hurricane Katrina, WWL-TV's website crashed as people from all over the world sought local information on the developing story. The same traffic overload occurred almost eight years later as the *Newtown Bee* website crashed, as people sought to learn more about the Sandy Hook Elementary School shooting in Connecticut.

The press has also been accused of being sensationalistic because of the knowledge that crisis commands attention from news consumers. After the Columbine High School shooting in 1999, seven hundred and fifty (750) news organizations converged on the small, Denver suburb. Upwards of that number of national and international journalists flocked to Ferguson, Missouri, population 21,000. Bentele said "thousands" of journalists came from all over the world. Almost a thousand took over Newtown, Connecticut. *Bee* reporter Kendra Bobowick, who had a nephew who attended Sandy Hook, said the town was overrun by reporters. "And that's how our town turned into not our town," she said (Miller, Roberts, & LaPoe, 2014). The sheer numbers of press can be overwhelming for a community and for the PR professionals who are providing information. But reporters know that covering crisis well can make or break a career. If a reporter is seeking a job at a larger or more prestigious news outlet, solid coverage of a crisis creates an impressive portfolio of work. Yet communication scholars have criticized that very work as being episodic and promoting victimization and stereotypes (Miller et al., 2014).

Crisis coverage in the press has also evolved with technology. Television used to be the go-to outlet, now the public is informed first about a crisis via Twitter or Facebook. After scanning social media, then perhaps the television is turned on or a local news website is accessed. With so many ways to get "news," the jobs of the journalists becomes more important because of their professional training that includes a commitment to accurate, well-sourced, and ethical information. This takes time, whereas social media is immediate. At the same time, the reputation of a client, whether it is a municipality or a higher education institution, often hinges on how the public relations practitioner manages the crisis communication. Journalism, as history, is about record, representation and meaning and its importance is increased in crisis situations (Kitch & Hume, 2008). PR is about relationships and reputation.

Public Relations Practitioners and Crisis

Public relations scholars and practitioners define crisis events in a variety of ways, but essential commonalities exist. For instance, Kathleen Fearn-Banks (2017) writes in her seminal book on crisis communication that a crisis is "a major occurrence with a potentially negative outcome affecting the organization, company, or industry, as well as its publics, products, services or good name." Crises disrupt "normal business transactions and can sometimes threaten the existence of the organization" (p. 1). Mitroff and Anagnos (2001), note that "in order for a major crisis to occur, it must exact a major toll on human lives, property, financial earnings, the reputation, and the general health and well-being of an organization" (pp. 34–35). A crisis can threaten an organization's reputation and damage the stakeholder /organization relationship (Coombs, 2007; Dowling, 2002). Timothy Coombs (2015) calls crisis simply a breakdown in a system that causes shared stress.

Crises can also be broadly categorized as (1) organizational, which professionals refer to as an issues management experience, and (2) disasters. Disasters such as hurricanes and floods are easy to distinguish as sudden, serious disruptions on a large scale and which require response by multiple agencies and governmental units (Coombs, 2015). Organizational crises are a bit more unpredictable and include health, safety and money, among others. These disrupt and violate important expectations of stakeholders (Coombs, 2015). Additionally, disasters can cause an organizational crisis. For example, in the Baton Rouge flood of 2016 that we discuss in this book, AT&T cell phone

service was disrupted, cutting off even vital basic communication and causing much stakeholder frustration. And vice-versa, an organizational crisis can
cause a disaster. That was the case with the explosion of the Deepwater Horizon oil rig in the Gulf of Mexico in 2013, which caused the largest maritime
disaster in U.S. history. In this book, we refer to all cases as crises, whether
disastrous, non-routine or organizational, for the sake of consistency.

Much of public relations history evolved in response to crises. The first
publicity firm was established in 1900 and quickly began to represent the
U.S. railroad industry to oppose regulatory legislation that threatened its ex-
pansion (Wilcox & Cameron, 2011). Ivy Ledbetter Lee, an early pioneer in
public relations, worked for the Rockefeller family. When 11 children were
killed during a strike at one of the Rockefeller mines in Ludlow, Colorado,
Lee counseled the Rockefeller family to be open with the public about the
crisis. He advised Rockefeller to visit the mining camps in person to see the
conditions under which the miners worked. We see many of the practices Lee
recommended still used in crisis situations today. Reputation management
and protecting organizational image remain important goals of practitioners
and the organizational decision-makers for whom they work.

A seminal crisis case study for students of public relations is the 1982
crisis Johnson & Johnson's Tylenol brand faced. Tylenol was the leader in
the painkiller market. In the fall of 1982, an individual removed bottles of
Tylenol Extra-Strength capsules from shelves in the Chicago area, replacing
them with bottles of cyanide-laced capsules. This resulted in seven deaths. For
a pharmaceutical company to be unknowingly selling bottles of poison, this
was potentially devastating. A Chicago news reporter looking for a comment
notified the company about the crisis. Johnson & Johnson's response to this
crisis has been widely lauded. The company swiftly removed all of its products from shelves nationwide. It demonstrated that it was placing a premium
on customer safety, although that amounted to a considerable financial loss.
Johnson & Johnson proactively communicated with the public. The mega
company was responsive to media requests and participated in a number of
interviews and news programs. This case is an excellent example of public
relations professionals and journalists working together to serve the public
interest in a crisis situation.

Journalists and public relations practitioners communicate with the public throughout stages of a crisis. PR practitioners define crisis communication
as "the dialogue between the organization and its publics prior to, during, and
after the negative occurrences" (Fearn-Banks, 2017, p. 2). Both journalists

and public relations practitioners provide citizens with information to help prevent crises and during crises to help navigate the situation. Where they often diverge in their goals is in the assignment or avoidance of blame. As part of the societal watchdog function, journalists are often seeking to discover which individuals and organizations are to blame for a crisis. After the deadly police ambush in the summer of 2016, East Baton Rouge Sheriff's Office Communication Director Casey Rayborn Hicks said the "blame narrative" was especially present when national reporters arrived to cover the crisis (personal communication, October 25, 2016). Because of its prevalence, journalism scholars study this narrative called the attribution of responsibility frame. In contrast, public relations practitioners often seek to protect their organization from blame during a crisis, while still attending to the communication needs of their publics. PR crisis communication addresses blame in strategies outlined in Benoit's (2015) Image Restoration (denial, evading responsibility, reducing offensiveness, corrective action, mortification) or Coombs's Crisis Response Strategies (attack the accuser, denial, excuse, justification, etc.). The goal of minimizing blame is often lost on journalists who believe that PR people only engage in spin, hype or other unethical behaviors to protect their organization (Macnamara, 2014). These conflicting roles often carry over into the post crisis stage. Journalists continue to seek understanding of what happened (and who is to blame), as well as next steps, while public relations practitioners see themselves more as facilitating the free flow of information (Bentele) and not as only working on behalf of the organization. Suffice it to say, practitioners also seek to rebuild and maintain organizational reputation. Coombs' (2006) Situational Crisis Communication Theory (SCCT) offers that while PR practitioners concentrate "on crisis response strategies that will maximize the organization's reputation . . . efforts to protect the organizational reputation are undertaken only after human safety is secured through instructing information" (Coombs, p. 187). According to Coombs, as "attributions of crisis responsibility increase, the crisis managers should use crisis response strategies that progressively accept more responsibility for the crisis" (p. 187). Scholars (Grunig, 2001; Grunig & Hunt, 1984; Ledingham & Bruning, 1998) agree that in order for excellent communication to occur, consideration of primary publics is and should be the goal. The media are also a public because they represent one of the vehicles through which PR professionals reach the public. Where they find themselves at odds is in how to best uncover and present the information. With this in mind, we will explore the development of a crisis from the perspectives of both sides.

Stages of a Crisis

Public relations professionals and journalists both serve the public interest with accurate, timely information. This is especially important in a crisis situation. The two sides already share a similar, predictive process when crisis strikes that opens up opportunities to work together (Fearn-Banks, 2017 Graber, 2002). In public relations, these stages are (1) the detection phase, which may be prodromal when warning signs are discovered (pre-crisis) or it may be when the first sign of the crisis is detected, (2) the prevention/preparation stage is when steps are taken to prevent the crisis or in cases it cannot be prevented, a plan is created or enacted to manage the crisis (3) the containment phase refers to the effort to limit the duration or scope of the crisis as well as keep it from spreading (crisis), (4) the recovery phase involves all the efforts to get the organization/entity back to a state of normalcy or business as usual (post crisis), and (5) the learning stage which is the evaluative stage that includes an examination of what was lost, how it can be gained back, and how the organization responded to the crisis.

The PR stages are like the stages of a news crisis which include detection, description, analysis, recovery/coping (Graber, 2002). We will argue the fourth stage of learning should be added as a final stage. As with PR, the crisis event must first be detected. Then in stage two, the journalist's job is to describe the event as it unfolds, giving the who?, what?, where? and when? to audiences. The third stage is analysis as the journalists correct wrong information, give perspective, and analyze what happened. This is the "making sense of it all" stage that often answers the why and how. The fourth stage that mirrors the PR stage is recovery. This is the stage that consists of stories about how the community can come together to get help and move forward. It is often in this stage that journalists provide the valuable services of social utility and linkage (Perez-Lugo, 2004). Social utility in the recovery phase gives the sense that we are a community and we are all in this together. Linkage does what only local news organizations can do, link the audience with information that can help with recovery, for example, where in the city FEMA officials are setting up space to meet with residents. And finally, we argue that the final stage should be learning. This phase includes finding where journalists who cover traumatic situations can get help and counsel, can talk about what they did well, what they did not so well, and how they can improve their coverage in the future. The learning aspect is often ignored in journalism. A communication scholar once said journalists have less continuing education than hairdressers. Post-crisis is the time to learn from coverage mistakes in order to improve the information transmission process the next time a crisis hits.

Public relations can act within these latter roles as well. Again, there is a symbiotic relationship between journalism and public relations. Both have to serve stakeholders—"People who are linked to an organization or who may have interest in an organization and are affected by the decisions made by that organization" (Fearn-Banks, 2010, p. 25). The decisions of public relations professionals can aid in recovery and rebuilding—rebuilding physically, but also reputational and emotional. The information from both sides helps foster resilience which "is the ability to cope with unanticipated dangers after they have become manifest, learning to bounce back" (Wildavsky, 1988)—an important end goal for both.

Inception of This Book

One of the authors of this book regularly teaches a crisis communication class. A goal of the class is to get students to view crisis from all different angles, from all stakeholders—thinking critically about the roles and perspectives of the victims, the press, the media audiences, and the PR organizations. The authors recognize that a text that merges the two perspectives is not available. For this class, case studies are pieced together using separate texts that focus on different stakeholders' stories. The second author, who has decades of experience in crisis—both as a journalist, PR professional and professor, recognized the need for both sides of crisis communication to be evaluated all in one place.

A good example of a stitched together case study is the 1999 Columbine High School shooting in Littleton, Colorado. The PR perspective is described in detail in Kathleen Fearn-Banks *Crisis Communication: A Casebook Approach*. On April 20, two students, Dylan Klebold and Eric Harris, shot and killed twelve classmates and one teacher and injured 23 more before they committed suicide in the school's library. Rick Kaufman, APR and Executive Director of Jefferson County Public Schools in Colorado, had been on the job for less than seven months when this, one of the deadliest mass shootings in a school setting, happened on his watch (Fearn-Banks, 2010). Seven hundred and fifty news organizations converged on the small Denver suburb. There had been plenty of prodromes—early warning signals—leading up to Columbine including the Pearl, Mississippi and Jonesboro, Arkansas school shootings. But nothing like this had ever happened before. The response from all stakeholders was and needed to be unprecedented.

When reviewing the different stages of crisis for both journalism and PR explained earlier in this chapter, the responses can be mapped. In the detection phase, there were warning signs from other school shootings. Again, Kaufman had only been in the community a short time and did not have time to prepare or make the necessary press and community connections that would help in such a circumstance. His staff also had no crisis training. But Kaufman and his staff went right to work to try and contain and manage the event (next stage) by establishing relationships with the local press, analyzing media coverage and offering information to counter and negate the bad images and information in a way to "take back our school."

In all stages, Kaufman and other school officials said they always kept the feelings of the victims' families at the forefront. This guided their decisions and interactions. In the recovery period, as the anniversary of the shooting approached, the school district arranged for a meeting of survivors and victim's families and the press. At this point, a PR firm was representing the victim's families. The group of survivors was asked questions by an appointed person while the cameras rolled. The event was to try and minimize the press' intrusion into the lives of the survivors and victim's families on the anniversary. The families also asked the media that the names of the two gunmen, along with any video from that day, not be used. The press could not honor that request countering that the story of what happened cannot be told without such usage. But the press did agree to not use the names outside of the first "nuts and bolts" stories that tell the facts of what happened that day. They also agreed to "pool" coverage for the memorial/remembrance ceremony outside of the school on the anniversary.

Columbine was a watershed moment in school safety for districts across the nation. Metal detectors were installed, zero tolerance policies went into place and crisis training was mandated. But beyond school policies, Kaufman and his staff had a steep learning curve and learned many lessons from that tragic time. First, cultivate relationships with the press before tragedies strike. Such a relationship establishes trust and an understanding of each other's duties and responsibilities. Second, train all of your staff—from those who speak to the press to those who answer the phone. All employees must be well-versed in how to respond to a crisis and what their duties would be in the event of another tragedy. And finally, always keep the victims and survivors at the forefront of the PR strategizing. Every action and reaction should honor and protect their memory.

The press, in the description phase, was guilty of disseminating much incorrect information as described in the Columbia School of Journalism DART Center for Trauma & Journalism's press documentary on the shooting, "Covering Columbine." Examples include a hoax phone call by someone who claimed to be inside the school that was aired on TV, an incorrect death toll of 25 that a law enforcement spokesperson gave, and one student, who had survived, was reported dead. Perhaps the most painful mistake was when the picture of a student lying dead on the sidewalk outside the school was published in the newspaper before the parents were notified of their child's death. The magnitude of this story seemed to have caused some ethical safeguards to go by the wayside (minimize harm) and the pressure to report information quickly in a competitive news town (at that time, Denver had two daily newspapers) may have played a role.

As the questions in the analysis stage became "how" and "why" did this happen, more mistakes occurred. The press assigned the gunmen as members of the "trench coat mafia," a group of misfits wanting revenge, which turned out to be false. To this day, ask people about Columbine, and many believe the trench coat mafia was to blame. Also in this stage, the anger toward the press was extreme. There was no place for the community to place blame. The gunmen were dead. There would be no trial and no confessions to answer why. Therefore, during the analysis phase and in fact into the recovery stage, the press became the villain and a constant reminder of what happened on April 20. The tension made it difficult for journalists to do their jobs. Also in the recovery stage, the differences between local press needs and national press needs become apparent. After the national press packed up and left, the local press continued to run stories related to Columbine and the town grew weary.

The press also learned some crucial lessons during this crisis and at least one mirrored a PR lesson. First, be correct and avoid quick conclusions or unsubstantiated information that may lay false blame or create stereotypes. Also, do not intrude on grieving families (PR lesson), but if you must, don't separate parents from their children—talk to them together. As always, wait until family has been informed to show crime scene pictures. And finally, recognize the process of grieving and when victims are in shock so they are not re-traumatized.

The above is a seminal case study for a crisis that changed procedure and policy across news and PR organizations across the nation. Could the two sides have worked together better? The answer is yes. First, the relationship between press and PR needed to be cultivated at the local level before crisis happened. PR professionals and local journalists are part of the community they serve and if they know each other, helping and understanding each other becomes more organic. Second, public relations professionals could have been more available to the press, because in the absence of people with authority to speak, the press goes to less-informed sources. The approach of and access to the victims' families was challenged by the press (with bad results) and in another stage controlled by the PR side, with more effective results. This crisis was unprecedented—both sides needed to learn together. Finally, one lesson both sides learned the hard way was that the victims and their families needed to be treated carefully—show victims dignity in death and the families respect in the grieving process. In modern society, PR professionals and journalists have bad reputations. They face a crisis of credibility that needs to be overcome in both professions. If they work together to make their processes and communication more helpful and effective, the result may be credibility or in the very least appreciation of their efforts in times where everyone is looking for comfort in information.

Overview of Chapters

This book features seven chapters focusing on eight crisis events that include a broad spectrum of entities—big business, family-owned business, a nonprofit, a university, an elementary school, a hospital, and state, national and local governmental authorities. The cases also cover different crisis categories—product safety, race relations, gun violence, police brutality, public health and natural disaster. In four cases, an unpredictable Mother Nature played the starring role (disasters), and in the last four, the crises were caused by man (organizational crises). In most case studies of events that concern tragedies, the cases are organized in pre-crisis, crisis and post crisis. However, the stages can be broken down even further to offer more specific information to researchers and practitioners who want to understand the nuances of crisis communication. All cases will be dissected according to the timeline of events that reflect the stages of crisis outlined above to see where mistakes were made and where cooperation could play a role in more successful communication in the future.

Panic and Outrage: Ebola in America

In 2014, outbreaks of Ebola in West Africa began making global headlines. On September 28, 2014, the first known case of Ebola was diagnosed in the U.S. at Texas Health Presbyterian Hospital in Dallas. Panic ensued as the Centers for Disease Control and Prevention (CDC) sought to communicate with healthcare providers and the general public about the actual risks of Ebola spreading in the U.S. This chapter will describe the communications efforts of Texas Health Presbyterian Hospital in Dallas and the CDC. Reporters had a fine line to walk in covering this story. In particular, reporters were faced with the challenge of how to get accurate and credible information out, while tempering public panic. Conflicting information came from the hospital while the media was shown as sensationalistic vultures. How do the media depict the horror of the disease without causing undue alarm and showing respect to the victims? The challenges for both sides when addressing this modern day plague will be explored.

Water, Water Everywhere…Again: Hurricane Katrina and the Baton Rouge Great Flood

Hurricane Katrina presented a unique crisis scenario for public relations professionals and journalists along the Gulf Coast. Many of these professionals were personally displaced and deeply affected by the storm and its aftermath. Despite their personal losses, the journalists still had stories to tell and the public relations professionals still had to advocate for their organizations while trying to accommodate their stakeholders. In this case, public relations professionals who had existing relationships with journalists had to find new ways to communicate with these journalists when cell phones and email were not functional. This chapter will focus on whether and how public relations professionals and journalists worked together to provide information to a public hungry for details. This chapter will also shed light on the unique ways these professionals communicated with one another in the wake of Hurricane Katrina in a place where the communication infrastructure was decimated. More than a decade later, this chapter will include new information from some professionals who have never spoken publicly about the tragedy.

Eleven years later, in the heart of Louisiana, historic floods submerged large portions of Baton Rouge and surrounding cities. Thirteen people died and 60,000 homes were damaged or destroyed when a 1,000-year rain dumped some two feet of rain in 72 hours. We will continue in this chapter with a comparison of journalism and PR communication from the great flood to Katrina. Many of those involved, just like Katrina, lost everything. What have we learned in the decade since Katrina in terms of communication efforts and digital changes?

Death and Brand Loyalty: The Sticky Case of Blue Bell Ice Cream

On March 12, 2015 the CDC announced five illnesses including two deaths from Listeria monocytogenes found in Blue Bell Ice Cream manufactured at the company's headquarters plant in Brenham, Texas. The company ordered a limited recall the next day, but after repeated failed testing, by April 3 all Blue Bell Ice Cream was off the shelves and thrown into grocery store dumpsters. This case is unique because of the strong brand loyalty that was the highlight of the communication effort, an effort not put forth by Blue Bell's PR team. This chapter compares the Texas ice cream giant case to the Denver-based Chipotle case. The multistate *E. coli* outbreak linked to Chipotle began in October 2015 also garnered extensive national coverage. No deaths were reported, but more than three dozen were sickened. The response to both brands' crises has been very different. The costumer took over the PR for Blue Bell, while Chipotle's PR professionals had their work cut out for them.

A Movement in the Heartland, Parts I & II: Ferguson & Mizzou

"One state—Missouri—stands out as the site of two of the most pivotal moments in the resurgent national discussion on race" (Marans & Stewart, *Huffington Post* [11–16–15]). These two chapters explore the unrest in Ferguson, Missouri, and the racial protests at the University of Missouri. On August 9, 2014, Michael Brown, an unarmed 18-year-old black teenager, is shot dead by a white police officer. Some witnesses claimed Brown had his hands up in surrender when he was shot. The next day in a press conference, police claimed Brown was killed because he was reaching for the officer's gun. That night the violence began and so did the Black Lives Matter movement.

Just one month later down the road some 120 miles in Columbia, at the University of Missouri, Student Government President Payton Head used Facebook to broadcast his frustration with what he said were bigoted, anti-homosexual and anti-transgender attitudes at the school. When school officials repeatedly did little to address the concerns, a series of protests by students and inaction by the administration led to the resignation of the president and the reassigning of the chancellor. These chapters take a look at a city and a university working to get their messages out in a highly charged environment. Many reporters covered both stories and focused, rightly so, on the injustices of the situations and ineptness of those in charge. We'll take a look at how PR professionals worked to build relationships that were frayed or non-existent and to save the reputations of a city and the state's flagship university—almost in complete contrast to the journalists' work.

A Divisive Issue: Susan G. Komen and Planned Parenthood

Toward the goal of promoting early detection of breast cancer, the Susan G. Komen Organization has long partnered with various organizations to offer mammograms and clinical breast exams for women. One of these organizations (since 2007) was Planned Parenthood. On January 31, 2012, in a divisive move, Komen stopped supporting Planned Parenthood. While Komen reversed the decision four days later, it still faced a substantial backlash. Founder and CEO Nancy Brinker resigned her position. The organization saw a 15–30 percent drop in participation in its Race for Cure from the previous year and it also experienced a drop in overall donations. For this chapter, non-profit crisis experts are interviewed to better understand the initial communications response and ongoing communications efforts after what some called a political move. Additionally, the Komen non-profit enjoyed extremely positive coverage since its inception. What was it like to suddenly be on the PR defensive? Did the relationships with reporters established for years help or hurt the PR effort? How did the reporters, who all of the sudden had to play an adversarial role, balance the positive with the negative?

A National Day of Mourning: Sandy Hook Elementary

On December 14, 2012, a 20-year-old gunman entered Sandy Hook Elementary School and fatally shot 20 children and six adult staff members. He later committed suicide. This tragedy shocked the nation and prompted a renewed discussion about gun control and access in the U.S. For the citizens of Newtown, Connecticut, the focus was more centered on mourning and recovery. For this chapter, the authors interviewed the former superintendent as well as a department of education representative. The relationship between local authorities and local reporters changes in a crisis of this magnitude. It also changes the way the story is covered and the actual content itself. Reporters at the local newspaper, the *Newtown Bee*, are entrenched in the community, as are those who handled PR for the various entities. The authors will talk to all of them, including the former editor of the *Bee*, to understand the nature of the changing relationship when unspeakable tragedy strikes too close to home.

The Authors' Access

In writing this book we met with unexpected challenges. With the exception of most public employees (Katrina, Sandy Hook, CDC), getting the private public relations professionals to speak to us about their crisis communication was difficult and in some cases (Komen, Blue Bell) not accomplished. More than a decade since Hurricane Katrina, communicators on both sides were more than willing to discuss their efforts, many of whom had plenty of time to deconstruct and reflect on their efforts. Limited time had passed for most of the other cases, and not yet enough, and they were therefore still unwilling to revisit their efforts. This was also indicative of their communication during the crises, they only reached out to the press in a limited manner. The rationales given over the phone or via email were that the event was in the past and they wanted to move on or they could not get permission to speak on the event. However, all responded to our requests, and were respectful, but their communication processes would not be discussed therefore the authors cannot directly discuss the motives and deliberations surrounding their communication. As one public relations professionals told us, it is difficult to be an armchair quarterback in a crisis and it is easy to criticize when you are not part of it or in the middle of it. The forensic evaluation after a crisis is crucial, but color commentary from the outside looking in, is often not productive. However, outside communication experts who have themselves worked extensively in crisis communication can rightly give their impressions of the observed communications. The authors seek here to discuss the end products, responses, and interactions with the press, which are the most visible effects. The case studies are not meant to judge their efforts, but simply to give a nod to ethics and best practices in both professions under very trying circumstances.

We can say we had the same issue with some journalists involved in the Baton Rouge flood, Hurricane Katrina and Ferguson. Many journalists did not return our calls and requests. However, unlike the small circle of PR professionals involved in each case, there were more journalists involved to contact, and we were successful in getting their sides of the stories.

Why Crisis Communication Is Important

This book is important because communication professionals do not work alone in a crisis vacuum. When crises strike, the mentality is all hands on deck, no matter which deck you serve on. Mass communication has a duty to transmit as much honest, accurate and helpful information as possible at a time when effective decisions are being made. The publics rely on media professionals to provide that service. People do not have the time, resources or inclination to go to the source of a story and gather information themselves. Therefore, there is a responsibility of public service attached to all mass communication professionals. And because of this responsibility, we present these cases in the voices of the mass communication professionals who were on the front lines. As scholars, we give a nod to theories and techniques that often underlie their work, but the real purpose of the book is to give practitioners real-world information, in laymen's language, that will hopefully aid in the next crisis.

In modern crisis and with advancing technology, the press and PR professionals sometimes lose control of events and stories. Technology has allowed "others," nonprofessionals, to control the crisis narrative via social media. Twitter erupted with anger at the mainstream media for not giving the 2014 Ferguson, Missouri police shooting story more coverage in its early stages. Twitter erupted with anger when information from Ferguson law enforcement was virtually nonexistent. And Twitter erupted when a white firm was engaged to manage crisis communication in a predominantly black city where a white police officer shot and killed an unarmed black teen. The narrative of that story was managed in 140 characters or less, one tweet at a time in the initial stages of the disaster. Journalists and PR professionals were playing catch-up because they were already behind in getting accurate information to the public. With an endless number of outside influencers with no ethical training, who can reach large numbers of people instantly, it just makes sense for the insiders, those "in-the-know" with the accurate information, to work together to serve those affected by crisis.

Many journalism and PR case study books are on the market. However, this book is the first to combine the stories of PR practitioners and journalists covering and managing crisis into single case studies. The goal is to use professionals' stories, social science theories and techniques to develop overall and crisis-specific strategies to help practitioners create better crisis communication that gives audiences what they need to function and sometimes, survive. Likewise, these strategies and tools will provide perspectives and guidance to professors who educate students who seek to work in either field. Tension exists between the two sides during crisis—if the press is not the bad guy, PR folks are to blame. Why at such a tense time, would we create more tension by not working together? Working together does not imply that the journalists or the public relations professionals will compromise their values, but it does imply that they will seek to understand each other's duties and goals and find common ground. Perhaps even a "happy-medium" information exchange that will serve both masters—the public and the publics. Never is there more of an important time to work together than in times of crisis. In order to have the most effective crisis communication possible and to feed the appetites of the public, PR professionals and journalists need to work together as if lives depended on it, and often in crisis, they do.

References

Abel, D. (2013, June 29). One fund to distribute nearly $61 million to victims. *The Boston Globe*. Retrieved from https://www.bostonglobe.com/metro/2013/06/28/one-fund-boston-raises-about/0K3aBfG6dZoMjZySr6qKTK/story.html

Benoit, W. (1995). *Accounts, excuses, and apologies: A theory of image restoration strategies*. New York, NY: State University of New York Press.

Berkowitz, D. (1992). Non-routine news and newswork: Exploring a what-a-story. *Journal of Communication, 42*(1), 82–94.

Berkowitz, D. (2000). Doing double duty: Paradigm repair and the Princess Diana what-a-story. *Journalism, 1*(2), 125–143.

Coombs, W. T. (2006). Crisis management: A communicative approach. In C. H. Botan & V. Hazelton (Eds.), *Public Relations Theory*, II (pp. 171–197). Mahwah, NJ: Lawrence Erlbaum Associates.

Coombs, W. T. (2007). Crisis management and communications. *Institute for Public Relations*. Retrieved from https://instituteforpr.org/crisis-manageent-and-communications/

Coombs, W. T. (2015). *Ongoing crisis communication: Planning, managing, and responding*. Thousand Oaks, CA: Sage.

Coombs, W. T. (2017). Protecting organization reputation during a crisis: The development and application of situational crisis communication theory. *Corporate Reputation Review, 10*(3), 163–176.

Dowling, G. (2002). *Creating corporate reputations: Identity, image, and performance*. New York, NY: Oxford University Press.

Fearn-Banks, K. (2010). *Crisis communications: A casebook approach* (4th ed.). New York, NY: Routledge.

Fearn-Banks, K. (2017). *Crisis communications: A casebook approach* (5th ed.). New York, NY: Routledge.

Graber, D. A. (2002). *Mass media and American politics* (6th ed.). Washington, D.C.: CQ Press.

Grunig, J. E. (1992). *Excellence in public relations and communication management*. Hillsdale, NJ: Lawrence Erlbaum Associates.

Grunig, J. E. (2001). Two-way symmetrical public relations: Past, present, and future. In R. L. Heath (Ed.), *Handbook of public relations* (pp. 11–30). Thousand Oaks, CA: Sage.

Grunig, J. E., & Hunt, T. (1984). *Managing public relations*. New York, NY: Holt, Rinehart and Winston.

Gudykunst, W. B. (1993). Toward a theory of effective interpersonal and intergroup communication: An anxiety/uncertainty management (AUM) perspective. In R. L. Wiseman & J. Koester (Eds.), *Intercultural communication competence: International and intercultural communication annual*, XVII (pp. 33–71). Thousand Oaks, CA: Sage.

Kitch, C. L., & Hume, J. (2008). *Journalism in a culture of grief*. London: Routledge.

Ledingham, J. A., & Bruning, S. D. (1998). Relationship management in public relations: Dimensions of an organization-public relationship. *Public Relations Review*, 24(1), 55. –65.

Longstaff, P. H. (2005). Security, resilience, and communication in unpredictable environments such as terrorism, natural disasters, and complex technology. Center for Information Policy Research, Harvard University, Cambridge, MA.

Macnamara, J. (2014). *Journalism and PR: Unpacking "spin," stereotypes and media myths*. New York, NY: Peter Lang Publishing.

Marra, F. J. (1998). Crisis communication plans poor predictors of excellent public relations. *Public Relations Review*. 24(4): 4361–474.

Marans, D. and Stewart, M. (2015). Why Missouri became the heart of racial tension in America: From Ferguson to Mizzou, the show-me state is now the focal point. *The Huffington Post*. Retrieved August 19, 2017, from www.huffingtonpost.com/entry/ferguson-missouri-racial-tension_us_564736eb)8cda3488f34d.

McCollough, C. J. (2012). *Pressures, centralization, economics, technology, and ethics: Factors that impact public information officers—journalist relationships* (Unpublished doctoral dissertation). School of Mass Communication. Louisiana State University, Baton Rouge, LA.

Miller, A., Roberts, S., & LaPoe, V. (2014). *Oil and water: Media lessons from Hurricane Katrina and the Deepwater Horizon disaster*. Jackson, MS: University Press of Mississippi.

Perez-Lugo, M. (2004). Media uses in disaster situations: A new focus on the impact phase. *Sociological inquiry*, 74(2), 210–225.

Public Relations Society of America (PRSA). (n.d.). Member code of ethics. Retrieved from https://apps.prsa.org/AboutPRSA/Ethics/CodeEnglish/index.html#.WKOBKBiZPVp

Stephens, M. (2007). *A history of news*. New York, NY: Oxford University Press.

Tuchman, G. (1978). *Making news: A study in the construction of reality*. New York, NY: Macmillan.

Wilcox, D. L., & Cameron, G. T. (2011). *Public relations: Strategies and tactics* (10th ed.). London: Pearson Education.

Wildavsky, A. (1988). *Searching for safety*. New Brunswick, NJ: Transaction Books.

· 1 ·

PANIC AND OUTRAGE

Ebola in America

Andrea Miller

The virus strikes fear in the hearts of all who hear its name. For decades, it has been the stuff nightmares are made of. Books have been written about it. Movies have shown its effects in full, disgusting Hollywood color. The virus attacks every organ and tissue in the body and the patient starts to bleed—and bleed and bleed. Insides turn to jelly and blood comes out of every orifice in the body—mouth, ears, eyes—nothing can stop it.

Author Richard Preston in his 1994 book *The Hot Zone: A Terrifying True Story* stated that we don't really know what the Ebola virus has done in the past and cannot predict what it might do in the future. But, in his book, he captured the effects on an Ebola victim who was traveling on a commercial airliner.

> He opens his mouth and gasps into the bag, and the vomiting goes on endlessly. It will not stop, and he keeps bringing up liquid, long after his stomach should have been empty. The airsickness bag fills up to the brim with a substance known as the *vomito negro*, or the black vomit. The black vomit is not really black; it is a speckled liquid of two colors, black and red, a stew of tarry granules mixed with fresh red arterial blood. It is hemorrhage, and it smells like a slaughterhouse. The black vomit is loaded with virus. (Preston, 1994, pp. 17–18)

The above description reads like a blockbuster movie script, but if you were writing a history of the factual and fictional accounts of Ebola, this would be pretty close. The Hollywoodization of Ebola has been seen repeatedly—it is in fact, most people's only exposure to the virus and what it can do. In October 2014, the stuff of fiction and fact hit home. During that long autumn, all eyes were on Dallas, Texas—the Ebola virus was in America. Limited knowledge of and sensationalized prior exposure to the virus presented an amazingly difficult communication challenge for anyone involved in the Ebola case. Journalists and public relations professionals likely knew little about the virus—so they overestimated the public's risk and underestimated the public's fear.

"I call it vicarious rehearsal," Barbara Reynolds[1] of the Centers for Disease Control (CDC), said (personal communication, April 27, 2016). At the time of the crisis, Reynolds was the Director of the Division of Public Affairs out of the Office of the Director of the CDC. "Where they are contemplating the threat, even though the threat is not imminent for them or may not be present at all." She continued that for the vast majority of the U.S. population, there was really no threat at all.

Reynolds, now senior advisor of crisis and risk communication, has worked for the CDC for 25 years. Because of her position and expertise, she had a role in the crisis response to the Ebola threat. Reynolds has spent a career around infectious diseases. She said most people do not understand the mechanisms of transmission in terms of their own perception of personal risk. "And so sometimes it's hard to separate your own knowledge of what the risk really is versus what people are feeling like it might be," Reynolds said. "And that complicates the communication process, not just for the communicators, but for the scientists and everyone."

Timeline of Events

The 2014 outbreak of Ebola in West Africa was not going so well. It was the largest outbreak since the virus was first discovered in 1976 (Loehrke, 2014). Until the World Health Organization declared the two-year epidemic over in January 2016, more than 11,000 people had died. At the front end of that outbreak, the disease also turned into a nightmare for Americans and the American hospital where the victims were diagnosed and treated. Until September 30, 2014, no cases of this disease, which has a 50 percent fatality rate, had been diagnosed in humans in the United States (Loehrke, 2014). This unexpected outbreak was a complex crisis that unfolded quickly.

Forty-two-year old Thomas Eric Duncan, the original victim, could have gone to any of the dozens of hospitals in the Dallas area. He had just returned from Monrovia, Liberia and was visiting family—who lived about a mile away from Texas Health Presbyterian Hospital Dallas. It is believed he was exposed in Liberia, but exact details of how or from whom are unclear. He landed in Dallas on September 19 and by the 24th, his family said he began to feel sick. Authorities say this is the day that he likely became contagious (Loehrke, 2014). The next day Duncan sought treatment at Texas Health Presbyterian Hospital Dallas and was sent back to the apartment where he was staying with antibiotics. Also unclear is when he was asked about his travels and who had access to the information that he had recently traveled from a West African nation. Three days later, on the September 28, Duncan is transported back to that same hospital by ambulance. He is critically ill and put in isolation in the hospital's intensive care unit.

On September 30, the federal Centers for Disease Control and Prevention confirmed that Duncan had the Ebola virus, becoming the first patient to be diagnosed in the US. In the coming days, all people who had contact with Duncan were observed for symptoms. Four family members were placed under quarantine and told they would face criminal charges if they did not stay in their apartment. Community fear started to take hold. On October 3, the four family members are moved to a private home for quarantine because no other apartment complexes would take them. Health officials took their temperatures twice a day as they continued to show no symptoms.

On October 8, Duncan died at Texas Health Presbyterian Hospital Dallas. Two days later, one of the nurses caring for him, 24-year-old Nina Pham, began to run a low-grade fever, reported the symptom, and was immediately isolated. On October 11, it was confirmed that Pham had Ebola, making her the second case confirmed in the US, but the first person to contract it within US borders.

A second nurse, 29-year-old Amber Vinson reported feeling feverish and was diagnosed with Ebola as well. To make matters worse, she had been visiting family in Akron, Ohio earlier in the week and had flown commercially both ways.

Conflicting Information

Matt Goodman, senior editor of *DCM Magazine* and *D Healthcare Daily* wrote an article for *D Magazine* looking at the public health aspects of the event, but also the business side. Goodman is no stranger to covering crisis, he was a reporter in Killeen, Texas in 2009 when the Fort Hood mass shooting happened. Revenue at Texas Health Presbyterian Hospital Dallas fell 25 percent and emergency room visits dropped by more than half during the Ebola outbreak quarter (Hethcock, 2014).

"There was a scary, scary new disease we haven't seen before, but it's also important to put that into context. The flu will kill more people this year than Ebola will, but it's just sort of that foreign aspect of it. So you had to kind of cover it really level-headed to not stir a lot of unnecessary concern," Goodman said (personal communication, September 1, 2016). Goodman interviewed the CEO of Texas Health Resources (THR), Presbyterian Hospital Dallas' parent company, Dr. Barclay Berdan for the article. According to Goodman (2015), Berdan had been on the job for just 25 days when the deadly virus landed in Presbyterian Hospital. Berdan told Goodman that he did not hear the news of the positive diagnosis from doctors or other hospital personnel, but from CNN.

> I think the thing that really also added to it [the fear] was that Texas Health was giving out different, different excuses for why this had happened because I mean obviously you've got a bad situation where a patient was sent home misdiagnosed then goes to this house, which is a communal home, with a family that essentially lives on top of one another while this guy is developing Ebola symptoms. And with the science, you know that you have to come into contact with the bodily fluids of someone that's showing symptoms, so you know, that in and of itself is like 'well we had 'em, and we lost 'em, and now who knows who had contact with him. (Matt Goodman, personal communication, September 2016)

All reporters interviewed for this case who covered the Ebola story confirmed that Texas Health gave out conflicting information. This may have added to the public's confusion and fear. But those involved from the hospital's side in the case claimed an early victory before the confusion set in.

"The one thing I can say with real pride, is that within two hours of a positive test result of Duncan in Dallas, we had a national press conference that included the hospital, the local health department or health representative, the state health department, and the CDC," Reynolds said.

After the press conference, communication victories would be few and far between.

Texas Health press releases during those first two weeks of October show the conflicting information the reporters referred to (Texas Health insiders call this the "October Event"). An October 3 release stated, "We would like to clarify a point made in the statement released earlier in the week… There was no flaw in the EHR [electronic health records] in the way the physician and nursing portions interacted related to this event." On October 9 they were again on the defensive, "In addition, we'd like to correct some misconceptions that have been reported about Mr. Duncan's first visit." On October 13, Texas Health press releases excerpted portions of a CDC statement for "clarification" to defend against allegations of a breach in protocol. Then on October 16, the release set out to "correct the record" after National Nurses United made allegations regarding improper protocol and equipment. But later in that same release they corrected an earlier informational mistake with "We regret the error." The press releases were confusing, conflicting and inconsistent. This also added to the reporters' frustrations in wanting to get this very important story right.

"Early on that [they] were just like 'okay, it's on EMR [electronic media records]. We'll get that out,' and then it was… 'oh, it was a nurse that didn't relay it to the proper individual. Oh, we'll put that out, and pull back on the other one. Don't bother explaining that,' so there was a lot of sort of chaos in the messaging, and as a reporter it was just like well you know you need to be really careful to understand your readers probably read yesterday that it was the EMR error, and today the message shift and address the fact that the message shifted, and it's not both anymore. It's sort of a difficult cross when you're getting those signals and THR (Texas Health Resources) wasn't really saying why they said the other thing to begin with…. When you're in the thick of it, it's like, 'what the hell's going on?'" Goodman said.

Mark Riordan, who worked for global crisis communication giant Burson-Marsteller, was brought in by Texas Health to lead the media team after the above series of press releases in mid-October. "Let's face it, there were the early mistakes, not only in the diagnostics around Mr. Duncan's visits to the emergency room, but also some significant missteps in how to handle the situation publicly, some of which were, I think, driven, well, they were all driven by the desire to do it right and to be transparent, but I think at a certain level, early on, they (Texas Health communicators) did not realize the enormity of the situation," Riordan said (personal communication, February 28, 2017).

Riordan, at the point of our conversation, served as vice president of stake-holder engagement for Texas Health.

Riordan has decades of crisis experience from the U.S. Senate to Florida government and Florida universities to Burson-Marsteller. He said that as is often the case in crisis, best practices are learned on the fly and then evaluated in order to apply, adapt and share with colleagues for the next time. But the missteps in the beginning from this unprecedented event made it difficult to gain traction for their message.

"Once they realized we had made a mistake, early on, it was as if anything that we said or did was tainted. And we were constantly trying to get out from behind that. And they had lots of air space to fill, because we had gone to the 24-hour news cycle, and it was easy to find people who were critical of our approach, and not just from the PR side, but just from the clinical approach. They knew nothing about it, but they spent hours on air talking about the mistakes that we made, even though they knew nothing about the actual mistakes, just that some were clearly made," Riordan said.

The press in crisis often frames stories in certain ways. News frames package meaning into organized ideas, allowing the media to shape the way it tells the story and even the way a story is perceived and interpreted (Auerbach & Bloch-Elkon, 2005). News frames can therefore define problems, identify causes, make judgments, predict possible effects, and suggest remedies (Entman, 1993). These frames influence public perception, yet they are typically unnoticed by the viewers (Bullock, Wyche, & Williams, 2001). The public's lack of awareness, along with their reliance on media for information and decision-making during times of crisis, makes audiences more likely to be influenced by framing (Auerbach & Bloch-Elkon, 2005; D'Angelo, 2002). The common frames used are the conflict frame (one versus one), the economic consequence frame (gains and losses), the morality frame, the attribution of responsibility frame, and the human-interest frame. The press releases early on from Texas Health fed in to the attribution of responsibility frame—commonly known as the "blame frame" as blame was shifted from issue to issue. The press picked up the blame narratives, then began to blame Texas Health for providing conflicting and confusing information.

Riordan said at this point no information was trusted, so the team decided to hunker down and just absorb the blows. Then, they began to strategically and selectively choose the members of the press they would engage with.

"So instead of stepping in front of the bank of cameras, we went to producers and correspondents who by the coverage that we had seen really were the people who were covering the issues most objectively," Riordan said.

Sensationalistic Information

The district that houses Duncan's family's apartment complex is diverse ethnically and economically and stretches from the affluent Preston Hollow in Dallas down to where Duncan was staying, Vickery Meadows. The latter community felt blame fall on it during the crisis.

"I think that some of the coverage was insulting to them, and so, that absolutely hurt our access," Diane Solis, a reporter for the *Dallas Morning News* and on the Justice and Race team, said. "I think that one of the things that really angered the family was the leap that folks made about whether the victim had lied to officials about being sick or, more precisely, having Ebola. Or having been near someone who, who was dying of it, before he left," Solis said (personal communication, September 1, 2016).

The actions of authorities in the first few days did not help the perception of a neighborhood to blame. Jeffrey Weiss, who at the time was an education reporter for the *Dallas Morning News*, said the assault on the apartment of the victim was purely for "PR purposes."

"They eventually took the family out of the apartment and destroyed everything in the apartment with guys wearing Hazmat suits," Weiss said. "Took about two weeks for me to figure out, from looking at the coverage, that if they had put a padlock on the door, turned the heat on and left for about four days, you could've held a dinner party in there without endangering anybody. By the time they took the family out, chances were pretty good there was nothing in there that was remotely dangerous. And yet, the, the iconic photo of those first days were the guys in hazmat suits coming in and out of that apartment... And the reason that they did it was that it showed that they were doing something. So, on the one hand, it's probably smart to show you were doing something, on the other hand what they were doing... needlessly raised fear" (personal communication, August 29, 2016).

The scene, again like out of a Hollywood movie, played out on screens across the globe. While Riordan acknowledged that Texas Health made mistakes early, he said the press was complicit.

"It [Ebola] had finally jumped the ocean. It was here, and it had been transmitted," Riordan said.

> I am going to lay this right on the media's doorstep; people were afraid that they could actually get sick and die, because of the overheated coverage in the media. What the media should have been doing was listening to us that we had this contained. They wouldn't let us tell that story. (Mark Riordan, personal communication, February 2017)

Local vs. National News

Solis said the national media camped out in the Vickery Meadows neighborhood and at times, were very aggressive with the residents. Ebola had taken over the airwaves—it was an inescapable 24/7 story. The local reporters interviewed for this book were cognizant of their duties during this time, and they took their jobs seriously. But communicating risk is a tricky line to walk sometimes in crisis, especially when the risk of contracting Ebola was so very, very low. Therefore, it was important, according to Goodman, to use experts in the field to address the perceived risk and the science behind it. "They could have used the story as a vessel for that information to . . . keep the unnecessary panic at bay," Goodman said, adding, "It's really important to be responsible in these situations instead of being sensational. Yet, it's so easy to fall into that trap."

And it was easy, Goodman said, for the national media to fall in to that trap. He was approached about doing a segment on a cable news show and talked to a member of the national press for about 45 minutes. It was a conversation with a producer that Goodman characterized as "fishing" and "narrative pushing."

In Goodman's view, the national media "had a very limited understanding" of the geography of the Dallas and Fort Worth area or how people there live. Noting that Dallas-Fort Worth is not New York City, he elaborated, "There is public transportation, but the vast majority of the way that we get around is very solitary." Because of that he said "you wouldn't set some sort of movie about infectious disease in Dallas necessarily. So, they were fishing for these kind of sexy answers of you know people aren't going out shopping," Goodman said. He even remembered laughing at the last question a reporter asked. "I felt kind of bad. She goes, 'do you think this is going to affect the attendance of this weekend's Cowboy's game?' and I was just like, 'are you fxxxing kidding me?'"

Local journalists also agreed that the national news was pushing certain narratives. By the way, the television segment featuring Goodman was cancelled.

The local press in this case looks different than the local press described in other cases featured in this book. While the local press is often involved in the community, in small to medium-sized media markets, such as Baton Rouge, reporters stay for a few years and then move on to larger markets. Dallas is the number five television market in the nation and is often a final destination in a reporter's career. Once you get to Dallas, you stay and put down roots. The average number of years on the job of the reporters we interviewed was 21.

Riordan said both sides (local and national) were co-opted by the intensity of the situation and lost some of their ability to objectively manage their coverage. However, when Riordan's team methodically targeted journalists they felt were doing fair work, as a local medical provider, they focused on local media. "But with that said, I think some of, probably all of the best coverage was at the local level."

Goodman said, "Whether you're promoting something or trying to get the word out about some initiative, or it's a crisis, your local media lives there. Your local media's part of the community." Although national media left within three weeks of the Fort Hood shooting, the *Austin-American Statesman* continued to send a reporter there weekly. At this writing the newspaper still had a presence there. "You know the area. It tends to be a little more responsible and kind of empathetic and understanding of what that community's going through."

Reynolds of the CDC also said that the Ebola coverage fit, if not mirrored, the popular national cultural narratives of the time, such as television's *Walking Dead* and Hollywood's World War Z.

"I think that's all we want to do is have a complete de-evolution of all of our society," Reynolds said. "It seems like that's the genre of our time? I think it's a great deal of helplessness, frankly, that our popular fiction and movies, TV and books, seem to be so focused on some kind of precarious loss of modern society as we know it right now."

The CDC also suffered an outbreak of criticism. Tom Frieden, the 53-year-old doctor, director and face of the Centers for Disease Control and Prevention, spent a day on Capitol Hill in mid-October getting grilled by lawmakers who asked: "Why not impose a travel ban? How can you be sure this won't happen again in another American city via an international traveler?" (Sun, Bernstein, & Achenbach, 2014). Frieden answered with a list of reasons including porous borders, untrained border and security workers and the inability to track and monitor travelers (Sun et al., 2014).

Reynolds said her boss had to defend himself because everyone felt helpless—they wanted to do something. She also said it was difficult to have a rational discussion of options on top of strong emotions. But a ban on international travelers coming in to the U.S. was not the answer. Reynolds said there would be too many unintended consequences such as mission trips or volunteer travelers being refused readmission.

"You know, what do I tell them to do? There's nothing to do. And that probably felt to them that we were being a little too laissez-fare, that we… and that's where I think border screening became a part of the response in the reaction that people are saying 'Do something! Do something!'… But it was difficult for many people, those on the site of the response and, I think, those outside the response looking in and wondering 'what the heck are you guys doing to protect us?'" Reynolds said.

The Difficulties in Communicating Science

Reynolds also stressed the complexity of such a story in terms of the science. While many newspapers and televisions stations still retain a health or science reporter, many outlets do not. When Reynolds traveled to Hong Kong in 1997 for the first reported cases of H5N1 bird flu in humans, the enormity of her communication task became apparent.

"I could tell within three questions at the press conference that I needed to help educate reporters that don't normally cover us, the difference between bacteria and virus. So, instead of me telling reporters what they need to do, I need to learn from them what I need to do to help them do their best possible job," Reynolds said. "We really did want people to know that we weren't hiding. You know, that we didn't want conspiracies to take hold because we were being as upfront with them as possible."

This has been an issue in many contemporary crisis cases. For example, in the 2010 Deepwater Horizon oil disaster, the science on the dispersant Corexit was mixed and misreported in the press. Hundreds of thousands of gallons were piped into the Gulf, yet no one really knew how it would affect the oil or the environment.

Explaining to the public how Ebola is transmitted was difficult according to Reynolds.

We may know the difference between something that's airborne versus a droplet, but try to explain that to the public. That's hard. And we had to think about those before the event itself. So, as we tried to tweak our messaging in response to people's misunderstanding of what we were saying, because we weren't communicating well, then they perceived us as changing the messages. And that is not something you want to do, unless you legitimately are changing the message. And that became a problem for us, too. (Barbara Reynolds, personal communication, April 2016)

The *Dallas Morning News* had a specialized reporter on staff, who gave it a major advantage in this realm. Dr. Seema Yasmin, trained as a medical doctor at the University of Cambridge in England and as a journalist at the University of Toronto, also served at one point as a disease detective in the Epidemic Intelligence Service at the U.S. Centers for Disease Control and Prevention. The newspaper hired her to cover public health crises and other science-related stories. As a local doctor, scientist, journalist and professor of public health at The University of Texas at Dallas, she served as a source for the newsroom as well as for other news outlets across the nation including a medical contributor for CNN and NBC Channel 5 in Dallas. She was able to explain the crisis, the virus, and the threat in a journalistic manner that carried much credibility and understanding.

Tom Huang, DMN Sunday and Enterprise Editor, who also has degrees in computer science and engineering from MIT, believed Dr. Yasmin's reporting, along with another DMN science beat reporter made the difference.

"I think our approach was definitely more in depth and with context and trying very much to tell the story in a responsible way," Huang said. "And it's difficult, because it's a fluid moving story and, we need to report that. There's a patient and then ultimately, a couple of patients with Ebola. But we also didn't want to create a huge public scare as well. So I think Seema, through her stories as well as going on television helped to keep people calm" (personal communication, August 29, 2016).

The PR Response Shifts

A few reporters did acknowledge that Texas Health had a big job to do. Goodman said they were unable to understand what Texas Health was going through until much later. That included "this incredibly complex analysis of this patient's medical record . . . which caregiver was in which place at which time, how information was transmitted . . . throughout the triage process. Later on, it made a lot of sense in terms of why things [conflicting information] were coming out the way they were."

As the immediate threat died down, Texas Health's communication went from being on the defensive, to being proactively on the offensive. On October 16, the first nurse who contracted Ebola, Nina Pham, was still in the hospital awaiting a transfer to a Maryland facility for further treatment. In an exclusive interview with *Dallas Morning News* court reporter Jennifer Emily (February 2015), Pham told the story of a doctor wearing a video camera under his protective hood coming into her hospital room.

"Thanks for getting well. Thanks for being part of the volunteer team to take care of our first patient," a man's voice said in the video. "It means a lot. This has been a huge effort by all of you guys" (Emily, 2015).

Pham said she was told he was filming for educational purposes. However, the video was released to the media, she told Emily (2015), without her permission.

Pham said she understood its purpose, telling Emily (2015), "They had just a PR nightmare with what happened with Mr. Duncan ... and then us being infected with Ebola. Not just one nurse, but two. People lost faith in them [Presbyterian], especially after we got sick."

Attorney Charla Aldous, who was one of the lawyers who represented Pham in the lawsuit against Texas Health Resources, told the DMN that they "used Pham as a PR pawn" in the video trying to renew faith in the hospital (Emily, 2015). Pham would also tell Emily that she was one of the last to learn of Duncan's diagnosis, similar to CEO Berdan's story.

Just two days after that hospital visit, on October 18, not long after Burson-Marsteller took over the communication response, Texas Health Resources CEO Berdan released a letter to the community. In it, he apologized for the initial misdiagnosis of Duncan and admitted making mistakes in handling "the very difficult challenge." This apologia effort moved the PR strategy from being on the defensive and shifting blame to being contrite and taking responsibility. Riordan said this approach is almost always necessary in a crisis. "In PR, if it's obvious, do it, right? Say the obvious things. When people have been harmed, apologize. When there's a reason to be sad, offer your regrets and condolences. When at all possible, engage the media so that you can begin to tell your story on your terms."

Berdan also declared Presbyterian a "safe place." The safe place theme was echoed throughout the press releases and actions going forward from this date. Five weeks after the crisis started, on November 7, former President

George W. Bush visited the hospital and the now-well nurse, Amber Vinson. Through hugs and handshakes (visual safety cues), the former president expressed his gratitude to the staff and told the press "I'm confident it [the hospital] is doing what is necessary to regain the community's trust."

Emily said in an August 2016 interview that when the exclusive Pham interview story came out, Texas Health was responsive to her requests for comment.

"I did want to say that... whenever I call Presbyterian Hospital or their parent company they always say something," Emily said. "I try to take them through every single thing so they can respond to everything if they want to, point by point, but they always had something to say and sometimes it wasn't much but I appreciated it."

The lawsuit involving Pham and Texas Health was settled in October 2016, two years after Ebola came to America.

But, Goodman said at the end of the crisis, even with the mistakes (for example, infected nurse flying to Cleveland), the event was contained. The reporters also in the aftermath recognized that it was a big story made bigger by the many entities involved (the public health department, which falls under the county, as well as the city of Dallas were also involved). While the reporters were perturbed by the initial response of the hospital, they recognized this after the fact.

"I think everybody started coming toward that realization that . . . this is literally a unique situation. There are no case studies. An American hospital...there are similarities, but not Ebola. What do you do?" In Goodman's opinion, "there was sort of an echo of that in the community," where even the competition realized it could have been them. He said that during off-the-record conversations with "any PR person in town [who] works for a hospital," they revealed "they were secretly just so relieved that that wasn't them" and wondered what they would have done if they faced that situation.

Why Misinformation or Lack of Information Matters

Texas Health made major communication mistakes at the beginning, trying to lay blame or deciding where the breakdown in protocol took place. First, it was the fault of the electronic medical records. Then, the breakdown was the nurse's fault. The mixed messages made reporters very upset. The reporters did not know what information to trust—and no explanation was given as to why the information missteps were made. Texas Health's Riordan, in our conversation, wanted to focus on what went right. In fact, he said, the two people who had ever contracted Ebola in America lived, when the death rate in Africa was higher than 50 percent. He said the outbreak was quickly contained and it could have been much worse.

But as ground zero for the outbreak, Texas Health took it on the chin, Goodman said.

As Reynolds explained, so did the CDC:

> I think that the wedge between CDC and the population as a whole started with the belief that what the director said was "Any hospital can manage a case of Ebola" and then we had two nurses become ill, and then there was the hoopla about the personal protective equipment and what would work versus what wouldn't work and um, the language that was used initially was "With proper training and procedures, any hospital can do this." And it got shortened, and I understand that it did, and it shouldn't have. And it was also done at a time when there were no, imported cases, cases that were sort of diagnosed here first of Ebola. And, I think that became a problem. (Barbara Reynolds, personal communication, April 2016)

Again, communicating risk, especially when the risk is minimal but emotions are maximal is difficult.

"We allowed for disconnect to occur between our messages and our empathy for people who were still frightened," Reynolds said. There is a need to respond to people's fears, even if the threat is not real, according to Reynolds, explaining "there's a difference between a real threat and real fear. And you can have real fear against a threat that's not real."

She said years of experience has taught that if the operational response of the organization or of authorities is questioned—you can usually blame the communication. Reynolds said, "If you look at any kind of emergency response, where people think of it as a horrible failure, I will guarantee you that they will have made these communication mistakes." Noting that in this country, "we have problems... But when we put it down in the record book as a really bad one, where it gives us a bad taste in our mouth and we're dissatisfied with the response itself, it will be because we had poor communication." She continued, "You can't save a bad [operational] response, but you could ruin a good response, if you can't respond with good communication."

Acknowledging that she might sound like a one trick pony, Reynolds expressed frustration "at the lack of resources and thinking that go to preparing for communication needs in a community." While attention is given to psychological needs and community resilience, everything, she said, comes down to "how do we communicate? And, if we don't communicate in the crisis, before the crisis, after the crisis, we're going to lose people, and it's going to be more difficult to succeed."

Reynolds has been a part of the response for many crises over her almost three decades with the CDC. She explained that by working for the government, the crisis becomes yours, as was the case with the anthrax letters that were sent in 2001 in which five people died. She said when the government and the CDC respond, they now own the threat. Therefore, it is their responsibility to mitigate or completely remove it. And, she said, that comes with professional, responsible and effective communication.

When Reynolds was interviewed in the spring of 2016, she was preparing to help tackle the latest health threat, the Zika virus, spread by mosquitos. The White House convened a summit at the CDC in Atlanta that included state, local and federal officials. Reynolds said while many will be ready with a logistical plan, they will not be ready for the communication challenges. She said her talk will focus on that fact that most of the decisions they will make will be related to the release of information.

"How you do it. When you do it. Who does it? It's not going to be the operational stuff. The operational stuff will be taken care of by good staff," she said. "You as the leader will be making the communication decisions more often than not. And I think it's just always a surprise to leaders when they're in a crisis, that they have to spend as much time as they do on communication."

Reynolds felt that overall, the hospital and all the local and state entities involved did a pretty good job with communication. She has observed media coverage of crisis over her decades in the field and has seen patterns develop.

"I will say that when the risk seems more remote, the coverage by popular media and even our exercise of our understanding of things, in social media are a little more dramatic," she said. She noted that during her extensive career with the CDC as well as the military, she has observed that the more imminent the threat is, the more sober the communication is around it. "So as long as the threat was more notional and not real, the coverage of the threat of Ebola in the U.S. was, how could I say... I don't want to say less responsible, but less precise," Reynolds said.

Riordan did not temper his opinion and said the press, at times during the Ebola crisis, was to blame for fear-mongering.

"To witness what I saw my friends and colleagues in the media become, which was truly out of control, the amount of hyperbole, the amount of breathlessness, the amount of, I think, of speed over accuracy, I have never seen before. And I would actually say the amount of irresponsibility among the media was the part that galled me and tested me and I think all of us the most," Riordan said.

Conclusion

Reynolds said for more than 40 years, the media and disease experts had created this "boogeyman of infectious diseases." The job of the journalist or the communications professional is not to make people afraid, but to minimize harm. Therefore, Reynolds said, be careful with the tone of your messaging—moderate the way you talk and write about the virus. "We talk about Ebola as that viral hemorrhagic fever, where people bleed from multiple orifices. And I said, if it's the organ lady from the church down the road or it's the used car salesman across the block, do you really want to be talking about that disease that way?" Reynolds asked.

Reynolds was key in the development of the model of communication known as Crisis and Emergency Risk Communication (CERC) that is used and studied by practitioners and scholars. The model merges standards in health and risk communication with research in crisis and disaster communication (Reynolds & Seeger, 2005). Reynolds approaches crisis communication based on this framework that has been taught by the CDC and put in to practice across the world. In the following takeaways from this chapter, some of the model's ideas, confirmed through our practical findings, will be discussed within this context.

Takeaways for PR Professionals

Get Accurate Information Out Quickly to Set a Tone of Transparency and Credibility

"Our first responsibility is to honestly communicate the risk. Now, the fact is, you can be doing that honestly and people will reject it, if others have what seems to be valid risk assessment and they think that you're not telling the whole story. So, it's not just, you tell people the truth, you have to do it within the context of having your own credibility and that's why most of my work at CDC has been dedicated to trying to build and maintain our credibility, so when we do have a crisis that we need people to look to us for recommendations and for actions, that they will find us to be a credible source for it. And we have over the years, pretty good success. I'd say it got bumpy during Ebola and I understand why it did, but people are still relying on us for their recommendations. It's not just telling people the facts, you have to tell the facts in a way that will be perceived as credible," Reynolds said.

Be Honest—If You Don't Know, Say You Don't Know. Don't Send Inaccurate, Mixed or Rushed Messages

"I don't want to treat people like children. I don't want to hide hard facts. If there's bad news, I want to put out that bad news. If you make mistakes, I want you to admit the mistakes and apologize for the mistakes as you should," Reynolds said.

Hold Joint Briefings

When many entities are involved such as in a public health crisis, a joint daily briefing to the media would be helpful. Texas state health officials held a daily briefing and reporters said that they found that helpful. The CDC also had briefings that provided supplemental information. Access and updates can help reduce wrong information or rumors from being reported. It also gives the reporters one-stop shopping.

"Every crisis has chaos. We need to be able to be flexible enough to recognize and not be thrown off by it and then communicate honestly about what we're doing. I… I know it's easy to say, 'Be honest.' And it's more difficult, but the best way to be honest is to quit thinking of people as 'them versus us.' And as us, altogether, trying to fix the problem," Reynolds said.

Internal and Cross-organizational Communication Is Key

Even with all of the entities involved, the internal stakeholders must be informed first of key information. The fact that Berdan and Pham both told reporters they felt they were the last to know about the positive diagnosis, emphasizes the need to pay attention to this crucial communication detail.

Use Positive Visuals in the Message

Ebola evokes frightening, Hollywood-style images. In the recovery stage, the visit of former President Bush to the hospital was all the reassurance the public would need. He hugged staff members and the formerly infected nurse. This photo communicated more than any press release or news story.

If the Message Is Not Getting Out, Adjust

Riordan said that when the press coverage became too hyperbolic, his team strategically sought out responsible outlets and reporters to talk to. This is a last case scenario only for when faced with a credibility crisis (because of Texas Health initial missteps) or when the threat is lessened.

Takeaways for Journalists

Put on the Cape of Facts and Accountability

> A journalist will, at different points along the way, be interested in the reputational side of the crisis. And, at different points, more interested in the messaging about what to do for the crisis. And I talk about journalists as having their public sector hat, their public health—or like safety, I think is what I call it—their public safety hat they put on early on in a crisis when they're just trying to gather the facts and share them with people. And then they're going to take that hat off and put on their journalism super cape and start looking at accountability. And that we need to expect both of those to happen from a journalist. So, they have to think about it in more than one way, too. (Barbara Reynolds, personal communication, April 2016)

Have an Organized Plan of How to Cover the Event and Who Is Going to Cover What

Determine possible crises to hit your community and have detailed plans to cover them. For example, a plan will include a contact list of authorities and experts, a list of supplies, who is covering the health department and who is stationed at the hospital, etc. Each plan will hold information specific to the crisis. For example, a plan for a plane crash at an airport would include a schematic of the runways and contact information for the National Transportation Safety Board (NTSB).

"I really thought about this a lot because once you're in it, you're sort of in it. If you know who you need to call or where you need to go or what you need to do. It's sort of…it becomes this weird adrenaline-focused sensation and you sort of have to direct in ways that will be best for gathering the information," Goodman said.

Resist the Sensationalistic and Hysteria of the Moment

Risk information is difficult to convey. Adhere to the Society of Professional Journalist's Code of Ethics that charges journalists to convey information in an ethical manner and minimize harm. Those who report in an unethical manner will get less cooperation from authorities and organizations because of fear of unfair or blame narratives. Don't let your own emotions or the emotions of the public affect your reporting.

Understand the Difficulties Facing the Other Side

The communication team for Texas Health was dealing with the medical records of multiple people, with the privacy of the patients at the forefront. Additionally, in this case, there wasn't much for the public to do to alleviate its fears. In crisis situations, it is suggested to give the public a list of things that they can do to minimize risk (create your evacuation route, throw out the contaminated food, etc.). But again, the risk was so minimal, the CDC even acknowledged there was not much that could be done. In the absence of a list, arm the press with additional information such as supplying expert interviews. And finally, the people on the inside are scared too. They too are resisting their emotions in order to do their jobs.

Takeaways for Both

Promote an Action—Give People Something to Do to Enhance Self-efficacy

"One of the key principles I teach in crisis and emergency risk communication, is that when people are facing a threat, promote an action. Give people things to do. It helps to reduce anxiety in the population," Reynolds said in terms of both journalists and PR professionals.

Reynolds and Seeger (2005), in a discussion of unique communication concerns during a crisis, stated: "The immediate communication needs are to reduce uncertainty, allowing audiences to create a general understanding of what happened so that they may act appropriately" (p. 50). This coincides with a communication theory, Berger and Calabrese's (1975) uncertainty reduction theory. When people are faced with a stressful situation (i.e., a crisis) they seek out information in order to assess risk and/or calm their fears. Research has shown that the public has an insatiable appetite for news when crisis hits—they want to know more. An immediate need is information and the public often goes to websites to find that information. During Hurricane Katrina, Sandy Hook, the Boston Marathon Bombing and the 2016 Dallas police ambush, websites of local news organizations crashed as people flocked to find out more information about these tragedies and overwhelmed servers.

Reynolds also said, a year later, facing the Zika virus threat, the communication around Zika she felt is easier than the Ebola case because the threat is more real and you can give the public something to do to prevent it. This case reminds journalists and public relations professionals again, that not all public health crises are the same. There will be specific communication nuances in every case.

Have Multiple Scientific Experts (or Experts Unique to Each Crisis) Ready to Explain

The press often needs help with difficult scientific explanations. Journalists and the public are going to ask what "that" word means—therefore, have someone who knows how to answer the questions. A press conference should not just be a spokesperson reading a statement. Have local experts (from local trusted universities) join you at the podium to answer those questions or available to be interviewed later. It is also a good idea to create a pamphlet or a one sheet that helps explain the virus and that contains your experts' contact information. Out-of-town reporters will especially appreciate this effort.

PR professionals and journalists can cultivate these relationships before crisis strikes. Again, part of a journalist's crisis plan will include the names and contact information of experts to go to to help explain complexities and give context for your stories.

"Have your subject-matter experts available. Be willing to answer questions is a big one too. It's always you know, understand that for me, making it up north to hear you read off a piece of paper is just sort of a waste, you know.

Just understand that there are questions beyond that, and you should be either prepared for them, or just say, 'we don't know at this time.' Because that's an important designation as well," Goodman said.

Communication May Be Necessary in Other Languages/ Cultural Contexts

The community where Duncan lived has many residents who are foreign-born and Hispanic according the DMN reporter Diane Solis, although most do speak English.

"I know that at the high school (near Vickery Meadows) there were a lot of kids who were scared and who were going to the nurse and were afraid to, to be there. And there was concern that people weren't getting information in the, in all the languages they needed," Solis said.

Plan for Multiple Agency Involvement

Crisis communication has to be balanced with the investigation that is being conducted in to what happened. So crisis plans for cases that involve multiple agencies, should include, in some regard, working with those other agencies.

For example, after Dallas officers were ambushed by a gunman in July 2016 and five were killed and seven more injured, the Dallas Police Department took over communication from Baylor Hospital where some of the injured were taken. The reason—it was an ongoing investigation. Journalists need to know who the players are in the information game.

For internal PR, when many agencies are involved, you must work together and DO NOT criticize another agencies response.

"It would be a shortcut, and it would be much easier to point out other people's mistakes as a way to gain our credibility back, but I won't do that," Reynolds said. "If we want our credibility the next time, we can't spend our time tearing down other people."

Work to Overcome Widely-held Frightening, Preconceived Notions About the Threat

"Ebola was pumped up as a big threat and then when it became a genuine possibility to have Ebola here in the U.S., we had to talk about a disease that, up to that point, had a pretty bad reputation. And, try to moderate people's understanding of it. It was just harder to do," Reynolds said.

Take Care Not to Victimize the Victims

The words we use and pictures we show to represent the victims may cause them additional emotional stress or facilitate or increase public perception of unworthiness. The implication that Duncan lied about his travels caused the attribution of responsibility frame to come in to play.

Continue to Cover the Story—Continue to Provide Information—Because You Are Local Media

For example, what about the other hospitals in the region? Are they ready to face such a threat? If Duncan's ambulance had turned right instead of left, how is that hospital preparing? What does infectious disease treatment training look like? Journalists, arm everyone with information to use at a later time. PR professionals, share what you have learned in the crisis with others.

Finally, Reynolds uses six principles in crisis communication that are supported by our findings. They are (1) be first, (2) be right, (3) be credible, (includes honesty and integrity), and then (4) promote action, (5) express empathy, and (6) show respect.

Crisis communication contains complex, sophisticated and nuanced messaging. But in a case like "the October event," as the Texas Health people call it, where fears and emotions were high, communication must also contain calmness and empathy. It is the only way, according to Reynolds, to achieve the Hollywood ending.

Note

1. Each journalist and public relations practitioner interviewed for this chapter was interviewed only once, unless otherwise noted; therefore, the first citation will provide that information. Individual in-text citations will not continue throughout.

References

Auerbach, Y. & Bloch-Elkon, Y. (2005). Media framing and foreign policy: The elite press vis-à-vis US policy in Bosnia, 1992–95. *Journal of Peace Research, 42*(1), 83–99.

Berger, C. R., & Calabrese, R. J. (1975). Some explorations in initial interaction and beyond: toward a developmental theory of interpersonal communication. *Human Communication Research, 1*(2), 99–112.

Bullock, H. E., Wyche, K. F., & Williams, W. R. (2001). Media images of the poor. *Journal of Social Issues, 57*(2), 229–247.

D'Angelo, P. (2002). News framing as a multiparadigmatic research program: A response to Entman. *Journal of Communication, 52*, 870–889.

Emily, J. (2015, February 28). Exclusive: Nurse Nina Pham after Ebola: Terrible side effects, lawsuit against employer. *The Dallas Morning News*, Retrieved from http://res.dallasnews.com/interactives/nina-pham/

Entman, R. M. (1993). Framing: Toward clarification of a fractured paradigm. *Journal of Communication, 43*(4), 51–59.

Goodman, M. (2015, March). How Texas Health managed its Ebola crisis. *D Magazine*, Retrieved from http://www.dmagazine.com/publications/d-ceo/2015/march/texas-health-ceo-barclay-berdan-ebola-crisis/

Hethcock, B. (2014, October 23). Presbyterian financial losses serious but contained after Ebola cases. *Dallas Business Journal*, Retrieved from: http://www.bizjournals.com/dallas/blog/2014/10/presbyterian-financial-losses-serious-but.html

Loehrke, J., & Carey, A. (2014, October 15). Timeline: Ebola in the USA. USA Today, Retrieved from http://www.usatoday.com/story/news/nation/2014/10/01/ebola-us-timeline/16541935/

Reynolds, B., & Seeger, M. W. (2005). Crisis and emergency risk communication as an integrative model. *Journal of Health Communication, 10*(1), 43–55.

Sun, L. H., Bernstein, L., & Achenbach, J. (2014, October 16). CDC director's challenge: Deadly Ebola virus and outbreak of criticism. *The Washington Post*, Retrieved from https://www.washingtonpost.com/national/health-science/cdc-directors-challenge-deadly-ebola-virus-and-outbreak-of-criticism/2014/10/16/f0109802-5547-11e4-ba4b-f6333e2c0453_story.html?utm_term=.c47b8f54e72a

· 2 ·

WATER, WATER EVERYWHERE...AGAIN

Hurricane Katrina and the Baton Rouge Great Flood

Jinx Coleman Broussard

Preparation: The Lead-Up

On Sunday, August 28, 2005, Sally Forman, communications director for the City of New Orleans and Mayor C. Ray Nagin, woke up, stepped into her slippers and walked to her front porch to retrieve the newspaper, as she did every morning (Forman, personal communication, 2016).[1] This morning, however, after glancing at the paper, she immediately checked the website of the National Oceanic and Atmospheric Administration (NOAA) and saw that forecasters were indicating Hurricane Katrina was serious; in fact, it was now a Category Five storm. She began to scream throughout her house, "Everybody up!" Then she quickly wrote a press release for the day and prepared her family to evacuate to the Hyatt Hotel on Poydras Street in downtown New Orleans. She headed to work at city hall across the street from the Hyatt. This was the day before the storm hit.

After Forman drafted her news release, Mayor Nagin soon issued the city's mandatory evacuation order. He declared the Louisiana Superdome a refuge of last resort for people who could not leave New Orleans. The city sent buses and police with megaphones into neighborhoods to tell people who could not evacuate they could go to the Superdome.

The doors of the massive structure opened Sunday at 8 a.m. for people with special needs, and 2 p.m. for everyone else. Roughly 20,000 people sought safety at the Superdome that day, while thousands of others disregarded the evacuation order and stayed in their homes to ride out the storm as they had done many times before. In the summer of 2005 alone, threats of direct hits on New Orleans had propelled many people to evacuate at least twice. This time, tens of thousands of New Orleanians chose to stay put.

During the past century, hurricanes flooded New Orleans six times.[2] Hurricane experts warned citizens for years about the impact a major hurricane would have on the below-sea-level, bowl-shaped city. Three years before Katrina hit, The *Times-Picayune* published a five-part series that predicted the impact of such a storm. "In Harm's Way," the first article in the series titled "Washing Away: Worst-case Scenario If a Hurricane Hits Louisiana" reported the levee system that protected the city from both Lake Pontchartrain and the Mississippi River "may turn against us" (McQuaid & Schleifstein, 2002). The *Times-Picayune* had experience covering hurricanes, crises and big events such as super bowls and major conventions where announced schedules were available and the newspaper could plan accordingly (Kovacs, personal communication, October 6, 2016).

On August 28, not only was a major hurricane brewing for the City of New Orleans. A PR crisis of monumental proportion also was brewing. Fearn-Banks (2017) succinctly defines a crisis as "a major occurrence with a potentially negative outcome affecting the organization, company, or industry, as well as its publics, products, services or good name" (Fearn-Banks, 2017, p. 7). "A crisis," according to Coombs, (2007) "is a sudden and unexpected event that threatens to disrupt an organization's operations and poses both a financial and reputational threat" (p. 164.) A crisis also "is a perception of an unpredictable event that threatens important expectations of stakeholders and can seriously impact an organization's performance and generate negative outcomes" (Coombs, 2012, pp. 2–3).

Although the city was expecting a hit from a hurricane, officials believed they were prepared for this threat in the same manner they had been for previous hurricanes. Officials were totally unaware of and unprepared for the colossal threat Hurricane Katrina and its aftermath posed to life, property and reputation.

After hours of heavy rain and winds, Katrina struck early in the morning on Monday, August 29. It had begun as a depression on August 23 over the Bahamas and gained strength as it traveled in the warm Gulf of Mexico waters to Florida, Alabama, Mississippi and Louisiana. It hit just to the east of the Crescent City, leading the *Times-Picayune* to declare that New Orleans had dodged a bullet. But the levee system and seawalls that surrounded the city and were supposed to protect it from flooding were no match for the storm surge. Water overtopped some levees and seeped under others, causing them the breach. Seawalls crumbled. News accounts first showed the ominous creep of water through the levees and then the steady flow that eventually flooded eighty percent of the city, with only the roofs of some buildings visible.

People had nowhere to go and no means to get where they might have wanted to evacuate. In the days after the catastrophe, forty-eight states accepted people who were evacuated via planes, buses, trains, trucks and cars. The psychological trauma was profound. Many New Orleanians had never traveled outside the city; in fact, many had not traveled beyond their immediate neighborhood and were now being placed on planes. The human toll was even greater than the psychological. More than eighteen hundred people who remained in their homes perished. Bodies floated in the streets and according to Andrea Miller (2014), images of people wading in the knee- and chest-deep foul water or pleading for help from rooftops remain etched in the minds of many. The city was brought to its knees; Katrina caused $81 billion in damage to property.

This, indeed, was "the big one" that hurricane experts and the *Times-Picayune* had warned about. New Orleans was in crisis. Before the storm, officials were aware that levees could overtop and they could expect short-term flooding, but no one expected or prepared for most of the city to go under water. Nor did city officials prepare for crisis communication management. Arguably, the city should have been aware that this unique event—another definition of crisis—could happen. As noted, the *Times-Picayune*—and other media—had periodically run prodromal stories about the potential for such a scenario as Hurricane Katrina and the accompanying levee breaches. Media organizations and journalists, although reporting on and warning of such a threat, would learn that in crucial ways they also were unprepared.

When the storm winds died down Monday, Forman encountered Fire Chief Charles Parent as she was walking to City Hall from the Hyatt where city administrators were staying. Parent informed her his fire fighters warned him of a breach in the 17th Street Canal Levee. Lake Pontchartrain was beginning to flood into the Lakeview area in the western part of the city.[3] Forman instantly turned around to find Nagin and communications deputy director Terry Davis to tell them they needed to disseminate a message to let people know what was happening. The mayor went down the hall from his suite in the Hyatt to where journalists were camped out and informed them of the unfolding situation. According to Forman, Nagin did not want people who had evacuated to panic and try to come back to save their property or check on family who stayed behind. He also did not want people who were listening to media locally to panic; therefore, he urged calm.

The heavy rain and the powerful winds that came with Katrina ultimately caused levee breaches. Phone and electrical lines went down. Homes, entire neighborhoods, grocery stores, pharmacies, schools and other businesses were destroyed. Katrina and its aftermath left people stranded on rooftops and others displaced across 49 states. There was a limited supply of food and water at the Superdome for evacuees, and for days, people at the Ernest N. Morial Convention Center had nothing but what they left home with.

The severity and nature of the storm and its aftermath disrupted normal operations of government as well as the media. Katrina posed a crisis of monumental proportion. Doorley and Garcia call a crisis "a non-routine event that risks undesired visibility that in turn threatens significant reputational damage" (2015, p. 301). The scholars also note the extent to which an organization "survives a crisis with its reputation, operations, and financial conditions intact is determined less by the severity of the crisis—the underlying event—than by the timeliness and quality of its response to the crisis" (p. 299).

Coombs (2006, 2007) and other scholars posit that the crisis influences the crisis response, and how an organization responds during the first twenty-four hours determines whether an incident becomes a full-blown crisis. Long-term negative consequences can occur if a crisis is not handled properly, according to Coombs and Fearn-Banks, among others. It would be difficult for Forman and the city to respond quickly or properly. The communications response was further complicated because of several factors. First, neither had ever been exposed to a crisis situation such as Katrina. None of Forman's past experiences related to natural disasters. Prior to becoming director of communications in 2004, she was chief of protocol in the city's department of international relations for one year. Moreover, she and Davis did not have a background in crisis management or crisis communication. Practitioners such as Forman and Davis (and the others we talk about in this chapter) are essentially public information officers who function in the role of public servants who facilitate communication, informing the citizenry and the media about the work and actions of government. PIOs coordinate communication and are official spokespersons for states, cities, counties, school districts, boards and commissions, and sheriffs, police and fire departments and other governmental entities. Employee, media, internal, external and community relations, along with image building and special events are areas these communications managers oversee (Broussard, 1986; Graber, 1992).

Second, and to complicate matters, most of Forman's staff evacuated. One woman was pregnant, some staff had young children, and some were "just terribly scared," according to Forman. She "thought long and hard" about letting staff who were deemed emergency personnel leave although traditionally they were required to stay, but concluded that if they were frightened and if their minds were elsewhere, they wouldn't be thinking clearly enough to work. Eventually, only Forman and Davis remained in the city. Ideally, the two would have functioned as communications managers who directed a staff while serving as the boundary scanners, communications facilitators, and problem-solvers. Absent a staff, they were almost relegated to becoming communication technicians trying to get the word out. Members of a public information team are essential personnel who should fulfill their responsibilities as public servants during crises. The city's PIOs were needed more than ever after Katrina.

In the first days following the levee breaches, Forman recognized that no information was just as bad as poor information. Rumors filled the information void. Within crises, miscommunication and rumors are problem areas, and official sources of information must be clearly demarcated and utilized (Lindell, 2013). PR practitioners should disseminate accurate information quickly before the vacuum forms (Coombs, 2006; Darling, 1994; Lukaszweski, 1997; Kempner, 1995).

The characteristics of the crisis influence the communication and actions of the manager (Benoit, 1995; Coombs, 2007). Because crises threaten an organization's image and reputation, crisis managers should have a goal of image repair and restoration. As the catastrophe unfolded and conditions worsened in New Orleans, Forman was not focused on that goal; instead, she sought to gather facts, assist the mayor and inform the community. She needed to convey everything known about the situation as well as disseminate what Coombs call instructing, adapting and adjusting information that would aid and direct the public regarding what they should do, and how and why. "Instructing information tells stakeholders what they must do to protect themselves from the physical threat," while "adjusting information helps people to cope with the psychological threat from the crisis," and adjusting information "is an expression of concern for the victims" (Coombs, 2007, p. 165).

However, with a depleted communication infrastructure, and lacking basic communication tools, Forman said she faced almost insurmountable challenges. She could not even produce fliers because printers were located in the flooded city hall basement. Twitter and Instagram did not exist in 2005, and even if they did, Internet and phone services were down in the majority of the city. Forman thought of tactics to disseminate messages to the mass of people still in New Orleans. One involved putting together "makeshift" press briefings in which Mayor Nagin walked from his room down the hallway in the Hyatt to a room where media were often gathered. From there, he gave periodic updates. Soon, "Paul Revere type of calls" began, according to Forman. That is, journalists who were not at the Hyatt walked to the hotel or sent people to deliver messages and make requests of the mayor or other officials there. Forman said she hoped whoever was in that "pressroom" at the time would pass the information on to other journalists they encountered. Although that was Forman's intent, local journalists who remained in the city and national journalists interviewed for this book indicated they did not interact with or rely on city spokespersons or public information officers for information. *The New York Times* reporters did not remember ever meeting Forman (Drew, personal communication, December 2016; Treaster, personal communication, December 2016).

Another tactic, Forman remembered, involved walking "through the superdome a few times" and letting small groups of people who gathered around her and Nagin know what was happening. However, the two lacked even a bullhorn that would have carried their message even a short distance. Requests that police commandeer a bullhorn proved fruitless, Forman noted. While in the Superdome, she learned that a large number of people inside the cavernous building, as well as in the convention center, had transistor radios. She would find a way to reach stakeholders through that medium.

Making a Connection

Meanwhile, in the days leading up to Katrina, veteran radio personality Monica Pierre was working in a news and a public information capacity for WQUE-FM, one of the Clear Channel New Orleans radio stations. Her job was to let people know the storm was coming and how they should prepare. She also provided news to sister stations WYLD-FM and WYLD-AM. Pierre provided updates until midnight, and, although she felt a professional obligation to remain in the city, she left New Orleans at 2 a.m. and arrived in Opelousas, Louisiana, hours later. After the storm hit, but before the city began to flood, all Clear Channel staff and operations moved to the Baton Rouge. Pierre travelled from Opelousas to Baton Rouge every day and became a part of United Radio Broadcasters of New Orleans.

From a broom closet-sized room outfitted with two chairs and two microphones at the Louisiana Radio Network, Pierre and other on-air staff from New Orleans Clear Channel stations and Entercom Communications radio stations "gave voice to the voiceless" (Pierre, personal communication, January 6, 2017). In the wake of the catastrophe, the two radio groups combined their "programming and engineering resources" and formed United Radio Broadcasters of New Orleans that also included Entercom's WWL-870 AM, the leading news, weather and sports station in the region. Other New Orleans region independent stations also were involved. At 10 p.m. Central Time on September 1, they began simultaneous broadcasting around the clock, providing "continuous news, information and coverage of local relief efforts" as well as "live feeds from street reporters and interviews and updates from local officials and relief coordinators."[4] Pierre referred to people who called in as "citizen journalists" who were still in the city or displaced. Often the conversation was about what happened in their lives. Arguably, this was what people in the Superdome listened to.

It is telling here to put the communication infrastructure in the context of 2005. Twitter didn't exist. YouTube had just come on to the scene and Facebook was a year old. The iPhone wouldn't be born for four years and the iPad for five years. There would be no pictures from citizens inside the Superdome or Facebook live reports from reporters walking through the floodwaters. In fact, Carl Arredondo, WWL-TV's meteorologist, admitted that he texted for the first time during the storm crisis because that was the most reliable form of communication. In this context, the journalists' and PR professionals work became beyond important, but necessary for survival. And radio, an "old" medium, became a lifeline within the city and for evacuees across the nation.

Forman contacted United Broadcasters. What soon followed was an interview Mayor Nagin gave to well-respected WWL host Garland Robinette.[5] The mayor used vivid language to voice his frustration and anger over the almost non-existent federal government response to the human tragedy unfolding in New Orleans. That interview was heard all over the country and even abroad. Clearly the White House and federal officials heard the interview, for assistance soon began to flow to the city.

While journalists had written the stories on "the big one" to hit New Orleans, they did not have a playbook on how to cover such an event that left an entire American city under water and the communication infrastructure decimated. With little official information from the city, journalists and photographers who remained in New Orleans or arrived right before the storm went out on their own or with law enforcement, talking to people and reporting what they observed. In fact, *Times-Picayune* reporters discovered the levee breach. Other journalists obtained information from first responders and politicians who often delivered a summary of the situation. Later, official PIOs sometimes filled in the details, according to Peter Kovacs, managing editor for news for the paper.

A View from the Capital City

Although Katrina did not hit Baton Rouge, the communications staff for then-Governor Kathleen Blanco was also besieged with managing media relations, addressing the crisis in New Orleans as it was unfolding, as well as the needs of the citizenry. Again, they were public information officers. Like Forman, Robert Mann was a former journalist before serving as press secretary to U.S. senators Russell Long and John Breaux and later becoming director of communication for Governor Blanco. Mann saw his share of crises and natural disasters during his career and had crisis management experience. Although Mann interacted with the press during Katrina, he did not do so every day and was not the governor's spokesperson. Denise Bottcher was the press secretary. Mann's regular role was to strategize, coordinate messages, coordinate and supervise the press office and constituent services, and handle the governor's scheduling and travel "to make sure everything we were doing was on message" (Mann, personal communication, March 2015).

Even before the crisis developed, Mann was proactive. Being prepared is Fearn-Banks' third stage of a crisis, following detection or recognizing the early warning signs, and engaging in two-way communications to build relationships with key stakeholders (pp. 5–7). A crisis communication plan reflects proactive public relations and crisis management and it can not only prevent the crisis, but also make "publics supportive when there is a crisis" (Fearn-Banks, p. 7).

Because of a previous "disastrous" evacuation out of the New Orleans area the year before Katrina, Mann used the following spring, fall and summer to lead a planning process that included executing evacuations—complete with printing and distributing one million maps throughout the state and to the media. In addition to outlining how agencies and areas would coordinate crisis communication management, the plan also included how the state would interact with the press during a crisis. This approach aligns with what scholars and seasoned practitioners recommend.

Accommodating the Press

As Katrina was approaching, state officials held initial press briefings in a small pressroom. After the storm hit, they decided against moving to a bigger location to accommodate the large number of media. Mann said moving the press would have "created such distrust" and the media would have "suspected ulterior motives." In addition, the electronic media were "camped outside on our front lawn . . . and would not have gone along with being moved away."

This action aligns with what crisis communication literature posit. For instance, Verrico (2015) stated that "building trust is at the forefront of government communicators' minds and priorities because of the current social and political environment."[6] Mann was cognizant of the trust factor and the extent to which it contributes to organizational legitimacy. His actions also revealed that the needs of a primary stakeholder—the media—were considered, as PR scholars and practitioners advance (Coombs and Holladay, 2010; Newsom, Turk and Kruckeberg, 2013).

Having the media nearby benefitted the four-person communications team, as Mann recalled for this chapter. He said he could see media such as FOX News and CNN report inaccuracies, and he could respond. "I could literally walk out the front door of the building . . . reiterate the facts" and ask the journalists to correct or clarify the information they presented. "The ability to communicate quickly and effectively is clearly an important component of successful and effective crisis management" (Marra, 1998, p. 461).

The media sometimes allowed the inaccurate reports to stand, Mann stated. Although *The Washington Post* eventually corrected its erroneous report that Governor Blanco had waited three days to declare a state emergency, according to Mann, *Newsweek* did not take corrective action. Similar instances occurred daily with journalists failing to call the governor or communication officers for clarification before running with the stories, Mann said. Bottcher is quoted as saying in 2014 that journalists could have verified the facts regarding the executive order by merely doing a Google search.[7] McCollough (2012) offers that "journalists who cover state government share a critical role in co-creating an enlightened citizenry through the body of information about state government that each group provides" (p. 8). Not correcting and seeking the truth reflected a lack of ethical behavior that is often at the root of a damaged PIO/journalist relationship.

During the first week of the crisis, the PIOs dealt with thousands of media. Public relations practitioners for the National Guard and the Louisiana State Police also disseminated accurate and pertinent information. Mann offered that they "were great, great sources" for their representative agencies, therefore, the governor's staff did not have "to do it all." As the crisis continued, a PR firm already on retainer to the state also assisted with communication.

The pace was so fast and media were "hungry for information," therefore, the PIOs did not have ample time to determine how to present it. In Mann's words, it was "the weirdest thing," because they were the "center of the news universe . . . where 99% of the world" was watching. Yet, he felt he "was often the least informed person in the world." He and the staff did not have the opportunity to even watch television.

After about a week, the communications director accepted the offer of a former congressional colleague to assist, telling him he could sit and watch TV all day and inform Mann of what was happening and what people were saying. That would then enable the PIOs to correct misinformation in real time rather than having to wait for the next news cycle. As noted above, Twitter did not exist and Facebook was in its infancy during and after Katrina. Even if they were available, the communications staff did not have the manpower to monitor social media or engage the public.

Telling the Truth: Fact Versus Rumor

A difference existed between how print and broadcast reporters approached their coverage of the crisis. In Mann's view, the former "were much more amenable to being told they were wrong," and were interested in accuracy. Therefore, the PIOs were able to place issues in context. The approach of print media was a nod, perhaps, to "acknowledging that what they were writing was part of the record," Mann said, adding "I really think there's a higher standard in print journalism." On the other hand, the broadcast reporter "looked at the accuracy of his or her reporting as a sort of work in progress."

It was as if the reporters were saying, "This is what we know this hour. Next hour we'll add to it . . . and if that was wrong, we just won't say it again." Their view appeared to be that their report "would just go into the ether, anyway," Mann said.

A difference also existed between how local and national media covered the crisis. In the view of the communications staff, the national media, with the help of "political operatives in Washington, D.C., were intent on a blame narrative," Bottcher told a conference of public relations practitioners in 2014. She praised local media, including the *Times-Picayune*, *The Advocate* and The Associated Press, for telling the "most accurate story . . . because they knew the most" (Bottcher, October 7, 2014). Botcher was referring to what communication scholars call framing, a theory that has to do with message transmission from the author to the audience.

As early as 1955 (Bateson) said frames occur when messages highlight the most "meaningful actions," while excluding others. Other scholars argue that journalists and other media personnel select and emphasize certain aspects of a topic or issue and ignore other attributes, thereby creating meaning for audiences (Entman, 1993; Tankard, Hendrickson, Silberman and Bliss; Goffman, 1974;). As Coombs noted in 2007, "The way a message is framed shapes how people define problems, causes of problems, attributions of responsibility and solutions to problems" (p. 167). Common frames include conflict (one versus one), economic consequence (gains and losses), morality, attribution of responsibility, and human-interest. The national news frame of this crisis was and continues to this day to be attribution of responsibility—who was responsible for the slow response?

PR Strategies and Tactics

The communications team utilized several strategies in interacting with the media. The first involved handling hundreds of calls from reporters who were not in that state but who wanted quotes or the governor or someone around her for an interview or show. The other strategy involved serving the "crush or reporters" . . . who "were just sort of hanging out in the lobby" and in the press room, and "seizing upon people" as they came and went to give interviews, Mann noted. U.S. Senator Mary Landrieu, Lieutenant Governor Mitch Landrieu and former U.S. Senator John Breaux were just a few of the individuals the media interviewed frequently.

Another strategy involved having the governor and officials provide up-dates during as many as four press briefings a day. As the crisis communica-tion literature indicates, frequent updates are crucial to avoid the informa-tion void or vacuum. Hence, that strategy worked better than issuing a lot of press releases because media were not really interested in releases, according to Mann. However, the briefings posed a challenge for the PIOs. Governor Blanco wanted a written statement each time, as opposed to talking points. "It was like writing four speeches a day . . . with a lot of crucial details" that had to be right, said Mann. The staff had to obtain the most accurate information from a variety of different sources.

Managing the governor's time was another strategy because "she was beset upon by the press in a way that . . . wasn't helpful," Mann said. Sometimes thirty minutes elapsed before the governor was able to get through the crowd when she arrived for work each morning. At that time of the day, she had not even had the opportunity to gather information. After several days, the PIOs used a back entrance to get the governor into the building. Not having to wade through a sea of reporters made managing media relations much simpler, said Mann.

The Local Journalists' Perspective

As Hurricane Katrina moved toward the Crescent City, the *Times-Picayune* believed it was prepared, Kovacs offered. The newspaper had generators, food, water and internet capabilities. Half of its 270 reporters were deployed to plac-es it usually covered during a storm, including the offices of emergency prepar-edness in each parish,[8] city hall, the Corps of Engineers, city departments and agencies, or "hubs where information was going to flow," according to Peter Kovacs, managing editor for news for the paper (at the time). The *Times-Picayune*, however, did not have anyone in the Louisiana Superdome, which Kovacs called one of the shortcomings of its coverage.

Even with such advanced crisis planning and action, for the *Times-Picayune*, which had covered crises and every hurricane that hit the city dur-ing the paper's history, Katrina was exponentially different. When the storm hit, "We ran a news organization under battle conditions," Kovacs said. Com-munications was "spotty," but "we marshalled the large staff at our disposal with the function of filling up the newspaper." Some of the staff remained in New Orleans, while others eventually wound up in Houma, Louisiana, and in

Baton Rouge and operating out of the Manship School of Mass Communication at Louisiana State University.

Gordon Russell was one of the *Times-Picayune's* city hall reporters who remained in the city. In the days leading up to Katrina, Russell covered Mayor Nagin, the city council, and press conferences regarding the storm. After the storm hit, Russell realized New Orleans was in the midst of a catastrophe when he accepted a ride Monday from New Orleans City Councilman Oliver Thomas to survey the damage. They headed east until they reached a point where the expressway was completely under water and Thomas's SUV could go no farther. When the pair stopped, Thomas looked out to the east with tears in his eyes and said to Russell: "It's all gone. It's all gone" (Russell, personal communication, 2016). That whole part of the city was under water.

Meanwhile fellow *Times-Picayune* writer and editorial board member Jarvis DeBerry had a similar experience when he and several other staff members tried to travel to New Orleans East in one of the newspaper's delivery trucks. They could not get far because the expressway was under water. When they returned to the *Picayune's* office on Howard Avenue, DeBerry wrote what he said remains his shortest piece ever. The blog post in its entirety read: "The service station at Franklin Avenue and the interstate are completely under water" (DeBerry, personal communication, 2016).

As he prepared to go to sleep Monday night, DeBerry saw the headline for the front page of the next day's online edition. Surely, "Catastrophic Breach in the 17th Street Canal Threatens to Drown Entire City" was hyperbole (DeBerry). The next morning he awakened to find fellow staff member Yohana Schindler shaking awake her husband photographer John McKuster and saying, "Come get your camera, get your camera. You have to see this!" DeBerry recalled that everyone at work ran to the windows, and as far as they could see, water was everywhere, He remembered saying, "It looks like we are in the middle of a lake, and are just surrounded by water." In that moment he realized the headline for the day wasn't exaggerated.

With limited resources, journalists were being forced to report as they never had before. Rather than writing stories to go out the next day in print form, they were writing them for immediate publication online, Kovacs said. Like almost everyone in the city, some of the journalists who remained lost their homes. Several stayed with Russell, whose uptown home did not flood and had a working landline telephone. Still, Russell recalled having to go through extreme situations. After compiling information, writing and editing each other's stories or writing pieces together, the reporters used the landline phone to call in and dictate the stories to a staff member who relocated to Houma.

Communication was so limited that Russell did not even know the Times-Picayune office evacuated to Houma. He found out when he stopped at a Wal-Mart to cover looting and ran into fellow *Times-Picayune* reporters. "They told me that everybody left except for us, so we're it," Russell said. Reporters who were embedded in various parts of the city were left behind, and Russell happened to be in that group.

Access to a landline phone that worked became an essential component for the reporters when it came to deciding where they were going to stay and work. Doug MacCash, *Times Picayune* art critic at the time, said the uptown home of fellow writer Stephanie Grace became the newspaper's "bureau" based in part on the fact that the landline was still working" (MacCash, personal communication, November 2, 2016).

Eventually all of the reporters worked out a strategy to communicate with each other or at least know where everyone was staying so they could find each other. The sports editor, David Meeks, oversaw the group. Every morning around sunrise, the group met and discussed what each journalist was doing that day and who was going where.

This lasted for about four weeks until the *Times-Picayune* was able to book rooms for about fifteen reporters at the Sheraton Hotel on Poydras Street, which had backup generators and power. Journalists from other news organizations were already staying there. Roles and beats no longer existed; everyone who was still there had one job, and that was to tell the story. DeBerry said, "It became an all-hands-on-deck type situation."

DeBerry recalled being frustrated with some of his colleagues at the "Laurel Street Bureau" because they were having what he called "professional envy." They were upset that *The New York Times* had a reporter "embedded" with city officials while local reporters were not. "They felt wronged. They didn't understand how an out-of-town reporter was able to have that sort of access and they weren't." This is a common issue within the journalism ranks when national reporters parachute in to cover crisis. But DeBerry had a different mindset and said he told them:

> Our readers don't give a damn about that. They want to know the status of their house. They don't care if you are sleeping on the floor of the mayor's office. They don't care if you have some extra access to some high public official. What they want

to know is... is my house okay? Is my kid going to be able to go to school? Will I still have a job?

—Jarvis DeBerry

DeBerry said he believed that the "hometown" *Times Picayune* reporters were doing a greater good and providing a greater service to their audience— Orleans residents—by providing them with the information they needed to make life-changing decisions.

Journalists Perspective:
The New York Times Covers the Crisis

The New York Times, indeed, had access. It was one of a handful of major news organizations with journalists in New Orleans during Katrina, according to Baranger (2015; Drew), (personal communication, December 2016) and Treaster (personal communication, December 2016). Its reporters were pro- active as the crisis unfolded. As soon as Christopher Drew saw the first report about the breach in the 17th Street Canal levee, he told his editors this would be a major event, and he asked for and received approval to cover the situa- tion. The native Louisianan who had once reported *for* the *Times-Picayune*, grew up not very far from the levee breach. Because the New Orleans airport closed while he was inflight, Drew and fellow New Orleans native and *The New York Times* reporter Susan Saulny flew to Baton Rouge poised to report on whatever unfolded.

In the meantime, Joseph B. Treaster, a business reporter for *The New York Times* who had covered hurricanes and crises all over the world, was already in New Orleans. He arrived in Florida before the weak Category 1 storm hit the state on Thursday. As the storm headed to Mississippi, Treaster and ap- proximately twelve journalists from the *Times* fanned out on the Gulf Coast. Treaster volunteered to go to New Orleans as outbound vehicles carried peo- ple who were heeding Mayor Nagin's mandatory evacuation order and leaving the city (Baranger, 2015; Treaster, 2005, para. 20). "A solid line of cars and trucks streamed out of Louisiana at a slow crawl," Treaster wrote in 2005.

After twists and turns, police roadblocks, following alternate routes, and getting lost a few times, Treaster arrived in the city Monday morning, the day the storm hit. He almost immediately contacted New Orleans Police Superin- tendent Edwin "Eddie" P. Compass. "I told him he was sitting on an historic event and that he ought to have me at his side to document the storm. He said, 'come right over,'" Treaster remembered in 2016. He and a photographer went to City Hall, where Chief Compass not only gave them "a spot on the floor to sleep" in the City's Emergency Operations Center, but two telephones and two computers and Internet access. Treaster and his colleague checked their equipment, "found some cardboard to make a little nicer bed and tried to get some sleep," and rode out the storm. Meanwhile, people all over the city did the same.

At some point after the storm, Treaster began to sleep on a cot that became available, sometimes rotating with other *New York Times* reporters. His colleague Christopher Drew told this interviewer: "We were the only news organization at city hall for the next three weeks and had unfettered and "easy access" to Police Chief Eddie Compass, EOC director Terry Ebert, and other officials in the EOC. At this juncture, Treaster had not attempted to contact the city's communications director, nor had Chief Compass referred him to Sally Forman or Marlon Defillo, one of the public information officers for the police department. Instead, the reporters said they found their own stories and located their own sources, many of whom were in the EOC.

Consistent cell phone service was unavailable in New Orleans, but *The New York Times* sent staff member Walter Baranger to Dallas "with suitcases of satellite telephones" (Baranger, 2015, para. 24). He rented a car, loaded it with camping equipment and drove to Baton Rouge where the newspaper had set up a temporary bureau. Reporters covered official announcements and Governor Blanco's news conferences, and they filed their stories from there.

During the first few days, Drew and Saulny attended some of the briefings the state's office of emergency preparedness held, but, more importantly, they interacted with city council members and other city and state officials who had evacuated to Baton Rouge, some 70 miles west of New Orleans. "We got connected with all of them and even had their cell phones," Drew said. He recalled riding to New Orleans to report one day with city Clerk of Court Arthur Morrell, who drove to the city every day. The reporter also obtained Sheriff Marlon Gusman's phone number. The sheriff became a valuable direct source for a while, according to Drew. Text messages were the best mode of communication because of sporadic voice call service.

Ideally, designated spokespersons should communicate with one voice on behalf of the organization during a crisis, but this was not an ideal or ordinary situation. The New Orleans public information staff of Forman and Davis were unable to play a facilitative role, and the media were on their own. "We did not need anybody to get through to them (officials)," Drew recalled, noting that reporters commented about "how open officials were, dealing with them one-on-one, with no filter." Although Drew and other reporters "appreciated the access," he said Chief Compass could have benefitted from a filter. He remembered the superintendent talking with him under a building overhang about rapes in the Superdome, which turned out to be an unfounded rumor.

On September 1, *The New York Times* ran Treaster's gripping account of what he had witnessed in the Superdome the day before. The voice of a woman he interviewed captured not only the misery of people who were hungry and thirsty in a sea of filth, but also the void created through their isolation: "'They're housing us like animals,' said Iiesha Roussell, 31, unemployed after four years in the Army in Germany, dripping with perspiration in the heat, unable to contain her fury and disappointment at being left with only National Guardsmen as overseers and no information about what might lie ahead" (para. 6).

This represented the kind of information void Forman recognized as a problem because it allowed for rumors and misinformation to take hold and diminish trust in the organization. Ultimately, a negative perception damages the organization's reputation. Roussell had lost faith in city government and felt abandoned. Public relations scholars and expert practitioners all note that organizations must always be aware of the wants and needs of their stakeholders and be responsive. Treaster and *The New York Times* became the voice for Roussell and the thousands of people in the superdome. At the same time, what the newspaper reported created a negative perception of the city that was deep in the crisis.

Unfettered access, in some instances, while creating some problems for the city, also created problems for journalists who accepted and reported what official sources conveyed as fact, but eventually had to correct the record. The rumors about rapes in the Superdome is one example.

One Visible PIO Maintains a Presence

Important to note here is that although the *Times-Picayune* reporters interviewed for this case study did not interact with Forman, Russell and several others quoted Captain Marlon Defillo, public information officer and one of the spokespersons for the New Orleans Police Department, multiple times in their stories following Katrina.[9] In fact, Defillo was featured in news articles in the *Times Picayune* and *The New York Times*, and he gave interviews to both print and broadcast media.

During Hurricane Katrina's aftermath, the New Orleans Police Department (NOPD) patrolled streets, rescued families and became a central source for national news—and even controversy. Defillo maintained a presence and was often a voice for the city. Just as the storm damaged the city, homes, businesses and families, it also ruined the police department's evidence and property room, "where thousands of documents and evidence" were housed (Defillo as quoted in Perlstein & Lee, 2005, para. 4). Defillo explained to two *Times Picayune* staff writers, "We lost everything."

The turmoil in the city seemed endless and was having an impact. In one article titled "7th DAY OF HELL—A week of horror ends with more evacuations and uncertainty," the captain said, "police morale had hit a low point in terms of the stress on officers, who had to try to keep the city safe without a working communications system amid increasing anarchy" (as paraphrased in Thibodeaux and Russell, September 5, 2005, para. 9). He dismissed reports that 60 percent of the force "had bugged out" and hadn't been heard from since the previous Monday. Inoperable communications prevented officers from checking in, he said as he also told Russell and Thibodeaux that officers who had been working non-stop were getting a bit of a breather.

On September 6, Defillo said he did not feel comfortable predicting the death toll, but told *The New York Times* that it would not be low (Applebome, 2005). Two days later, he conveyed the desperation of the situation. Telling *Times-Picayune* writer Brett Anderson that approximately a dozen corpses were taken out of the Superdome, he added, "We're getting to the point where this environment is not safe. We're getting to the point where there are bodies floating on the water" (Defillo, quoted in Anderson & Duncan, 2005). And two days after that, while former Mayor Ray Nagin stated the number of deaths could reach 10,000 for the region, Defillo explained to yet another *Times-Picayune* staff writer that residents were still calling for rescues (Filosa, 2005).

As illustrated above, Defillo talked with reporters almost every day, sometimes providing updates and explanations (Warner & MacCash, 2005), and other times trying to address rumors. It did not appear any topic was off limits. He commented on continuing rescue attempts, accusations of police officers stealing cars from a dealership (Varney, 2005) and additional law enforcement personnel in town to assist NOPD (Baker, 2005). Defillo even commented on the suicide of a fellow police PIO in the days after the storm. For instance, he told an Associate Press reporter: "A public information officer turns the senseless—murder, rape, mayhem—into something orderly for the public. It's like dominoes scattered across a table and putting them in order" (Cain, 2005).

One article referred to Sergeant Paul Accardo as "the public face of the New Orleans Police Department, the spokesperson who went in front of the TV camera on a regular basis . . ." (O'Brien, 2005). The *Times-Picayune* quoted and the reference to Sergeant Accardo as a "public face" reveals that while reporters may not have had access to city communications director Forman or did not remember talking to any PIOs, many journalists, indeed, had access to the spokespersons for the NOPD.

Prior Relationships: Keys to Successful Communication

Literature over the years points to an "antagonistic" relationship existing between practitioners and journalists (Kopenhaver, 1985; Macnamara, 2014; Pincus, Rimmer, Rayfield, & Cropp, 1993). McCollough (2012) argues that "Institutional pressures" impact both sides. "High levels of centralization in state government communication limit the ability of PIOs to meet the needs of journalists, fostering journalists' antagonism and a more combative working relationship" (p. vi). However, in more recent years, more symbiotic relationships are evident because of economics resulting in shrinking newsroom staff who are more reliant on PR practitioners, technology, and to some extent, crises. Yet, crisis or the threat of crisis, has aided in that relationship because both sides know they need each other.

In many instances, prior relationships with local media benefitted Forman, such that although she did not interact with journalists and did not provide timely updates, they understood the effect of the storm on the city and on communication. That is how Russell explained his view. He and Forman had always had a good relationship; however, he said once Katrina hit he no longer had access to information he was accustomed to having. "Everything sort of went haywire and we were all just sort of roaming around trying to figure out what was going on generally."

During the days following Katrina, Russell meandered around the downtown area. City officials were scattered about, and, as Forman noted above, there was no set place for media to get information. "It seemed like the stories were more out on the street, and the city folks didn't seem to have that good of a fix on what was going on, honestly. So, it was more like one of these things where we were just all spanning out around the city trying to figure it out for ourselves," Russell noted.

Forman, recognizing the existing "great relationship" with local media, said she made them a priority for updates. Although that might have been Forman's goal, none of the local journalists interviewed for this chapter remembered ever interacting with Forman or obtaining information from her.

As stated above, staff of United Broadcasters interacted with city officials and became a valuable conduit. In Pierre's view, prior excellent relationships with Forman and Defillo was beneficial for Pierre and colleagues as well as the spokespersons. "We knew them and their caliber of expertise. We knew we could trust their information." In addition, United Radio Broadcasters of New Orleans "did not have the luxury of time." Therefore, they "had to trust" Forman and Defillo "when they called in to disseminate crucial information and updates or arrange interviews for the mayor or police chief. "It was live and raw," Pierre remembered, noting she did not envy the city's public information people who had limited means of communication and had to perform a difficult job against a backdrop or rumors.

In Pierre's view, the trust factor was not evident when interacting with spokespersons for such national entities as the Federal Emergency Management Agency (FEMA) or the Red Cross. They were "too attached to their scripts, their talking points. . . We challenged them because we knew some of what they said was happening, indeed, was not happening. Local people were telling us that contrary to what official spokesperson were saying on the air, call wait times might have lasted hours or distribution centers were not open when and where spokespersons said they were." Echoing what many journalists said, Pierre added, "We had a lack of tolerance for spin." The reference to *spin* confirms a long-standing perception journalists have of public relations practitioners, that is, that they are unprofessional and unethical, do not understand news value, and lack objectivity (Macnamara, 2014).

It is understood that PIOs should behave ethically by telling the truth and facilitating the timely flow of information to and between the citizenry. This involves recognizing and respecting the media's role as the conduit through which information is disseminated. Failure to do so results in the lack of trust and damaged relationships with journalist Pierre alludes to. It goes without saying that journalists must work cooperatively and respectfully with PIOs in seeking the facts and reporting them accurately and without bias or placing blame. Relationships based on trust will lead to enhanced accessibility of journalists to public information officers and the latter's greater success in message dissemination (Broussard, 1986).

Recovery: A Year Later

Forman left city government in February 2006. Six months passed before Ceeon Quiett, communications director for the city of Detroit, arrived in New Orleans to assume that role during the emergency response period that was still going on. The full-time staff consisted of a special events coordinator, a writer and a publicist. An intern from a local university rounded out the team. Some were personally still dealing with the effects of Katrina. Some were commuting to work from other cities or had the majority of their family located in another city.

Securing technology resources was at the top of Quiett's agenda, especially because only a week before her arrival, the full-time technology person resigned (Quiett, personal communication, 2016). Quiett ascertained whether and how she could gain access to e-mail, blogs and a website. Determining exactly to whom they were communicating and where they were located also was a major priority. Quiett needed to understand the budget to address the need for communicating with New Orleanians who were scattered all over the nation. The city was operating with emergency funds, but Quiett knew she needed communication tools and additional staff.

Understanding the media landscape was equally important. Local media were still covering the crisis and national news organizations had opened bureaus in the city. USA Today, CNN, the Associated Press, the Atlanta Journal-Constitution, and others assigned journalists to cover what was taking place every day during recovery. Lastly, the one-year anniversary of Hurricane Katrina was quickly approaching (Quiett).

Faced with a full agenda and limited resources, Quiett said she relied on her past experiences to navigate the new landscape. From her work in Detroit, she understood federal funding, economic development funding and municipal budgets. She also had experience with planning major national events, including playing an instrumental role in planning the funeral of civil rights icon Rosa Parks. The new communications director sought input from people she worked with previously, including the White House parliamentarian.

Quiett methodically developed strategies to tackle the items on her agenda. Email was the best tool to facilitate the flow of information between administration and city officials because many of them were still displaced and working from multiple cities. Knowing that displaced residents needed to have information to make relocation and/or rebuilding decisions, Quiett and her staff developed and kept current a fact sheet on such items as the status of lights, debris removal and state of street signage.

To tackle communicating with people living in other cities, Quiett co-ordinated with mayors of those cities, city council members, communication directors and other administrators to develop what she called "a roadmap of clusters." She learned that large numbers of New Orleanians were in cities throughout Louisiana, as well as Houston, Dallas, Atlanta, and as far as Detroit. The cluster was so large in Houston that its mayor had a designated space for people to obtain information about human resources and fill out various applications. Quiett and other administration officials drove to some cluster cities to hold meetings to update residents on progress being made, and steps they should be taking to prepare to move back.

In January, Quiett successfully added people to her team. She gained permission to "borrow" people from the city's planning and economic development departments. Their positions were already being funded, and their backgrounds in planning and business was useful. They were able to interpret the FEMA planning and funding and communicate it in "very simple easy-to-read terminology." By 2007, Quiett had hired two additional people. The first was a former journalist and communication director for the mayor of Indianapolis. Quiett said she hired him to assist with writing official testimonies city officials needed to deliver at congressional hearings on Katrina and the levee failures. The other hire was a technology person whose main job was to manage the city's website.

One of the most important strategies was the grassroots initiative, Quiett noted. The most important aspects of this strategy were being consistent, having information and making sure city and communications officials had a regular schedule of traveling to area cities to meet with residents if they were planning to come back. The grassroots movement had four levels. Connecting with displaced residents was first. Second, holding small neighborhood meetings at the home of residents. These meetings were called "Conversations with the mayor," and happened in two different types of groups. The first type consisted of 10–15 people in somebody's house with the mayor, police chief and whoever could attend. They would talk about what was happening in ravished neighborhoods and in the city and would also answer displaced residents' questions. The third level involved community groups and small businesses. For example, meetings took place with restaurant owners, beauty shop owners, teachers, and other groups. The final level included city council people by districts.

As noted above, servicing the media is a crucial role of public information officers and in keeping with public relations and crisis communication literature. Quiett understood that and implemented several approaches to accomplish that goal. One included off-the-record informational meetings with media. Hughes and Palen (2012) suggest that the role of PIOs has shifted from gatekeeper of information to translator, making information able to be understood by a larger or different audience. Quiett did exactly that by coordinating with FEMA and local attorneys to create a book she called *FEMA for Dummies*. The book explained key aspects of FEMA such as how federal money flowed, and other information reporters would need to understand to accurately write about the recovery stage. To disseminate the book, the communications director invited news directors, publishers, and all key personnel at all the media outlets in to explain the book's contents. It was important to her to provide them with everything they needed and to keep an open flow of information, she explained. She also held an off-the-record training meeting for media as soon as the city's website was restored. The aim was to demonstrate to media where and how to access information they might need.

Quiett said being prepared for a crisis was very important. Therefore, as the next hurricane season following Katrina approached, she gathered the local media for a meeting. If something were to happen that year, she wanted to know ahead of time who from the *Times-Picayune* and other outlets would remain in the city. She made them a part of the preparation process, obtaining their contact information and where they could ideally be located. "It worked really well," Quiett recalled, noting that the city's communication during the first hurricane a year after Katrina received an "A" from CNN's Anderson Cooper. Offering that she taped and saved that report, Quiett stressed, "We were so well coordinated because we started talking to them (the media) a year out and made them part of the process." She combined her past experience as well as observations of what happened during Katrina to create a strategic plan to aid in the city's recovery.

That fits in with what crisis communication expert Gerard Braud suggests. He says cities and organizations should prepare for unforeseen crises, planning on a "clear and sunny day," before a storm is at their front door (Braud, personal communication, October 2016). He stressed that one has to communicate before, during, and after the crisis, but before is crucial because a plan prior to a crisis happening means the organization doesn't have to figure things out during the crisis. It also allows for PIOs and journalists to share what they learned about crisis communication with other professionals if a similar event happens in another city—and especially when that city is less than 100 miles down the road.

Another Ground Zero:
The Baton Rouge Great Flood of 2016

In many ways, the flooding that occurred in Baton Rouge in August 2016, mirrored the catastrophe Katrina wrought in New Orleans almost eleven years to the day. Although almost 2,000 people died during Katrina, and less than 100 perished in the flooding in the Baton Rouge metropolitan area, the toll in property and misery was similar. The area was not below sea level or shaped like a bowl but three days of nonstop rain proved too much for the rivers, canals and drainages. For instance, in Livingston, the hardest hit of the parishes surrounding Baton Rouge, a whopping 86.6% of the homes flooded (Gallo & Russell, 2016). Fifty-eight percent of homes in Baton Rouge were impacted. Both events displaced people and businesses. Even the basement of the Governor's Mansion flooded and caused Governor John Bell Edwards and his family to relocate.

Similarities were also evident between the two major newspapers for New Orleans and Baton Rouge—the chief being that Peter Kovacs was in a leadership role for both events. He was managing editor for news at the *Times-Picayune* during Katrina. For the Great Flood, he was editor of *The Advocate* in Baton Rouge, which he joined in 2013.

As with Katrina, journalists were negatively affected. One quarter of *The Advocate*'s approximately 400 employees were flooded, according to Kovacs. Likewise, all of the public information officers in the Baton Rouge area interviewed for this book had some connection to Katrina. Richard Carbo, the director of communication for Governor John Bel Edwards, worked for former Louisiana Governor Kathleen Blanco during the storm, and for Louisiana U. S. Senator Mary Landrieu during hurricanes and the BP Oil Spill. He pointed out, however, he had only a small communication role in those crises, but gained valuable insight into how the disasters were handled.

Michael Steele was a seasoned television journalist before becoming a public information officer. As the lead communications person for the Governor's Office of Homeland Security and Emergency Preparedness (GOHSEP), Steele was part of a fifty-five person leadership team engaged in planning and response for crisis situations.

In the nine years Casey Rayborn Hicks had been serving as the public information director for the East Baton Rouge Sheriff's Office, she handled crisis communication during hurricanes, shootings, prison escapes and numerous other incidents. Hicks almost single-handedly was responsible for all external communication from the office to the public and the media, including interviews, press releases, press conferences, videos, social media and speeches (Hicks, email communication, October 11, 2016). Her staff consisted of a secretary who also assisted with public information.

Like Carbo and Steele, Hicks was involved in crisis communication for the two major incidents that occurred in Baton Rouge weeks before the flooding. The first was the police shooting of Alton Sterling, an unarmed black man. The second was the ambush shooting that left three Baton Rouge officers dead and three injured.[10] Two officers with the Baton Rouge Police Department and one with the East Baton Rouge Sheriff's office were killed.

Those crises arguably gave Steele, Carbo and Hicks practice in working together and with media during the flood. Collaboration was the word they used to describe the strategy they employed. The state had a crisis plan and team in place and practiced regularly for emergencies. "Our state Crisis Action Team (CAT) stands up for response during any major emergency," Steele stated (Steele, email communication, October 2016). As soon as it became clear that the flooding was going to be of crisis proportion, the state activated its Joint Information Center (JIC) composed of communications/public information officers from all state agencies; therefore, the governor's team of five, two of whom were seasoned reporters who also had covered storms, reported there.

The PIOs saw a crisis coming the "first day of the weather event,"[11] but it was difficult to determine how severe the conditions and impact would be, largely because the damage occurred in phases after the initial flooding (Steele). Carbo concurred that they were monitoring bad weather, but certainly could not predict "the magnitude of the flood" (Carbo, personal communication, August 2016).

Although the continuous rain caused damage unlike any storm before, it was not called a tropical storm, which, in turn, did not garner the kind of attention a major storm would have. Yet, Carbo offered, "It was so historic and touched places we had never seen before." The gauges that measured

flooding were under water in some places. The governor's concern went beyond the metropolitan Baton Rouge area because the rains and flooding affected "nearly half of the state," Steele noted. (Steele, email communication,
October 2016). According to news reports, seven areas near Baton Rouge
were affected, and flooding reached southwest into Lafayette and New Ibe-
ria (Burgess, 2016; Gills, 2016; Laborde, 2016). Damage spread more than
two hundred miles (Broach, 2016;). Many people did not have access to any
form of communication. The failure of a large cell phone network (AT&T)
further exacerbated the situation (Steele). The GOHSEP's email system also
was down for a while.

During the first week of the crisis, the JIC staff interacted with national and
local media about the same on a first-come, first-served, according to Steele.
They fielded dozens of calls for live radio and TV interview, or for statistics and
other data. However, obtaining data of the "overall scope" was bit challenging,
Steele pointed out, because the flooding was consistently affecting new areas of
the state, and that, in turn, constantly caused the stats to change.

The PIOs operating out of the JIC employed a variety of strategies and
tactics, including press releases and media alerts to proactively communicate
information the public needed to know and to engage the public, Hicks said.
Although one person from the governor's staff monitored news, all of the
PIOs paid attention to the coverage, although that was difficult because there
was so much initial coverage on the local level, however. Others on the communications team responded to media queries. Carbo was with the governor.
All members of the team wanted to disseminate the correct information and
messages "as quickly and effectively as possible" and to "give the public an
outlet and instructional," in Hicks's view.

Information included instructions about how, when and where people
could obtain assistance. Initially, the governor held daily press conferences
that agency and other officials attended but that tapered off gradually. Keeping the media and, by extension, the public informed, was a priority. As Carbo
offered, "We were initially just talking with folks about evacuating or staying
where they were as the storm made its way across south Louisiana." However,
in the aftermath and moving into the recovery phase, press conferences and
briefings disseminated information about where people could obtain assistance
and shelter, register with FEMA. In Steele's view, ". . . some communication
went well . . . but there were still some challenges getting information to all."
Major damage to a cell provider's network disrupted communication. This
was similar to Hurricane Katrina, but this time, users could not text either.

During the immediate aftermath, the inability to provide pictures and videos to support messages was another limitation. As Steele remembered, the state encountered a challenge when it initiated a housing program but did not have pictures or videos to show what people could expect. Once pictures and video became available, the problems decreased (Steele).

Social media also was beneficial in communicating with stakeholders. Facebook Live became an invaluable vehicle to "tell our own story particularly during the flood when we weren't getting the national coverage we needed," Hicks remembered, adding that applied primarily to national media. Calling local media "great," Hicks said they grabbed and used the Facebook live videos in real time (Hicks, personal communication).

Many local journalists were also upset at the surprising lack of attention by the national media. The national media did not take notice of the crisis until late in the week after 6.9 trillion gallons of rain had fallen on Louisiana (Pallotta, 2016). One of the reasons, they argued, was the fact that the storm was unnamed. Mike Scott of the *Times-Picayune* told CNN that the story had been relegated "a secondary story at best" (Pallotta, 2016). Even FEMA administrator Craig Fugate was critical of the national press, saying lack of media coverage in the beginning of a crisis hurt the recovery donations later (Pallotta, 2016). The Twitterverse erupted with citizen pleas and criticism via #batonrougeflood. Local media and local PIOs were joined in their belief that the national media should have done more to help bring attention to this crisis.

Relationships Matter

As this chapter illustrates, scholars and public relations experts argue that a healthy understanding of reciprocal roles decreases antagonism between the two sets of professionals (McCollough, 2012). The PIOs agreed. Prior "strong" relationships with local media enabled the "smooth flow of information to the public," according to Steele. Because of familiarity, "the media knew more about our role and what this office is responsible for," Steele offered. Carbo concurred and Hicks explained.

> Our local media are really great in that they are a part of our community.
> They are invested in our community, and they want to see our community
> succeed and thrive. They still have a job to do, which sometimes include sensation-
> alizing information. So, there's a balance that we try to keep.
> —Casey Rayborn Hicks

Steele said the coverage was "mostly fair" during the emergency phase, but "challenges in the recovery phase" were still difficult to resolve at the time of this writing. Hicks expounded on this by pointing out that everything might be going well in the recovery; however, one person might call the media to complain about an issue. The media would take that one complaint and make it the focus of extensive coverage.

Interacting with national media during the crisis was not as positive as with locals. As mentioned, the national media did not pick up on the magnitude of the flooding and crisis it caused; therefore, the dire situation received minimal national attention "until after the President came, unfortunately," according to Hicks. President Barack Obama toured Baton Rouge on August 23, eleven days after the flooding began (Schleifer, Malloy, & Valencia, 2016). Presidential candidate Donald Trump came on Friday, August 19 (Gray, Schleifer, & Diaz, 2016).

When national journalists finally arrived, according to Hicks, they had a preconceived narrative and only framed their "loaded questions" that pointed to their assumptions. "It's really hard when you are dealing with a media outlet or reporter that has their story already pre-packaged prior to even talking to you." Steele said that relationship with national media is not strong because "many times you are not dealing with the same people from event to event." As Hicks stated, "The national media is here today gone tomorrow and they do not have the same stakes in the success of our community."

Local Journalists' Perspective: Partnerships Are Advantageous

Maya Lau of *The Advocate* covered the Great Flood on the heels of reporting on the shooting and ambush crises. She acknowledged the "chaos," but said she believed PIOs "were doing their best to get pertinent information out" and "there was a more clear [*sic*] sense of partnership in being part of the media to get the word out" (Lau, email communication, October 2016).

The Associated Press's Melinda Deslatte also agreed that the relationship with the PIOs was beneficial. She had covered at least five hurricanes going back to 1999. For Katrina, she was based in Baton Rouge and covering the response of then-Gov. Kathleen Blanco and other state government leaders and agencies to the crisis. She was an Associated Press reporter working and living in Baton Rouge during the Great Flood of 2016.

The AP moved into action on August 12 as the threat of severe weather for the Baton Rouge area became evident. The next day, stories about overnight flooding and water that continued to rise revealed the magnitude of an unfolding natural disaster. Deslatte and another Baton Rouge colleague became the two primary reporters covering the flooding, while staff from the New Orleans bureau also traveled to the area to assist. The AP's team also included photo journalists and editors in New Orleans and Atlanta. (Deslatte, email communication, January 3, 2016).

Because she covered state government, Deslatte knew many of the first responders, as well as Louisiana State Police leaders, local lawmakers whose districts were devastated, and the public information officers who worked for them. She became even more familiar with those communication professionals when she interacted with them during the volatile events earlier in the summer.

During the Great Flood, Deslatte's colleague primarily worked with the PIOs for the Baton Rouge Police Department, and she mainly covered the Louisiana State Police, the governor's office, GOHSEP, and the Department of Children and Family Services, which was in charge of sheltering. Deslatte noted that the PIOs for the East Baton Rouge and Livingston parish sheriff's offices were very helpful; although, her contact with them was not as frequent.

Prior relationships with PIOs served both the reporter and the practitioners well. As Deslatte offered, the more familiar a PIO is with you, the easier the working relationship during a crisis. Knowing the communications directors, press secretaries and other public relations professionals before the flooding was helpful and made access easier. She said they exchanged cell phone numbers and email addresses. Authorities would just call or text her when they had information.

"Having worked with these people before gave them a sense of comfort that they knew the AP could get the information out quickly, in a widespread fashion with accuracy and fairness," Deslatte said.

Another positive aspect of the relationship is the fact that although the AP is an international news organization, officials and their PIOs often view it as local because the reporters live and work in the Baton Rouge area. "The AP was one of the only national press organizations that continued to follow the flooding and its aftermath on a daily basis."

Conclusion

Public communication is an essential aspect of crisis management for governments. This is particularly true of local governments, which are first into an event response and last out, and on the front lines of response and recovery. According to Arpan and Pompper (2003), during crises, proactive communication can improve how journalists perceive practitioners.

Hurricane Katrina was an organic event that illustrates failures and some successes of principals involved in communicating about the crisis. Both public information practitioners for the city of New Orleans as well as local and national journalists learned valuable lessons. Being prepared for any kind of crisis was a main takeaway. As this chapter has shown, the city and its communication office were unprepared and reactive. Based on the city's history with hurricanes, government officials and those who spoke for them should have anticipated that a storm could knock out power and infrastructure, cause massive flooding and disrupt communication.

Forman said in many ways the city failed two major sets of people: the individuals in the Superdome, and the individuals at the Convention Center. Whether they were tourists who fled from a hotel to the convention center, or locals whose home was flooded and they ended up at the Superdome, they didn't know for a long period of time what was going on. They were desperate for information, there was a serious void and the professional communicators failed to fill it.

In Russell's view, several factors exacerbated the crisis. Those included a lack of preparation on the part of the city, as well as failing to understand what was going on, and a lack of understanding of the actual crisis once it began. Russell recalled sitting in a meeting right after the storm hit. He said one of Police Chief Edward P. Compass' main concerns was getting televisions for the Superdome because people were getting bored and restless just sitting there.

"I always think of that because it was one of those moments, in hindsight, that it was clear people didn't really understand what the real problems were yet. It hadn't dawned on everybody that the real problem was going to be the city was flooded and getting everybody out of the city was really the problem," Russell said.

According to Braud, the main problem was that officials failed to plan and were in denial. Calling Nagin the "poster child for bad leadership," Braud said the mayor waited eighteen hours—and only after surrounding parishes acted—to issue mandatory evacuations because he "was in denial about how bad the storm was going to be." The "delayed response and calls to action led to much of the devastation."

Forman confirmed that view when she noted she did not fully realize the crisis that Katrina posed for New Orleans was a national story until she received her first phone call Thursday night, three days after the storm hit. It was the White House saying President George W. Bush was coming to New Orleans and would like to meet with the mayor. The president's staff had heard the WWL interview and told Forman Bush wanted to talk directly to the mayor about some of the negative things he said during the interview.

During Katrina, Mann and the communications team did not have the infrastructure and communication challenges their counterparts were up against. They did face the crush of media, the unrelenting demand for information, specific statistics, requests for interviews and more. Yet, they successfully strategically managed journalists/PIO interactions and relationships.

Mann, as a seasoned crisis communication practitioner, recognized the important role in the media in the unfolding tragedy, placed a value on relationships and trust early on as he considered where to locate the media. He and the team understood that they had to not only service the media, but maintain credibility to ensure the smooth flow of information. That is not to say the Forman did not recognize the need, but, as local journalists noted, circumstances hampered her ability in some ways.

In the case of the Great Flood of 2016, eleven years removed from Katrina and just weeks after two major events that garnered international attention, the state, municipal and parish PIOs were well-prepared and successfully executed crisis communication management and communication. They also benefitted from previous relationships with local media, although they did not have a positive experience with national media.

Coombs and Holladay (2010) argue that, "Managers anticipate crises but they cannot predict a crisis. We might not know when a crisis is likely to happen . . ., so we must be prepared for one at any time" (p. 238). Just as Louisiana residents took what they learned from Hurricane Katrina and applied it to the Great Flood (contact the Cajun Navy to rescue a stranded relative from high water and gut your house within hours of the water receding), so too did the journalists and public relations practitioners. The following are important lessons both learned as well as advice they provided for colleagues and others. The authors also recommend crisis strategies. Again, much of the literature on crisis communication and crisis coverage is based on qualitative and quantitative research that scholars conduct. The information in this chapter, and especially the takeaways, are based on our direct contact with the PR practitioners and journalists in the heart of the crises.

Takeaways for PR Professionals

Create and Execute a Thorough Crisis Plan— Think Worse-case Scenario

Be proactive. Read books, cases studies, playbooks and manuals about crisis management and communication. Then write a plan that maximizes efficiencies, avoids mistakes and considers what will happen when "the big one" hits. As Lukaszewiski (1997) notes, corporate and individual crisis communication standards are crucial. Implement the plan prior to, during and after the event. As part of the plan, conduct planning and training exercises, including regular drills. Make sure the roles of the staff are clearly delineated in the plan. Breaux suggests limiting the number of decision makers in one room to no more than five who serve as representatives from different entities. The team should expect to assume different roles and to manage its time efficiently in order to provide information people need and want to know. Some roles will be in the plan, some will not. Understand that during a crisis, practitioners will have to be flexible and "courageous," Pierre said.

Make Sure the Leader of the Organization Is Prepared for Each Media Venue

Mann remembered what he called a poor strategic decision that ultimately made Governor Blanco look unprepared. He advised her to go to a network or cable TV interview with James Lee Witt, a former FEMA administrator whom the state hired as a consultant to help guide them during the crisis. Witt did 80 percent of the talking because he knew more about dealing with a crisis such as Katrina, while she stood there. That made the governor "look weak and not… not particularly informed," Mann said.

However, according to Mann, his communication team probably spent too much time preparing the governor for the press briefings. She wanted and needed to know everything that was happening to present accurate information.

Braud had two suggestions for the leaders. First, be a leader who is supportive and will let the staff do what is necessary to be successful. And second, certain messages, such as condolences and sympathy, are best coming from the leader—the governor, mayor or official organization spokesperson.

Use All Forms of Media to Quickly Release Accurate Information

Prepare template news releases in advance. Trying to write a release during a crisis can be difficult. However, know when to use news releases prior to, during and after the crisis. Remain cognizant that social media, especially Twitter, can be more successful as emerging details of events change quickly and as the public turns to social media for information. The media attend to social media constantly during a crisis, therefore, assign appropriate staff to monitor and engage media on various platforms. Utilizing pictures and videos on social media is critical to help some understand the scope of an emergency.

Utilize radio. That medium filled an information void during Katrina. Talk radio stations in Baton Rouge provided timely information during the Great Flood of 2016. Radio aired voices of people actually experiencing the flood in certain areas to other people needing information about traffic, flooded streets, shelter location and hours—and how to stay safe. Officials could not always provide this rapid flow of information, but average citizens on the ground could.

Answer phone calls or text message—even if you don't have all the information. It's always better to respond, than to ignore because a piece of information isn't available. Obtain as many facts as possible and as much information as possible then make a statement and share information with media. All practitioners interviewed for this book stressed that misinformation can not only cause confusion, but contribute to the magnitude of the crisis.

Finally, across all forms of communication, do not forget journalists' needs. "Journalists are trying to break a story fast! When PIOs do talk to media, they should keep in mind that the media is looking for three things, a headline, synopsis and a quote," Braud said.

Establish a Command Center and Get to Know Your Fellow PIOs

For government entities, establish a Joint Information Center before the crisis and ensure departments and agencies are staffed and can provide timely information to the PIOs. That would eliminate the need for the PIOs, as Carbo said, "to chase it so much." Establish an ongoing cooperative relationship with other PR professionals who have similar jobs, such as working for varying levels of government. That will facilitate ease of working together during a crisis. Hold regular joint press briefings and/or conferences from this center because reporters want to hear from official sources frequently. A major goal of the joint information center should be convenient accessibility.

Cultivate Relationships, Especially with Local Press

While this is a takeaway for both sides, we will elaborate for each. Establish and cultivate relationships with media personnel prior to a crisis. Make the media part of your crisis communication plan. As Quiett and other professionals have suggested to us, sit down with local journalists to ascertain who has specific beats and in the event of a natural disaster, who would be covering what. Don't wait until a crisis happens; find out who will be the contact and obtain their information ahead of time. And do not view the reporter as the enemy. They too live in your community and can help you help yourself. For example, if a journalist tells you he or she is working on a piece about your company or organization's deputy director... work with the reporter. Talk to that person so that you and the reporter can share information. Such interaction allows you to be fully aware and have some input. Establishing trust and mutual respect will go a long way in a crisis situation.

Go to Where the Reporters Are...Digitally and Literally (or Invite Them to Come to You)

Even if communication technology is unavailable, go out and find where reporters are clustered, exchange phone numbers or the best means of contacting you and then provide frequent updates. As Drew noted, such a proactive stance facilitates the dissemination of information and relationship building that could benefit the spokesperson and the journalists. It also could facilitate the free flow of factual information, as opposed to rumors or misinformation.

Finds ways to contact the national desk of major national news organizations and ask how to contact reporters in town covering the story. Then, reach out to those journalists. Such a proactive approach should go a long way in improving interaction with national journalists who parachute in to cover the crisis.

Allow reporters and photographers to go on rescue missions with first responders, to see first-hand the work that is happening. Remember that jour-

nalists and media organizations are trustworthy vehicles to get accurate information out to the public during a crisis. Social media is not always accurate.

And finally, engage the media on social media regularly and more frequently during a crisis—don't just use the platforms to release information.
Keep in mind the media monitor your organization's social media regularly,
but constantly attend to it during a crisis. Shin and Cameron (2003) predicted technology was showing promise regarding cultivating a professional and
productive mutually beneficial relationship for public relations practitioners
and journalists work in different directions (pp. 253–272). That prediction is
now a reality.

Takeaways for Journalists

Have a Crisis Plan That Includes Potential Community Crises

In addition to obtaining background information about the locale where you
work to help you prepare the plan, keep abreast of issues or concerns in specific regions, such as safety concerning nuclear power plants, weather, education
and poverty. If you live in Dallas-Fort Worth, a crisis plan for a plane crash
at DFW Airport or Love Field is a must. If you live in Baton Rouge, how to
cover a chemical plant explosion would serve the news organization. Once
you have identified potential crises, meet and get to know stakeholders in the
area who will be affected and part of an emergency response. This includes
emergency personnel, first responders, public information officers, business
leaders, those that live near the affected area (airport or plant), the mayor or
chief elected official and other local leaders and officials. That could make the
difference when something happens and PIOs have to select media to embed
in the command center, Quiett maintains, adding, "You want to be the one
selected."

Learn the Specific Roles and Responsibilities of Governmental Agencies and Key Businesses

It is not sufficient to just have a list of authorities—find out how local, state,
and federal agencies operate in the area. Yes, this should be a part of your
routine as you do your job; therefore, during a crisis, you should be able to
call the correct offices responsible for the inquiry you are making. However,
do your homework and become knowledgeable about all aspects of the area

you cover. Various agencies fulfill different functions, and knowing that information in advance saves time and lessens the chance of inaccuracies and frustration. This applies to key businesses in the area as well. Find out their hierarchies, background information, leaders, etc. This will help you be respectful of their time when a crisis situation hits. You will have background information and know their roles; therefore, you will be able to understand the time constraints and other pressures the elected official or PIO is working under and refrain from asking such questions that could put them on the defense.

Maintain Ethics and Accept Responsibility by Acknowledging Inaccuracies, Then, Make the Corrections

In the early hours of a crisis when information is trickling in, mistakes are made. However, they need to be corrected and reported in a timely manner. In the days after the Columbine shooting, it was reported the "Trenchcoat Mafia" was to blame. This is false, yet remains part of the story conversation to this day. Mistakes happen. Confirm everything before it is reported and correct anything that is wrong so that the public will not continue to perpetuate untruths. Ethically accepting responsibility also helps build credibility and trust.

Refrain from Blame

A constant across cases has been the request for the press to refrain from focusing solely on what PIOs (and scholars) call the blame narrative. Practice writing different narratives that contextualize the impact of the crisis on people. As Quiett noted, in addition to writing about the problem-blame narrative, cover the accompanying social impact. For instance, ask whether minorities are disproportionately impacted or how education, transportation are affected. Again, this complaint mainly targeted national media. Therefore, if you're from out of town covering a crisis, try to embed with local journalists who can help you, who can tell you where to go, what things mean and who's who in order to give context and add to the storytelling beyond fault. Recognize that each situation has a different set of dynamics and that reporters also have "to talk to real people as the source material, not just people in positions of authority," Deslatte said. While a sheriff's office or a governor's office can provide the "big picture" information, the people who experienced the losses can better convey the impact of the devastation.

Build Relationships with Public Relations Professionals

"The more familiar a PIO is with you, the easier the working relationship," according to Deslatte. Working with PIOs before the flooding was helpful because Deslatte obtained cell phone numbers and email addresses. When the flooding occurred, she did not have to search through office phone directories. She and the communications officers called and texted when the PIOs wanted to disseminate information and she did the same when she needed information. "Having worked with these people before gave them a sense of comfort that they knew The AP could get the information out quickly, in a widespread fashion with accuracy and fairness." However, be patient and understand the circumstances communications professionals are working under. They may not be able to immediately access the information journalists are seeking.

Takeaways for Both

Prepare a "Go Bag" and Keep Emergency Supplies and Equipment

Always have a kit of supplies and equipment that will get you through days or weeks without communication, food or water. Even a change of clothes would be useful. Hicks told us she keeps a "go bag" in the trunk of her car that contains a rain jacket, boots or tennis shoes. She also always has a portable charger for her phone.

For organizations, keep a stock of essentials for living during a crisis for employees who must remain to manage or cover a natural disaster or other crisis. Essential items include sleeping bags, bottled water, food, and toiletries, extra clothing, at least two cell phones and portable cell phone chargers, and extra batteries, disposable waterproof cameras and other technologies that will enable communication professionals to do their job.

A Plan Is Not Enough

Practice, practice, practice. Be proactive in crisis coverage, planning and drilling so that the responses become learned. In 2017, according to Drew, *The New York Times* still held regular monthly Katrina meetings to discuss how it can continue to deliver the news during an emergency. Drew continued that although satellite phones enabled journalists to dictate their stories to staff in a recording room in New York, the newspaper learned immediately after the storm "that telephone dictation is not acceptable in a web-powered news cycle." Therefore, continually purchase and update technology, providing the necessary equipment and mobile tools to more people in the newsroom.

Take Care of Yourself and Control Your Emotions

Realize that everyone is under tremendous pressure and don't let emotions add to that tension. Mann said he regrets "until this day" a verbal exchange he had with a reporter he had known for years.

Another aspect not addressed fully in this chapter is that local professionals were victims as well. Many professionals from both sides lost their homes during both crises, including WAFB's Kiran Chawla who returned to work every day to report from flooded neighborhoods knowing she did not have a home to return to each night.

Therefore, take care of yourself. If you don't, self-control becomes more difficult and you will not serve your organization. "You've got to eat," Russell said, "and you've got to drink water, and you've got to try to sleep. It's hard when something like this is going on, but if you're sick and not feeling well you can't even do your job.

Notes

1. Each journalist and public relations practitioner cited in this chapter was interviewed only once, unless otherwise noted; therefore, the first citation will provide that information. Individual in-text citations will not continue throughout.
2. For reference, see the National Atmospheric and Oceanic Administration Fact Sheet. Retrieved from: http://oceanexplorer.noaa.gov/backmatter/faqs.html
3. Parent was identified as the fire chief in the following story. "New Orleans firefighter: Hurricane Katrina eyewitness account made me 'Billion Dollar.'" WDSU, Retrieved from: http://www.wdsu.com/article/new-orleans-firefighter-hurricane-katrina-eyewitness-account-made-me-billion-dollar-man-1/3379212
4. For reference, see "Clear Channel Communications, Inc. (2005, September 2). Radio Groups Come Together to Form United Radio Broadcasters of New Orleans." Retrieved from: http://www.csrwire.com/press_releases/26169 Copy also retrieved from the personal papers of Monica Pierre
5. For reference, see the transcript of the interview under the title "Mayor to feds: Get off your asses." CNN, Retrieved from http://www.cnn.com/2005/US/09/02/nagin.transcript/; Also see, Walker, D. (September 2, 2005). Robinette interview with Nagin was unforgetta-

ble radio. NOLA.com/The *Times-Picayune*. Retrieved from http://www.nola.com/katrina/index.ssf/2005/09/robinette_interview_with_nagin_was_unforgettable_radio.html

6. John Verrico, a veteran government relations expert, made those remarks when he was serving as president of the National Government Communications Association in 2015.

7. A *Times-Picayune* article quoted Denise Bottcher, Governor Kathleen Blanco and Robert Mann as they reflected on their crisis communication experience during a discussion at the Public Relations Society of America's 2014 Southwest District Conference.

8. In Louisiana, counties are referred to as parishes.

9. Captain Marlon Defillo was not available to discuss his experience for this chapter. Information herein in based on print articles that quoted him. This author did not consult broadcast transcripts, believing that the flavor of his activities is captured in the print copy.

10. Gavin E. Long killed three police officers and wounded three polices officers on July 7, two days after Alton Sterling's death. The 29-year-old Kansas City, Missouri resident sought revenge for Sterling and another victim slain by police in Dallas. Long was killed at the scene (Sahagun, 2016).

11. It rained continuously for more than seventy hours, beginning on August 12.

References

Anderson, B., & Duncan, J. (2005, September 8). Rescuers face fight from those who won't leave—Nagin says use force to remove holdouts. *Time-Picayune*, p. A04.

Applebome, P. (2005, September 6). In small town, huge morgue takes shape. *The New York Times*, Retrieved from http://www.nytimes.com/2005/09/06/us/nationalspecial/in-small-town-huge-morgue-takes-shape.html

Aronoff, C. (1975a). Credibility of public relations for journalists. *Public Relations Review, 1*(3), 45–56.

Aronoff, C. (1975b). Newspapers and practitioner differ widely on PR role. *Public Relations Journal, 31*, 25.

Arpan, L., & Pompper, D. (2003). Stormy weather: Testing "stealing thunder" as a crisis communication strategy to improve communication flow between organizations and journalists. *Public Relations Review, 29*(3), 291–308.

At Last Communications. (2015). Government communication and public affairs through the eyes of John Verrico. Retrieved from http://www.atlastcommunications.com/our-observations/government-communication-and-public-affairs-through-the-eyes-of-john-verric/ Baker, A. (2005, September 11). Storm and crisis: The police; Duty binds officers who have gone to help after storm. *The New York Times*, Retrieved from http://query.nytimes.com/gst/fullpage.html?res=9F04E3DE1031F932A2575AC0A9639C8B63

Baranger, W. (2015, August 26). Katrina: A turning point at the Times. *The New York Times*, Retrieved from http://www.nytimes.com/2015/08/25/insider/how-we-covered-hurricane-katrina.html?_r=0

Benoit, W. (1995). *Accounts, excuses, and apologies: A theory of image restoration strategies*. New York, NY: State University of New York Press.

Bottcher, D. (2016). Quoted in Lane, E. (2014, October 30). Politics and rumors: Lessons from Hurricane Katrina PR failings. *Times-Picayune*, Retrieved from http://www.nola.com/politics/index.ssf/2014/10/politics_rumors_and_access_les.html

Broach, D. (2016, August 25). Louisiana flooding range shown in new interactive map. *Times-Picayune*. Retrieved from http://www.nola.com/environment/index.ssf/2016/08/louisiana_flood_map.html

Broussard, J. C. (1986). *Establishing a public information office for the city of New Orleans* (Unpublished master's thesis). Louisiana State University. School of Journalism. Baton Rouge, Louisiana.

Burgess, R. (2016, August 16). Lafayette Parish flooding impacts more than 1,500. *The Advocate*. Retrieved from http://www.theadvocate.com/acadiana/news/article_bbbd5382-640f.-11e6-aab1-db50a16c15fd.html

Cain, B. (2005, September 6). Chaos of Katrina drives police officer to suicide. *Associated Press*. Retrieved from https://www.policeone.com/healthfitness/articles/118576-Chaos-of-Katrina-drives-police-officer-to-suicide/

Coombs, W. T. (2006). Crisis management: A communicative approach. In C. H. Botan, & V. Hazelton (Eds.), *Public Relations Theory*, II. Mahwahm, NJ: Lawrence Erlbaum Associates.

Coombs. W. T. (2007). Protecting organization reputations during a crisis: The development and application of situational crisis communication theory. *Corporate Reputation Review*, *10*(3), 163–176.

Coombs, W. T. (2012). *Ongoing crisis communication: Planning, managing, and responding* (3rd ed.). Thousand Oaks, CA: Sage.

Coombs, W. T. & Holladay, S. J. (2010). *PR strategy and application: Managing influence*. Malden, MA: Wiley-Blackwell.

Darling, J. R. (1994). Crisis management in international business: Keys to effective decision making. *Leadership and Organizational Development Journal Annual*, *15*(8), 3–8.

Doorley, J. & Garcia, F. (2015). *Reputation management: The key to successful public relations and corporate communication*. New York: Routledge.

Entman, R. (1993). Framing: Toward clarification of a fractured paradigm. *Journal of Communication*, *43*(4), 52.

Fearn-Banks, K. (2017). *Crisis communications: A casebook approach* (5th ed.). New York, NY: Routledge.

Filosa, G. (2005, September 10). Door-to-door searches turning up … not much—Empty homes hint at fewer deaths in Lower 9th Ward. *Times-Picayune*, p. A-11.

Gallo, A., & Russell, G. (2016, August 19). Sobering stats: 110,000 homes worth $20B in flood-affected areas in Baton Rouge region, analysis says. *The Advocate*. Retrieved from http://www.theadvocate.com/louisiana_flood_2016/article_62b54a48-662a-11e6-aade-afd357ccc11f.html

Gill, S. (2016, September 28). Zachary Chief David McDavid recounts August flooding, provides update. The *Advocate*, Retrieved February 08, 2017, from http://www.theadvocate.com/baton_rouge/news/communities/baker/article_e7a5cffe-8423-11e6-9cf1-578d465772fc.html.

Gitlin, T. (1980). *The whole world is watching: Mass media in the making & unmaking of the new left*. Berkeley, LA: University of California Press.

Goffman, E. (1974). *Frame analysis: An essay on the organization of experience*. Cambridge, MA: Harvard University Press.

Graber, D. A. (1992). *Public sector communication: How organizations manage information*. Washington, D.C.: Congressional Quarterly, Inc.

Gray, N., Schleifer, T., & Diaz, D. (2016, August 19). Trump, Pence tour flood damage in Baton Rouge. Retrieved February 06, 2017, from http://www.cnn.com/2016/08/18/politics/trump-pence-headed-to-baton-rouge/.

Hughes, A. L., & Palen, L. (2012). The evolving role of the public information officer: An examination of social media in emergency management. *Journal of Homeland Security and Emergency Management, 9*(1), 1–20.

Kempner, M. W. (1995). Reputation management: How to handle the media during a crisis. *Risk Management, 42*(3), 43–47.

Kopenhaver, L. L. (1985). Aligning values of practitioners and journalists. *Public Relations Review, 11*, 34–42.

Laborde, L. (2016, August 23). Louisiana floods: Mapping the impact across the state. *Curbed New Orleans*, Retrieved February 6, 2017, from http://nola.curbed.com/maps/2016-louisiana-floods-damage-map

Lindell, M. K. (2013). Disaster studies. *Current Sociology Review, 61*(5–6), 797–825.

Lukaszewski, J. E. (1997). Establishing individual and corporate crisis communication standards: The principles and protocols. *Public Relations Quarterly,42*(3), 7–14.

Macnamara, J. (2014). *Journalism & PR: Unpacking 'spin', stereotypes, and myths*. New York, NY: Peter Lang.

McCollough, C. (2012). *Pressures, centralization, economics, technology, and ethics: Factors, that impact public information officer-journalist relationships*. Unpublished doctoral dissertation. School of Mass Communication. Louisiana State University, Baton Rouge, LA.

McQuaid, J., & Schleifstein, M. (2002, June 23). In harm's way. *Times-Picayune*, Retrieved from http://www.nola.com/environment/index.ssf/2002/06/in_harms_way.html.

McQuaid, J., & Schleifstein, M. (2002, June 23–27). Washing away: Worst-case scenarios if a hurricane hits Louisiana. *Times-Picayune*, Retrieved from http://www.nola.com/environment/index.ssf/page/washing_away_2002.html

Miller, A., Roberts, S., & LaPoe, V. (2014). *Oil and water: Media lessons from Hurricane Katrina and the Deepwater Horizon disaster*. Jackson, MS: University Press of Mississippi.

Newsom, D., Turk, J., & Kruckeberg, D. (2013). *This is PR: The realities of public relations*. Independence, KY: Cengage Learning.

O'Brien, K. (2005, September 5). Amid horror, 2 officers commit suicide: 'World can't understand'. *Boston Globe*, Retrieved from http://archive.boston.com/news/nation/articles/2005/09/05/amid_horror_2_officers_commit_suicide/

Pallotta, F. (2016, August 18). National media criticized over Louisiana flooding coverage. *CNN*. Retrieved from http://money.cnn.com/2016/08/18/media/louisiana-flooding-media-coverage/index.html

Perlstein, M., & Lee, T. (2005, September 1). As evidence floods, criminal cases likely collapse: Court basement also housed thousands of appeals. *Time-Picayune*, p. 6.

Pincus, J. D., Rimmer, T., Rayfield, R. E., & Cropp, F. (1993). Newspaper editors' perceptions of public relations: How business, news, and sports editors differ. *Journal of Public Relations Research*, 5(1), 27–45.

Sahagun, L. (2016, July 18). Baton Rouge police shooting updates: Gunman had been in city for several days before attack, police say. *Los Angeles Times*. Retrieved February 06, 2017, from http://www.latimes.com/nation/la-na-baton-rouge-police-killed-live-updates-htmlstory.html

Schleifer, T., Malloy, A., & Valencia, N. (2016, August 23). Obama tours Louisiana amid criticism that he's late. *CNN*. Retrieved February 06, 2017, from http://www.cnn.com/2016/08/23/politics/obama-louisiana-tour-criticism/

Shin, J. H., & Cameron, G. T. (2003b). The interplay of professional and cultural factors in the online source-reporter relationship. *Journalism Studies*, 4(2), 253–272.

Steele, M. 2016, October 16). email communication.

Tankard, J., Hendrickson, L. Silberman, J, Bliss, K., & Ghanem, S. (1991). *Media frames: Approaches to conceptualization and measurement*. Paper presented at the meeting of the Association for Education in Journalism and Mass Communication, Communication Theory and Methodology Division, Boston, MA.

Thibodeaux, R., & Russell, G. (2005, September 5). 7th DAY OF HELL—A week of horror ends with more evacuations and uncertainty. *Times-Picayune*, p. A01.

Treaster, J. B. (2005, September 1). Superdome: Haven quickly becomes an ordeal. *The New York Times*, Retrieved from http://www.nytimes.com/2005/09/01/us/nationalspecial/superdome-haven-quicklybecomes-an-ordeal.html

Treaster, J. (2015, August 26). The hard road to the Big Easy [Web log post]. Retrieved from https://www.nytimes.com/2015/08/25/insider/september-13-2005-the-hard-road-to-the-big-easy.html.

Varney, J. (2005, September 29). N.O. cops reported to take Cadillacs from dealership: Foti investigating looting allegation. *Times-Picayune*, p. B01.

Warner, C., & MacCash, D. (2005, September 26). N.O. moves past setback from Rita—Power restored. *Times-Picayune*, p. A01.

· 3 ·

DEATH AND BRAND LOYALTY

The Sticky Case of Blue Bell Ice Cream

Andrea Miller

If you live in the South and Southeast and celebrate birthdays, graduations, Fourth of July, Memorial Day, Labor Day or any other holiday or milestone, you know the summer of 2015 as the summer of NO Blue Bell Ice Cream. Consumer memes took over social media feeds, conveying frustration with the brand's absence:

> Let me break this down for Northerners who can't understand the tragedy of recent events: The Blue Bell recall doesn't mean we're down a brand of ice cream. We don't BUY other brands of ice cream. The Blue Bell recall means WE ARE OUT OF ICE CREAM.

> I had no Blue Bell ice cream to drown my sorrows after watching Grey's Anatomy last night.

> Blue Bell. Ice cream so delicious that we killed people and you don't even care.

"I don't think I've ever seen anything like this in my career," Dr. Lance Porter,[1] former advertising professional and current professor in digital advertising at Louisiana State University said referring to the rabid brand loyalty. "They are kinda the Disney of ice-cream… You know, there's ice-cream and there's Blue Bell" (personal communication, October 10, 2016).

Timeline of Events

Blue Bell had been a family owned business for more than 108 years when the crisis hit. The logo of the company is a little girl in a dress and a hat leading a dairy cow by a rope. Its television advertisements feature open countryside and delivery men wearing bow ties. The ad conjures up smiles and melancholy as the voiceover sings "Blue Bell, the best ice cream in the country." Based in Brenham, Texas, it has production facilities in Brenham, Broken Arrow, Oklahoma and Sylacauga, Alabama. In early 2015, it had plans to expand its reach to a 23rd state.

But by mid-March of 2015, Blue Bell announced its first-ever recall after five people in Kansas developed listeria after eating its ice cream products. Three of those people died. But what was not communicated to the public was that a month earlier state health officials found Listeria monocytogenes, the germ that causes listeria, in products during routine sampling at its South Carolina distribution center (Levin, 2015). According to the Centers for Disease Control and Prevention (2018), listeriosis is a serious infection that primarily affects pregnant women, newborns, older adults, and people with weakened immune systems who have eaten contaminated food. Symptoms can vary depending on who is infected, but most common include fever and diarrhea. However, it can be life-threatening for those special populations (CDC, 2018). A quiet withdrawal had already been taking place at some retailers and hospitals (Levin, 2015).

Business reporter Karen Robinson-Jacobs of *The Dallas Morning News* (June 28, 2015) reported, "The March 13 recall notice came as a terse, six-paragraph statement that pointed the finger at a specific production line that put out a 'limited' amount of product. The release noted that 'all products produced by this machine were withdrawn. Our Blue Bell team members recovered all involved products in stores and storage.'" After this information came to light, Robinson-Jacobs said getting answers to any questions from Blue Bell was very difficult (personal communication, August 31, 2016). For example, Robinson-Jacobs said in a response to an email inquiry, Blue Bell challenged criticism that it should have notified the public about the health threat and quiet recall sooner.

On April 3, Blue Bell shut down the Oklahoma plant after tracing back the outbreak. Ten days later Blue Bell assured grocery stores that its products were safe and large chains moved to restock shelves. But the move proved premature. On April 20, more samples tested positive for the bacteria, all Blue

Bell products were recalled and consumers were told to throw away all ice cream in their freezers. And the memes began:

> I see you're still eating Blue Bell ice cream after the recall. I too like to live dangerously.

> It's been raining in Texas since Blue Bell closed… because God is crying.

The following day CEO Paul W. Kruse released a 32-second video apologizing to loyal fans and customers saying he was "heartbroken." He continued by saying "we are committed to fixing the problem" and that "we're going to get it right."

In May, Blue Bell announced it would shut down all of the company's ice cream plants to conduct comprehensive cleaning programs and new worker training, but that did not hold off the inevitable. A massive round of layoffs and furloughs followed for Brenham employees. Thirty-seven percent of its workforce was let go and more than 1,400 furloughed (Heneghan, 2015). Also in May, the first lawsuit was filed.

> But Blue Bell… Summer is coming!

Karen Robinson-Jacobs is a business reporter for *The Dallas Morning News* who has worked in journalism for about 30 years. Her beat includes the food sold at grocery stores and public health issues, so the recall fell into her purview.

"As time went on, there were more tests done by more health departments and it became clear that the problem was more widespread than what they had initially thought and that lead to… shutting down all production at all four plants and recalling all product, which was pretty unprecedented in the consumer packaged goods space," Robinson-Jacobs said.

In July, after all plants were cleaned and procedures were put in place to test product on a regular basis, test production began at Blue Bell's Sylacauga, Alabama plant. At the same time, a $125 million investment by prominent Texas billionaire Sid Bass was announced. Bass now owned 33 percent of the company.

After receiving approval from Alabama health officials, Blue Bell began shipping ice cream from its Sylacauga facility and Blue Bell products returned to stores in limited parts of Texas and Alabama. And the meme creators rejoiced:

> Hallelujah!!! Blue Bell is back!

> Brace yourselves. Photos of people eating Blue Bell are coming.

While back in most major markets by October of 2016, Blue Bell's sales remained down by half from the same time the previous year and the company was issued an $850,000 fine from the Texas Department of State Health Services for the listeria outbreak (Blunt, 2016). In 2014, Blue Bell was the nation's fourth largest marketer of ice cream, with an estimated $680 million in sales (Porjes, 2015). The company was still working to regain its title as the third highest-selling brand of ice cream in the country when it found itself in another sticky situation. When it reintroduced the fan favorite cookie dough earlier in the year, it contracted with a small Iowa company named Aspen Hills to make the cookie pieces. A discovery of the listeria bacteria in some Aspen Hills unopened packages of cookie dough triggered yet another recall (Aspen Hills denies it was source). The recall included all half gallons and pints of Chocolate Chip Cookie Dough and Cookie Two Step sold to retail outlets in 16 states (The latter was a new and heavily-promoted flavor) (Chamlee, 2016).

The Communication Response, or Lack Thereof

Robinson-Jacobs said throughout the crisis, getting information from Blue Bell was like pulling teeth. "I would have to say [Blue Bell] was not the most forthcoming company that I've ever dealt with," Robinson-Jacobs said. "One of the big challenges, I would say, is they still thought of themselves as a small company, so they essentially had two people doing media relations, and for a little while they brought in an outside consultant who was not all that great frankly... I believe they underestimated this from start to finish. They underestimated how big the problem was. They underestimated how much they needed to communicate." She continued that most of their communication consisted of posting press releases on the website and that they did not have much of a social media presence.

Mass communication scholars as well as professionals would argue this is a technique called stonewalling, where there is an effort to either hide or delay the release of information. In a case such as this, the PR practitioners, whether intentional or unintentional (overwhelmed with requests) are not operating within the public's interest. Stonewalling also erodes any trust or relationship the PR side has with the media. It should be noted here, that a formal written request and a telephone request for an in-depth interview for this book were declined.

Robinson-Jacobs said Blue Bell insisted that she send questions via email. She would send ten questions and maybe a day later they would return answers to three questions and not address the other seven. She said this became a regular "little dance" she went through to get information.

"I think part of it was they just weren't used to the media, and part of it was it became an international story and they're like getting calls from like Sweden, you know, all over the place and they basically had two people dealing with it, and it was not sufficient. It was not sufficient. The people that they had didn't understand sort of really how to get out in front of the message and there weren't enough of them. So you know, I understand that they were working you know around the clock, but, you know (claps hands and sighs), this is a public health issue, and I felt like they really…it was just maddening sometimes, especially on deadline it was just maddening."

And she was very annoyed to find the answers to her email questions in other media outlets—mostly in national outlets, such as *The Wall Street Journal*. "What is up with that?" she said. "I mean from their standpoint, I guess they're figuring, 'Hey they have a national audience so we need to get to them first.' But I mean the fact of the matter is the vast majority of their sales still come from Texas, and I'm Texas."

She said in other crises and events she has covered the same scenario plays out. The public relations people become enamored by the interest from the national press. But she said, it is important to not leave out the local press. "I would remind them as I remind other people, I will be here when *The New York Times* is gone. I will still be here, and you will still have to deal with me because I'm not going away," she laughed.

Robinson-Jacobs said Blue Bell often fell back on the excuse that there was only two of them handling communication for what turned out to be an international story. "They were not ready. They, they truly underestimated every single aspect. They underestimated how much they were going to have to communicate, they underestimated how many people they were going to need, they underestimated the (times 3) media savviness of the people they had delivering the message," Robinson-Jacobs said.

The Role of the Consumer in Communication

Blue Bell, however, as the event progressed, was quite cognizant that it had a number of other effective communicators on its team. A crisis is a major occurrence with potentially negative outcomes affecting the organization, company, or industry, as well as its publics, products, services, or good name

(Fearn-Banks, 2012). The perception of an unpredictable event threatens important expectancies of stakeholders related to health, safety, environmental, and economic issues, and can seriously impact an organization's performance and generate negative outcomes (Coombs, 2015). Initially, it appeared that Blue Bell did not recognize or understand that it was an organization in crisis or how to manage one or communicate effectively. A company needs to seek to understand its situation. It may take time, but follow the fact-finding phase with information, transparency and accountability. Crisis communication is the dialog between the organization and its publics, in this case ice cream consumers, prior to, during, and after the negative event. Blue Bell did not understand it was in crisis and by the time it did, an alternative strategy had already been formed. Crisis communication response should be used to lessen the effects, these negative outcomes, but for Blue Bell, the communication cross was taken up by another constituent. As shown earlier through meme examples, customers flooded the internet via social media with unprecedented support. It was an unexpected *positive* outcome for the company, but not for the media. The social media response from their loyal customers helped the brand survive, but it also appeared to enable the company's limited release of information and noncooperation with the press. Robinson-Jacobs said she struggled with the social media reaction just as she did with the company's response. She felt as if journalists and those involved in food safety were the only ones seeking more information about the cause and resolutions of the recall.

"There was not a great clamor on social media for a lot more transparency on their part. It was much more like, 'Oh we just love you, Blue Bell.' You know stuff like 'hang in there,'" Robinson-Jacobs said. "And so absent a big outcry from the public, I don't think they felt as compelled to move as quickly and to be as transparent, as if there had been a big groundswell. WE needed to nudge them a little more, but, you know, they could just say, 'Hey look see they love us.'"

Digital Advertising Professor Porter agreed. He said Blue Bell may have taken advantage of the consumers' goodwill and used it to not respond to the press. "After they saw the power of it, after holding the product out for so long and then bringing it back and the reaction of it coming back, [it] could have given them a false sense of 'oh well we really don't have to respond and you know people love us so much that why should we talk to these reporters they're only going to print bad news," Porter said.

Robinson-Jacobs said in terms of business numbers, the company also relied on the fact that it is a privately held company and are not required by law to disclose sales numbers. She said because the public was so invested in the brand, she felt more of a responsibility to get all the questions answered.

Crisis communication scholar at Texas A&M University Timothy Coombs said family-owned companies see crises differently. He said for them crisis is personal because it is the family business, and not just a simple financial stake. He said the brand and the business are seen as a part of the owner's identity (personal communication, September 29, 2016). In this case, it appeared the consumers felt the same way.

Robinson-Jacobs continued, "I struggled with that the entire time... Even though people were, deaths were linked to their product, the public was like, 'well we love Blue Bell, and we don't know those people. We know Blue Bell.'"

Unprecedented Brand Loyalty

Branding expert and Professor Porter said there are not many brands that could survive a total recall of product. But Blue Bell, he said, is different. He equates the popularity as being tied to sentimental attachment to region and the culture of the region—similar to Coca-Cola in the south or Ben and Jerry's ice cream in New England. If you show up at a party with another brand of ice cream, you will be made fun of or chastised. Blue Bell is a lifestyle, tied to all feel-good moments.

"I think that there's something at play here with the company being local and southern and family owned and tied into its ice cream. So, you know, a symbol of being an American and all the things that people really care about in this region so it fits into that whole situation so the brand is really tied up in all of that," Porter said.

Robinson-Jacobs said the people she interviewed for stories after the total recall surprised her. When asked if they had Blue Bell in their freezers, she said they responded, "heck yeah" and planned to eat it. She said many even said they were buying more and stocking up and were comfortable with taking the chance that it was contaminated.

Because of that intense brand loyalty, Porter said the company would have to intentionally harm its customers to make these super fans switch brands. In terms of crisis communication research, the consumers perceived the crisis as an accident, not intentional. Therefore there was a low attribution of crisis responsibility attributed to Blue Bell. Situational Crisis Communication Theory (SCCT) says that fact makes it easier to forgive and move on (Coombs, 2007; Coombs & Holladay, 2002). For the consumers, there was little damage to reputation. However, the company did issue an apology, which according to SCCT, is usually a strategy reserved for high perceived crisis responsibility. An apology is also an accommodative strategy used to begin rebuilding the relationship. PR Institute President Tina McCorkindale said in terms of textbook crisis cases and in terms of PR theory, the Blue Bell brand should have been ruined or in the very least, tarnished. She said when you add in the human element, it muddies what people are willing to accept and how far they will go to remain loyal (personal communication, June 22, 1016).

Advertising brand expert Porter said that you cannot top the kind of brand loyalty that is driven by the customer. He said the grassroots effort had nothing to do with Blue Bell's crisis communication or again, lack thereof: "So many people waiting with bated breath for the product to recover and be back in stores and you know all the photos of empty spaces within stores and you know there's been some, it's just amazing," Porter said. "When I look at what was there it is purely people with true fandom for the product and so it didn't appear to be seeded by Blue Bell or encouraged by them in any particular way from my perspective. It was actually real love for the product. You can see the power of that brand as they were able to recover quickly from this."

Blue Bell vs. Chipotle

The PR professionals we talked to, have never seen such brand loyalty. Chipotle, a publically traded company, went through a food illness crisis the same year as Blue Bell. Even though its communication efforts were visible and more widely praised, the brand took a serious financial hit. We wanted to compare both cases, because the negative and positive outcomes have been very different.

In November of 2015, Chipotle temporarily shut down dozens of West Coast locations after public health officials linked the Denver-based burrito chain to an outbreak of E. coli (Czarnecki, 2017). In the months following, separate outbreaks linked to the chain occurred—norovirus in California and salmonella in Minnesota (Czarnecki, 2017). Chipotle responded to the crisis appropriately by mapping out, in a statement, its solutions to the problems such as sanitizing restaurants and replacing all food items (Czarnecki, 2017). On

December 10, founder Steve Ells went on the *Today Show* and apologized to those who got sick (Carufel, 2015). Less than a week later, he apologized in full-page ads in newspapers across the country (Carufel, 2015). These steps follow textbook crisis communication response that often begins with an apology, then informs stakeholders what happened and what steps are being taken to ensure this will not happen again. Blue Bell also apologized, but has never, according to Robinson-Jacobs, addressed the deaths. But less than a week after Chipotle's efforts, the restaurant chain was blindsided with a second, smaller E. coli outbreak and in the same month faced a norovirus outbreak at Boston College that sickened at least 120 students (Czarnecki, 2017). In February 2016, the company halted lunch operations at all locations to host a nationwide retraining session on food-safety procedures held via video conference (Czarnecki, 2017). But in March 9, another positive test surfaced and perhaps became a nail in the coffin. A Chipotle location in Massachusetts closed after yet another employee tested positive for norovirus (Czarnecki, 2017). The coast to coast, repeated outbreaks had caused sustained damage to the company. The financial ramifications of this extended food safety crisis bled in to 2017. Crisis communication scholar Timothy Coombs said that crisis in the food industry operates on a different timetable. He argues that the communication response can be slow because the company, in conjunction with governmental food safety experts, have to track the problem and find its source. The process takes time. He said he believes Blue Bell did the best it could given that it was the company's first big food safety issue. "There's nothing stellar in their performance," Coombs said. "I don't think they were bad either. In terms of what they did, I think it was a pretty normal response in what they did as a food company."

But Susan Porjes, a food industry analyst who has been writing about the consumer packaged goods market for 25 years, felt Blue Bell was a little more humble than many companies that face outbreaks (personal communication, Aprils 27, 2016). In fact throughout the crisis, Porjes wrote, most media—and even the FDA and state health agencies—went easy on Blue Bell, citing the company's cooperation and "humility and accountability" (Heneghan, 2015). She also pointed to the fact that it was the company's first recall in its 108-year history and that the federal government declined to press criminal charges.

In contrast, the response to Chipotle Mexican Grill's series of food safety problems in that same year, did not enjoy the consumer or institutional support. In fact, according to Porjes, even though the founder apologized, the company's top executives developed a cocky, antagonistic relationship with the media and even the U.S. Centers for Disease Control (CDC). She said serious health violations seemed to be ignored and the company's "Food with Integrity" mantra was questioned and excoriated. While Blue Bell appeared to have turned a corner, Chipotle's stock value and revenues continued to plunge.

According to Porter, the problem with Chipotle was that the negative outcomes were tied to the company's brand identity. Chipotle prides itself on no preservatives and an open air restaurant, so the problem, he said, was a legitimate flaw in the design. Unlike Blue Bell, Chipotle has brick and mortar spaces.

> Their brand is that it's fresh and it's small farms and it's organic and all those things. And then all of a sudden people start getting sick because it's those things that's a problem. And so they had to go back and reconfigure publicly and they are also a retail establishment so you walk into their place of doing business and you see whether or not they have those safeguards, the problems that the way that the system was set up was causing the issues. So it's still, when you go in there, you still kinda think well is that really that different than it was before? And what have they changed? And it's not visually apparent that they had and so the retail part of Chipotle is part of their brand and Blue Bell doesn't have those problems they can fix it on the back end. (Lance Porter, personal communication, October 2016)

Robinson-Jacobs argued that Blue Bell's brand is tied up in its family-owned, homespun, little kid with a cow, Texas pride. "Whereas Chipotle I don't believe the people in Denver or Colorado have the same feeling. Nobody grew [up] with Chipotle. There are generations here that Blue Bell is part of, has been part of every 4th of July celebration, Memorial Day, blah, blah, blah. Kids' birthday parties—it's been part of their…they're sort of associating Blue Bell with their own life story in a way that does not apply to Chipotle at all. Chipotle was a source of food. People talked about Blue Bell as a source of comfort, and that was the difference," Robinson-Jacobs said.

But it has not been all meadows and cute dairy cows for Blue Bell either. *The Dallas Morning News* considered the Blue Bell recall a business story mainly because at first, no one knew how bad it was or was going to get. The health reporter at the time Sherry Jacobson (now retired) said the problem with Blue Bell was that they did not report early on contamination that was widespread. Jacobson said the company did a poor job of testing it products and was hesitant to believe the company had a problem. "They believed their own PR," Jacobson said. "They started out by saying it was just the institutional products, you know, the stuff that went to hospitals and nursing homes, which is terrible. Because those are the most vulnerable people eating it. Okay. And then, it wasn't until later that they admitted that it was everything and… my daughter was pregnant at the time, and we had Blue Bell ice cream… She was at risk, eating that at my house. And so I was absolutely upset that it took so long for them to acknowledge how widespread the issue was. And that everybody needed to stop eating everything."

Back on the Shelves

Social media can also play an important role in later crisis stages (after a crisis is already well-known and widely spread) by providing emotional support to consumers (Liu, Austin, & Jin, 2011). In this case, the consumers on social media were rabid even asking for prayers for Blue Bell, like the company was a sick family member who needed help. All were feeling the loss. Less than two weeks before Blue Bell began restocking stores in a strategic and geographic roll out, it unveiled the flavors in what it called the "starting line-up." Perhaps recognizing the power of the picture and the meme brought to the forefront of the visual agenda by their customers, the announcement appeared on social media. The announcement was made on the company's newly created Instagram page on August 21, 2015, ten days before the August 31 rollout.

"It's a continuing challenge that every brand faces which is how do you decide who to respond to and when because of the nature of the communication field now," Porter said. "It's a challenge to really get your arms around who to talk to and when and through what channel. So they have to continue to, because of the precarious situation they're in right now with this second situation, they have to be even more interactive with their audiences rather than thinking about okay we're releasing this information and then we're done. They have to actually be forthcoming to their audiences."

Food analyst Porjes said, because the recall was about food that we all consume, it is more than being interactive. Blue Bell had a special obligation, a responsibility, to communicate and did not do so. Stakeholder expectations are simple according to Coombs, when you fly commercially, you expect the plane to take off and land safely. If you buy food from the grocery story, you expect that food to taste good and not harm you. Porjes continued that retailers, manufacturers, restaurants and food services have an obligation because they affect so many consumers directly. "If you're studying something about education, for instance, that may affect only the students who go to one university," Porjes said. "But if you're studying something about food poisoning— that is widespread. That can affect anyone in any part of the country."

Takeaways for PR Professionals

Take Advantage of Your Customer's Positive Branding Efforts (Unique to This Crisis)

The rabid customer loyalty displayed in the memes featured in this chapter, is what makes this case study so unique. When the brand loyalty is at this influential level, PR professionals need to take full advantage of the customer's goodwill and build on their efforts to help save the brand. The positive branding is coming from the consumers, not the company, and can be strategically harnessed as one part of a crisis communication strategy.

Don't Hide Behind Your Customers' Goodwill

However, a company should not hide behind their customers, relying on the goodwill to shield them from scrutiny or transparency. Withholding information hurts the relationship with the press and destroys any goodwill that the company will need from media outlets in the future. Again, repeated attempts to interview Blue Bell representatives for this book were ignored, but eventually declined.

Have a Crisis Plan in Place That Includes a Staff That Can Handle the Increase in Requests

In the cases explored in this book, organizations never have enough staff (or experienced staff) when crises hit. But if you have a plan in place and if you assess the enormity of the crisis early on, the staff will have a playbook to follow that will help in the response. Be transparent with the media about the overwhelming response. But just as companies should not hide behind customer goodwill, they should not use a lack of staff or resources as an excuse not to respond. Again, there is never going to be enough staff to handle thousands of media requests. Both sides acknowledge this. Don't allow it to paralyze your efforts. Keep moving forward by using strategies and techniques offered in this book to handle the communication duties necessary in crisis. For example, find mass ways to answer reporters' questions with press releases or website information and press conferences. But go beyond a typical press conference by including topic experts (food safety scientists) who join the communication professionals at the podium.

Open the Lines of Communication Early

A quick response (right out of the gate) must be part of that communication plan.

"I think they need to communicate fully and fast," Porjes said. "That's what people want. 'We are horrified to find out that… whatever' and 'We will do our best to make sure that we track it down and that it never happens again.' They have to take action fast, because, especially, with social media… the word gets out very fast. There has been a crisis. They can't wait a week to respond to it."

Respond in a Thorough and Timely Manner

If reporters do not get the information from you in hours or days or weeks, they will seek other, perhaps not as well-informed sources. In the case of a food safety issue, where everyone has a chance to get sick, information is of the utmost importance. If you do not know the answer quite yet, tell them you will find out and get back to them. This is an acceptable response. Again, radio silence or a delayed, half-attempted response is not acceptable.

Takeaways for Journalists

Be Persistent and "Nudge"

As we have seen with other cases, and as PR experts have told us, in a crisis situation, the first instinct is to shut everything down and not talk. That is the worst idea for a company because as Porter said, journalists can "can smell that a mile away." Reporters must be persistent and continuously nudge public relations professionals to get the information not only that they need for their stories, but that the readers and viewers need to make good decisions.

Robinson-Jacobs said, "They felt like they could wage a war of attrition, and, you know, well if we don't answer these questions, she'll just stop asking. And I said this to them, I am not going away (claps for emphasis). I am not going away. I am here. I'm going to send you back these same questions over and over and over again until I get something that looks like an answer."

Stand Up for Local Media

This has been a crisis constant across all of the cases. Companies tend to want to work with national media outlets first, leaving the local or statewide media on the back burner. Stand up for your community (perhaps reminding them that most of their sales are in the state you cover) and remind the company of the importance of the local media to get the story and the context right and sent to the right audience.

"Work with the local media first because they're going to be there, and we're always objective but, we're probably going to come at from a different angle than the national press. So, I think they do themselves a disservice by running to the national press first," Robinson-Jacobs said.

Crisis Outcomes Can Guide Your Storytelling

Instead of a simple story on the recall, a food safety crisis contains many story avenues to be pursued by reporters. For example, a food crisis can turn in to stories about public health, restaurant processes, financial losses, reputation losses, and sometimes unexpected, fanatical brand loyalty. The latter helped Blue Bell get out of a sticky situation with less financial melt and helped put the ice cream back on store shelves to a meme generator's delight.

It's my Blue Bell and I want it now!

Note

1. Each journalist and public relations practitioner in this chapter was interviewed only once, unless otherwise noted; therefore, the first citation will provide that information. Individual in-text citations will not continue throughout.

References

Blunt, K. (2016, October 12). At Blue Bell, new questions after a business decision: Outsourcing leads ice cream maker to more recalls. *Houston Chronicle*. Retrieved from http://www. houstonchronicle.com/business/article/At-Blue-Bell-new-questions-after-a-business-9967802.php

Carufel, R. (2015, December 21). The worst- and best-handled crisis communications of the year revealed by CrisisResponsePro: NFL's "Deflate Gate" is top clunker. Retrieved from https://www.bulldogreporter.com/the-worst-and-best-handled-crisis-communications-of-the-year-revealed-by-crisisresponsepro-nfls-deflategate-is-top-clunker/

Centers for Disease Control and Prevention. (2018, March). Listeria: Questions and answers. Retrieved from https://www.cdc.gov/listeria/faq.html

Chamlee, V. (2016, October 11). 16 states affected by latest Blue Bell ice cream recall: Listeria concerns persist. *Eater.com*. Retrieved from http://www.eater.com/2016/10/11/13242122/blue-bell-cookie-dough-ice-cream-recall-Listeria

Coombs, W. T. (2007). Attribution theory as a guide for post-crisis communication research. *Public Relations Review, 33*, 135–139.

Coombs, W. T. (2015). *Ongoing crisis communication: Planning, managing, and responding*. Thousand Oaks, CA: Sage.

Coombs, W. T., & Holladay, S. J. (2002). Helping crisis managers protect reputational assets: Initial tests of the situational crisis communication theory. *Management Communication Quarterly, 16*(2), 165–186.

Czarnecki, S. (2017, January 5). Timeline of a crisis: When Chipotle's new crisis met its old one. *PRWeek*. Retrieved from http://www.prweek.com/article/1419873/timeline-crisis-when-chipotles-new-crisis-met-its-old-one#dHpSs1ZTImBjvREu.99

Fearn-Banks, K. (2012). *Crisis communications: A casebook approach*. London: Routledge.

Heneghan, C. (2015, September 3). Inside the Blue Bell recall—and what happens next. *Fooddive.com*. Retrieved from http://www.fooddive.com/news/inside-the-blue-bell-recall-and-what-happens-next/404795/

Levin, M. (2015, April 21). Timeline of the Blue Bell recall: A listeria outbreak has led to a total recall of all products from the Texas-based ice cream maker Blue Bell. *Houston Chronicle*. Retrieved from http://www.chron.com/business/slideshow/Timeline-of-the-Blue-Bell-recall-107965.php

Liu, B. F., Austin, L., & Jin, Y. (2011). How publics respond to crisis communication strategies: The interplay of information form and sources. *Public Relations Review, 37*(4), 345–353.

Porjes, S. (2015, December). *Consumers and Food Safety in the U.S.: Implications for Marketers, Retailers and Foodservice*. Excerpts from Packaged Facts report.

Robinson-Jacobs, K. (2015, June 28). Food safety experts question initial Blue Bell listeria response. *Dallas Morning News*. Retrieved from http://www.dallasnews.com/business/business/2015/06/28/food-safety-experts-question-initial-blue-bell-listeria-response

· 4 ·

A MOVEMENT IN THE HEARTLAND, PART I

Ferguson, Missouri

Jinx Coleman Broussard

The body of Michael Brown lay on a Ferguson, Missouri, street for about four hours after a white police officer shot him on a hot August Saturday in 2014. People, primarily African Americans, gathered. In the view of many, the hours the uncovered body remained in the sun may have seemed an eternity. The fact that the African-American teen was unarmed and that so much time elapsed before he was taken away stirred outrage. Tempers flared. Eyewitnesses and those who arrived on the scene after the shooting voiced their indignation to each other, and they gave differing versions of what had transpired to media that were gathering quickly. Protests began. Narratives emerged about long-simmering problems and deep-seated racial tension. According to the *St. Louis Post-Dispatch*, the state chapter of the NAACP had filed a federal complaint on November 2013 against the St. Louis County police department over racial disparities in traffic stops and arrests, and that racism was "rampant in the department's hiring, firing and discipline" (Byers, 2014, para. 1).

With a population of 21,000, Ferguson is a small city[1] in St. Louis County and is approximately ten miles from St. Louis, the state's second largest city. At the time of the shooting, the city's police force lacked racial diversity. Ferguson had its own police department. Of its 53 officers, only three were black in a city that was 67 percent African American. Many officers did not reside in the city. Darren Wilson, the officer who shot Brown, lived 30 minutes south of Ferguson in the town of Crestwood.

Brown's death was the latest in a series of killing of young black males after run-ins with law enforcement in such places as Staten Island, New York; Cleveland, Ohio; and North Charleston, South Carolina (Capehart, 2015; Hudson, 2014). Much of the world already knew about the killing of Trayvon Martin in Sanford, Florida two years prior when George Zimmerman, a white man who called himself a neighborhood watch representative, shot the un-armed teen who had gone to the store in his father's upscale neighborhood to get snacks. The *St. Louis Post-Dispatch*, while covering the on-going breaking news of Brown's death, deployed "six or seven" reporters to look hard at "why in the hell this happened here? Why was Michael Brown shot here in Fergu-son, Missouri?" (Bogan, personal communication, October 2016).[2]

Timeline of Events

The timeline of events of this sustained crisis began on August 9, 2016 with a police call of a theft at a Ferguson convenience store. Darren Wilson, a white officer, responded, alone in his police vehicle. Speaking through his window, he told two men, 18-year-old Michael Brown and a friend, to move to the sidewalk. The officer noticed that Brown fit the description of the suspect in the convenience store theft. There was an altercation between Wilson and Brown, who was standing at the window of the police car. The officer fired two shots from inside the vehicle, one grazed Brown and the other missed him.

Brown attempted to run away and Wilson gave chase on foot. Some-time during the chase, Brown stopped and turned to face the officer. Wilson fired again, and Brown fell dead. Witnesses gave conflicting statements as to whether Brown was moving toward Wilson when he was shot and killed. Television stories ran interviews of some witnesses who said Brown had his hands in the air, while others said he did not. All agreed Brown was unarmed.

On Tuesday, August 12, President Barack Obama issued a statement ex-pressing his deepest sorrow, acknowledging that "the events of the past few days have prompted strong passions," and urging everyone in Ferguson and the United States to remember Brown through "reflection and understand-ing." The police department had initially promised to release the name of the officer on that day but indicated on Monday that it would not meet its self-imposed deadline. *Time* magazine ran the following on August 12: "Citing threats lodged on social media, Ferguson police spokesman officer Timothy Zoll said, 'We are protecting the officer's safety by not releasing the name.'" This did not go over well with Ferguson residents. The crisis escalated. Zoll's statement violated a cardinal tenet of crisis communication, that is, to show empathy toward those affected by the crisis. An organization that fails to communicate compassion and concern damages its reputation and standing with its stakeholders and may never regain their trusts.

Protests and riots ensued that almost completely shut down the area for days and weeks. Dozens of businesses were vandalized and looted, schools were closed, and residents and protesters were arrested and / or injured. The authorities' aggressive response with military-style tanks and weapons drew criticism from community leaders, civil rights advocates, and media pundits immediately afterward and in the US Justice Department's report of March 4, 2015. Media were still writing about it well into the next year and beyond. For instance, major newspapers such as the *Los Angeles Times* (June 30, 2015) cited the government's report regarding the inappropriateness of the response. So did NBC's Pete Williams (September 3, 2015) and broadcast and cable networks that covered the riots and response.

On November 24, 2014, the St. Louis County prosecutor announced that a grand jury decided not to indict Officer Wilson. The announcement set off another wave of violent protests. Four months later, on March 4, 2015, after weeks of investigative reports by news outlets and the government, the US Department of Justice Department issued a report that called on Ferguson to overhaul its criminal justice system, declaring that the city had engaged in constitutional rights violations.

By the time the reports were issued, Ferguson had been in crisis for months—some might argue decades—because simmering problems between it and its constituents led to distrust, animosity, and other issues that almost irreparably damaged relationships. Timothy Coombs (2007) defines a crisis in public relations as a significant threat to operations that can have negative consequences if not handled properly. "A crisis can create three related threats: public safety, financial loss, and reputation loss" (p. 1). Fink (1986) notes that for an incident to qualify as a full-blown crisis, the situation must be "escalating in intensity, falling under close government or media scrutiny, interfering with normal business operations, jeopardizing public image and damaging a company's bottom line in anyway" (p. 15). That was exactly what was happening in Ferguson.

The city had failed to recognize the five stages that Fearn-Banks (2017) assigns to a crisis: prodromes, preparation/prevention, containment, recovery, and learning. Prodromes are warning signs organizations must notice and heed in every effort to avoid a crisis, most notably a series of police shootings of African-American males. The preparation or prevention stage occurs when organizations plan for a possible crisis. Both stages illustrate proactive strategies that can help avert a crisis or mitigate its effects. The third stage, containment, happens when a crisis occurs and the organizations devote their efforts to minimizing its duration and impact. This and the following two stages—recovery and learning—are reactive, although learning can be proactive. During the recovery stage, organizations try to normalize operations. Learning involves evaluating the crisis, its management, and communication, and using that information as prodromes and preparation for future crises.

The civil unrest surrounding the Michael Brown shooting and the media attention created a volatile and classic crisis situation that would require strategic and nuanced communication. The city of Ferguson had virtually no response. Explanations by Zoll and others proved inadequate. As Wilcox and colleagues (2013) say: "How an organization responds in the first 24 hours… often determines whether the situation remains an "incident" or becomes a full-blown crisis" (p. 175). The city did not have a public information office, and to complicate matters, the phone lines at city hall had been cut. Both the city and St. Louis County's internet had been hacked, thus inhibiting basic communication.

Ferguson's reputation—how people evaluate the organization—was in tatters with its key stakeholders. As scholars note, stakeholders who are latent publics often become active publics when a triggering event occurs. James E. Grunig (1997 argues that five stages comprise the development of publics: non publics who are unaware of the problem or issue; latent publics, who share an issue with organization but don't recognize the situation or its potential; apathetic publics who face and know the issue but do not care; aware publics, who recognize they share the issue but are not organized to discuss or act on it; and active publics, who discuss or act on the shared issue. Brown's death and the response to it had clearly led residents to that last stage –and they were acting. This did not bode well for Ferguson. It desperately needed crisis management and communication.

Journalists Provide Context

Media on the scene almost immediately began to give context to the situation. Seeking to answer the *why* question, to go beyond the *who, what* and *where*, the reporters looked in to housing, diversity, poverty and other issues (Bogan, personal communication, October 2016).

On August 15, CNN reported on Ferguson's racial divide: "To locals and longtime observers, the tension has been brewing since the 1970s, when Ferguson underwent a racial transformation" (Sanchez, 2014, para. 4). *The Washington Post* addressed the police department's record on race-related issues. Along with problems with officer training and racial sensitivity, the newspaper reported that in 2013, the Missouri attorney general's office concluded the following in an annual report: "Ferguson police were twice as likely to arrest African Americas in routine traffic stops as they were whites" (Lowery, Leonnig, & Berman, 2014). Reports also indicated traffic tickets were a major source of revenue for Ferguson and placed an onerous burden largely on the poor and black population. The investigative story that ran Sunday, August 17, eight days after the shooting, documented that of the 5,384 traffic stops in Ferguson in 2013, only 686 involved whites, while the other 4,632 involved blacks.

The *St. Louis Post-Dispatch* also found that Canfield Green, where Brown lived with his grandmother, and other nearby complexes had over time become a cluster of apartments characterized by poverty and crime. An analysis of crime data the *Post-Dispatch* obtained from St. Louis County revealed "The area accounted for 28 percent of all burglaries, 28 percent of all aggravated assaults, 30 percent of all motor vehicle thefts, and 40 percent of all robberies reported in the city of 21,000" (Bogan, 2014, para. 15).

Residents of this isolated part of the city believed police stopped them for no reason, and that they were being targeted. One nineteen-year-old young man who would soon leave for college told the *Post-Dispatch*: "If you stay here, they basically think you are a thug." Over time, police had closed off practically all access points to the area with concrete barriers and fences, often leaving residents only one way in and one way out. "I am wondering if it is for safety or just to cage us in," resident Rochele Jackson told the newspaper. This view reveals a deep distrust that over time delegitimized the police department and local officials. Wilson and Ogden (2015) say that trust is "an emotional judgment of one's credibility and performance on issues of importance" (p. 1). Suchman (1995) noted that legitimacy is "a generalized perception or assumption that the actions of an entity are desirable, proper, or appropriate within some socially constructed system of norms, values, beliefs, and definitions" (p. 574). Along with communication, these two factors are crucial elements in creating and maintaining harmonious relationships between organizations and their stakeholders Liu, Horsley, & Yang, 2012). Arguably, they are more essential in the public sector because government exists to serve the public that must have confidence in it (Broussard, 1986; Heise,1895; Ledingham, 2003).

The situation in Ferguson aligns with what an Institute for Crisis Management report (2013) terms a "smoldering crisis" in which an organization knows of a potential disruption to business as usual long before the public learns of the situation. The study also revealed that an organization's management is responsible for the crisis 76 percent of the time. Documents that one of the *Post-Dispatch*'s reporters uncovered showed Ferguson knew about the potential crisis but was concerned about bad publicity four years prior to the shooting (Bogan, personal communication, 2014). An effort to avoid negative publicity had now transformed into a worldwide negative perception of the small suburb in Missouri. It was now what Kathleen Fearn-Banks (2017) calls "a major occurrence with a potentially negative outcome affecting the organization, company, or industry as well as its publics, products, services, or good name" (p. 1).

While protests continued and media were arriving on the scene in the first days after the shooting, information from police and other Ferguson officials was slow in coming, creating a vacuum that enhanced feelings of distrust and a perceived lack of transparency as well as disrespect of African Americans. Rumors swirled in the information vacuum and gained traction. The rumors were sometimes reported as facts by media from all corners of the nation and world. Representatives of Britain's *The Guardian*, the British Broadcasting Corporation (BBC), and the *Daily Mail* joined hundreds of journalists from Canada and as far away as Turkey, Germany, and the Netherlands. Multiple personnel from state and national media added to the numbers (Bentele, personal communication, 2016; Deere, personal communication, 2016). PR practitioners and scholars note that information should be disseminated accurately and quickly before the vacuum forms (Lukaszweski, 1997; Coombs, 2007).

PR Remains Silent and Stumbles

The civil unrest surrounding the shooting as well as the media attention created a volatile and classic crisis situation that required strategic and nuanced communication. Scholars (Coombs, 2007; Fearn-Banks, 2017) agree that crises can threaten and disrupt organization if proper action is not taken. Timothy Coombs (2007) defines a crisis in public relations as a significant threat to operations that can have negative consequences if not handled properly.

Again, the city of Ferguson had virtually no response. And without the ability to make phone calls or even use social media, there was "almost no way to respond to citizen's needs," public relations professional Denise Bentele (personal communication, 2016) recounted for this chapter. The crisis escalated as the public believed officials were not being transparent. John Verrico (2015), head of the National Government Communications Association, offers the following assessment: "When a government official refuses to be transparent, tries to hide information that makes them (sic) look bad, or gets caught misrepresenting the facts, it becomes harder to sell anything that comes out of their mouths in the future."

It was well into the second week of the crisis before the City of Ferguson hired Bentele's firm to handle crisis communication. Common Ground Public Relations is a full-service firm in the St. Louis suburb of Chesterfield. Shortly after the crisis erupted, a board member of the St. Louis chapter of the Public Relations Society of America referred Common Ground to Ferguson city manager John Shaw[3] because Bentele had extensive experience in crisis communication. She had worked for such major clients as Amoco, Monsanto, Disney, Eli Lilly, and UnitedHealth Group.[4] Common Ground already was working on economic development, enterprise zones and small business promotion throughout the region for the St. Louis Economic Development Partnership. When she signed on with Ferguson, Bentele told city officials she would not be their "long-term solution" because the fact that she was white and from Chesterfield would not be perceived well. She recommended that the city partner with a minority firm to handle ongoing community engagement. That move would enable Common Ground to put in place a system to field media calls and coordinate media relations, according to Bentele.

The hiring created a controversy for the very reason Bentele noted—an all-white agency engaged to represent and communicate on behalf of the city to a predominantly black community during a time of racial tension. This further reinforced the negative perception of a lack of sensitivity and transparency by the city. Efforts to mitigate that situation created yet another PR firestorm when a minority firm was hired. Shortly before the shooting, the St. Louis Economic Development Partnership had hired the Devin James Group to market Ferguson and other North St. Louis county cities.[5] The city awarded Devin James a $100,000 contract on August 27, 2014, to be the city's public relations representative. The Economic Development Partnership would pay his fee. Nevertheless, media still contacted Common Ground for assistance although the agency was no longer under formal contract with the city.

In an exclusive interview with MSNBC's Trymaine Lee that was posted to the network's website on October 2, James told the correspondent that as soon as he was hired, he began organizing a series of town hall meetings intended to discuss the city's racial tensions. He also said he met behind closed doors with black community leaders and went out to shake hands with protestors and gang members. Police Chief Thomas Jackson and Mayor James Knowles could not do those things, James said, because they had made racially insensitive remarks and had responded negatively to protesters (Lee, 2014). Because James already was working with the partnership, city and county officials arguably viewed him as a bridge between them and the majority African American community. In his enhanced role, James helped coordinate chief Jackson's September 24 video apology to Brown's family and to protesters. Lee appeared as a guest on MSNBC's The Reid Report the day after his story was posted. Host Joy Reid opened the segment titled "New PR headache hits Ferguson police," by showing a clip of what she called Chief Jackson's "awkward apology." She said members of Ferguson's black community "scorned" the apology, Brown's family "definitely" did not accept it, and the media ridiculed it. Even more damaging, Reid said "the video marked the beginning of the end for the relationship between the police and the PR firm hired to fix Ferguson's PR nightmare" (O'Connor, 2014).[6]

While serving as the PR face of Ferguson, James became the center of his own controversy. His interaction with reporters covering the crisis led to another PR blemish for Ferguson, albeit not of the magnitude of the shooting and protests. The negative exchanges also reinforced the perception that journalists have of PR professionals as flacks, and untruthful, unethical hacks.[7] Research backs up this view. For instance, a 2007 Institute for Public Relations article based on reviews of multiple academic studies found the following:

> Many critics argue that there can be no ethical public relations because the practice itself is akin to manipulation and propaganda. An unfortunate belief among many journalists, policy makers, and laymen is the belief that the term "public relations

ethics" is an oxymoron: either an unreal possibility, or smoke and mirrors to hide deception. (p. 1 of article posted online)

Likewise, the Public Relations Society of America (PRSA) ethics pledge indicates that members must conduct themselves "professionally, with truth, accuracy, fairness, and responsibility to the public."

As noted, that was the view of *St. Louis Post-Dispatch*'s Stephen Deere, who called James "a disaster," adding the consultant did not return his phone calls, sent rude and "disrespectful texts" to reporters, and complained when clearly untruthful information he provided did not appear in Deere's stories. Toler (2014) said a "Twitter tussle" occurred between James and James Campbell, a national reporter, when the latter tweeted that James spent more time tweeting about his fashion sense instead of answering his phone calls.[8]

Those actions put James "on everybody's' radar" and got everybody in the newsroom thinking about "this guy," Deere recalled. Even the terminology (this guy) conveys the negative perception the journalists had of the practitioner, which translated into a lack of credibility. His and Ferguson's standing with the media devolved when the Devin James Group took credit for releasing the police chief's apology. "What PR person brands an apology from a police chief or any public official?" Deere asked. "Most PR people want to be invisible, and they want to be directing things behind the scenes." The fact that James was not "struck everybody as bizarre," Deere said. The press wanted to know "who the hell is this guy."

Deere's reporting found that the Devin James Group probably only existed on paper because some of the people listed as employees on the firm's website were not connected to the agency. Deere and another reporter decided to do "a profile on this guy because something was not right" (Deere, personal communication, 2016). About 20 reporters who were conducting Google searches about James found he had purchased the 25,000 Twitter followers he claimed to have. "Then we learned about his arrest for involuntary manslaughter," Deere said. Exhibiting a distrust of both James and Mayor Knowles, Deere and another reporter called the PR representative and the mayor simultaneously because "we didn't want to give them a chance to get their story straight, to come up with a narrative." The reporters' action also showed distrust that resulted from a perceived lack of the practitioner's credibility. James, nevertheless, met with the journalists.

On September 25, 2014, Deere broke the story that in 2006 James was convicted of reckless homicide in Shelby County, Tennessee, for shooting and killing an unarmed man. The newspaper reported that Ferguson officials knew of James' conviction before the county signed the contract with him. However, the county's partnership agency, which was paying James' fees, said it was unaware of his conviction, and only found out when the story broke. Shortly thereafter, it rescinded James's contract because of what it termed his lack of transparency. Headlines read, "Fired Ferguson rep Devin James public relations nightmare" and "Ferguson PR man was convicted of reckless homicide; loses contract." The headline on a story by Jeremy Kohler (2014) went directly to the heart of trust and credibility: "Ferguson PR consultant told city he had a college degree; now he says he doesn't." Untrustworthiness on the part of the PIO not only damages relationships with the media, but also negatively impacts the reputation of the organization he or she represents. Hence, while attention should have been on crisis management and communication, the public relations representative was a part of the story for about a month. The journalists also did not believe public officials' version of what they knew about James's past, and when. This also indicated a lack of trust.

Ferguson and, arguably, St. Louis County faced multiple crises in the days and months following the shooting of Michael Brown. E. Little Communications Group, an African American public relations firm, took over in November. Crisis communication expert Gerard Braud (personal communication, 2016) argues that organizations and even cities as small as Ferguson should have a public relations practitioner and a strategic communications plan that includes proactive crisis communication. Successful crisis communication hinges on transparency and trust, in addition to successfully implementing other crisis strategies. None of that was occurring in Ferguson. Therefore, the city experienced a cascade of crisis situations, one after another.

Prior to Devin James, Bentele and a senior Common Ground staffer who also had multiple years of crisis communication experience, had established the basic lines of open communication with media. They physically set up operations in Ferguson City Hall and stayed there for several days, primarily handling media queries. Bentele assessed the situation and talked with city officials about their lack of communication. A next step involved reaching out to contacts in St. Louis County and the governor's office, asking for and ultimately "imploring for a proper, appropriate regional response to handling the crisis, and approval to enact a communications effort" (Bentele, personal communication, 2016). That proved difficult because, as Bentele recounts, "the higher powers"… were not going to "let that happen." Crisis management and decision making for Ferguson and Clayton initially were directed to the Missouri State Highway Patrol that reported to Governor Jay Nixon. In the days immediately following the shooting, protests were not just happening in Ferguson; several hundred demonstrators seeking criminal prosecution of Officer Wilson, also gathered in Clayton, the county seat about 11 miles south of Ferguson. Bentele said the governor did not seem to view communications as vital, and this inhibited a strong, coordinated communication effort.

In Bentele's view, Common Ground sought to reverse the "negative" media relations as journalists continued to cover the tension in Ferguson that was getting "to a boiling point." The firm's representatives tried to disseminate the correct information to the right reporter and to send media to the appropriate places. Twenty-hour days were the norm initially. But before beginning, Bentele used two cell phones the city had purchased, and dedicated one of the lines solely to what she called "triaging" or receiving and documenting calls, working through queries, and responding to media messages. She and her staff members also set up the media@fergusoncity.com email account just for media queries. Next, the pair printed and distributed to the media at different locations a basic alert that notified journalists of the telephone number and the voice and email accessibility.

They fielded approximately 1,200 messages and queries during the first forty-eight hours. Those first steps were necessary because a construct did not exist for handling "random" and "different" calls that came in. As Bentele recalled, people were showing up with their press credentials and "just walking into city hall, grabbing the chief of police, grabbing the mayor, grabbing the city manager, grabbing anybody on the city council."

Francis Marra noted in 1998 that most crises immediately trigger a deluge of questions from an organization's many different publics. Reporters, employees, stockholders, government officials, and local residents all want—need—to know, what happened? Who did it happen to? When? Where? How? Why? Organizations that wait to answer these questions often suffer unnecessary financial, emotional, and perceptual damage. The ability to communicate quickly and effectively is clearly an important component of successful and effective crisis management (p. 461).

Common Ground referred questions about the shooting to St. Louis County, which was handling the investigation. Many other phone calls involved Freedom of Information Act (FOIA) requests that had to be handled within the required timeframe. Some of those went to Ferguson, while others went to St. Louis County.

The media were reporting about and voicing on social media their frustrations over the lack of responses from the City of Ferguson. In Bentele's view, some reporting was erroneous and unfair because it did not take into consideration that it was almost impossible for the city to even respond absent basic communication tools. Other media expressed gratitude that they were finally getting a response. Nevertheless, handling media relations was difficult.

Bentele cited one example where six to eight different producers for different programs on one particular network were competing with each other to get sources and guests for their individual shows. The "deluge of media" kept increasing because the protests made for "fabulous television."

She noted that crisis communication strategy dictates that the organization transmit cohesive messages with a "unified communication response." The "inability to pull together who we needed to pull together . . . was . . . such a huge barrier." Meetings between elected officials presented this major challenge. Bentele recalled being in meetings where they "were unable to get along," disrespected each other and disregarded differing opinions. One particularly acrimonious meeting involved religious, local and surrounding county leaders; a group of African Americans; and out-of-town individuals who "saw this as a stage for them. . . The fighting in that room was as verbal and as emotional as the disagreement between elected officials in a more open area. So it really was disappointing to see how hard it was to get alignment for the greater good in some of those early days." Such behavior was "unfair" to the residents of the region, Bentele lamented.

PR professional and crisis communication expert Gerard Braud advises that during a crisis no more than five people should be in the room to respond to and manage a situation. "Most organizations make the mistake of putting too many decision makers in one room." The five become a kind of concentric circle that has a team of five more in the next circle. "If you need to communicate with your team of five, you leave the room and go to the room where that five are and communicate with them."

A Rocky Relationship in a Trying Time

The crisis in Ferguson presented a classic storm in which to explore the relationship between journalists and public relations practitioners. Although editors, reporters and other media gatekeepers rely heavily on sources to enable them to tell the story, to provide information and to explain, many journalists do not acknowledge that reality (Macnamara, 2014). In a comprehensive book on the subject, Jim Macnamara cites numerous studies that show journalists have negative views and descriptions of public relations practitioners. For instance, Grunig and Hunt argued journalists believe PR people thwart efforts to get "the truth" (Grunig & Hunt, 1984, p. 224). Others use pejorative terms such as spin, hype, and flack when referring to PR practitioners. Macnamara (2014, p. xii) also cites studies by Robert McChesney's 2013 book that called attention to the extent to which journalists now "increasingly" overly rely on "unfiltered public relations generated surreptitiously by corporations and government" (McChesney, 2013, p. 183). According to some estimates, as much as 80 percent of news content originates from public relations practitioners on behalf of their clients or the organizations for which they work. Churnalism is the term Nick Davis coined in 2009 and argued that media merely "churn out" or "regurgitate" material from public relations practitioners/sources and wire service reports. (Macnamara, 2014, p. 9). Contrary to the view of many journalists, PR practitioners view their work as a service in which they facilitate communication and foster dialogic and beneficial relationships that address the needs of stakeholders and the organization. "Honest broker" is the term Hohenberg (1973) coined to describe that role (p. 137).

In the opening days of the crisis in Ferguson, Common Ground PR embraced that role. Bentele said her firm has an excellent reputation among journalists with whom it interacts regularly, and it earns the respect "pretty quickly" of those with whom she normally does not engage. All her team are journalism school graduates who operate based on professionalism grounded in transparency, trust, truth, and giving media what they need or helping them to get it. She believed relationship building helped deflect some of the criticism Ferguson received when she was hired. That line of questioning was probably "a direct result of media looking for other side stories and creating narratives," Bentele added, and suggested that a lot of the media did not care that she was white. "They just wanted me to get them whatever they were asking for."

The Journalists' Perspective: On Our Own

While Common Ground and Devin James—until he was terminated—were engaging in their respective PR-related activities, Deere, Jesse Bogan, and other *St. Louis Post-Dispatch* reporters were trying to cover the chaos. Deere had covered all manner of crises—hurricanes in Florida, two high-profile kidnappings—one where a child was rescued, and another in which a child who had been missing for years and presumed dead was found alive. Bogan had seen his share of crises, also. But Ferguson was different not only because of the shooting, but because of the intense media interest—a fact Bentele stressed. As a grand jury convened from the end of October through December to investigate the shooting, protests continued. Deere commented, "There would be more cameras on the marchers than there were marchers" . . . as if they were "performers.'"

The local paper, the *Post-Dispatch* did not rely on public relations practitioners. Instead it relied on its own resources and enterprise reporting. Bogan recalled there was a "lull in the beginning," because the crisis caught the newspaper off guard (personal communication, 2016). The *Post-Dispatch* "didn't have a plan in place for something like this," Deere remembered, adding "to be fair, I don't think we would have because this was . . . a once-in-a-lifetime deal." The newspaper was under "unusual pressure . . . to have to cover everything," to be "story detectives" who competed against hundreds of outside media that often had multiple journalists.

The *Post-Dispatch* sprang into action and almost immediately set up a team of reporters to "investigate the key players," including the police chief, Officer Darren Wilson, Michael Brown, and the shooting itself. Journalists used their own judgment as they got up close and placed themselves—or were thrown in the middle—of "some dangerous situations" to interview witnesses Deere said. They were not at full staff because some editors were on vacation. Those factors and the belief they had to do as much or more than the national reporters affected how journalists were able to report the story. "We were calling in quotes and things from the scenes." In the beginning, coverage involved editors and reporters determining the theme of the day and figuring out how they were going to wrap the story around that theme. Deere said they were in "survival mode" for the first week, but that changed as time went on. The paper soon deployed approximately fifty metro, business, and other reporters and photographers to cover Ferguson.

Deere recalled the lack of forthcoming information from the government during the three-month period the grand jury met that "made everything worse" and "infused with drama," as journalists were vying for any kind of original story. Bentele also said her job was complicated for the same reason Deere cites and because so many journalists had difficulty even "understanding that Ferguson was one part of St. Louis County, not its own big city some place." *St. Louis Post-Dispatch* reporters again relied on themselves.

The Crisis Continues

E. Little Communications Group joined the communications team on the second day of unrest following the grand jury's decision not to indict White. Based in the central west end of St. Louis, the firm has a small staff. In the early days after Brown's death, some reporters assumed Little "had the account" because not only had he once lived in Canfield Apartments for two years, he had been handling crisis and other communication in St. Louis for seven years and still was under contract to the nearby Normandy School District in Missouri (Little, personal communication, 2016). However, Ferguson officials did not reach out to Little. That action reflected Ferguson's unawareness of public relations and crisis communication tenets, which dictate that the source of the message should relate to the audience. Ki and Hon (2009) maintain that "a positive relational outcome is dependent on an organization's effort to cultivate and sustain positive relationships" (p. 3). Because of Ferguson's racial makeup, in a perfect world, it would have had relations with Black firms. "Being prepared means thinking about your audience," Bentele said.

Following the James controversy, Little contacted Bentele and offered assistance. She informed Shaw of Little's desire to become involved. Once hired, Little took over completely, assessed the situation, as Bentele had done months before, and continued to utilize the email and phone system Common Ground already had in place. He also implemented a coordinated crisis communication plan. The new firm's chief goal, according to Little, was to "assist" and "represent the client," by communicating constantly with the mayor, city council and police department while filling all media inquiries and requests quickly. A second priority was to assign a staff member, Jeff Small, as the full-time public relations representative on the ground in Ferguson. Small had worked at one of the local television stations in St. Louis, and Little had worked for at least two stations. Because of this, both men enjoyed good media relations, Little said.

The first day on the account was just as hectic as Bentele's months before. Little only had one hour of sleep in the first 24-hour period as the team responded to all media queries. They categorized queries according to print, television, radio, national, international and local media, and responded within a day. Plans also took shape for a 1 p.m. November 25 press conference during which the mayor and approximately thirty pastors would appeal for "peace and calm." Little said city officials also wanted to convey compassion.

Bentele described the press conference as a turning point because before it occurred, the governor had taken authority away from local decision makers. Now, local authorities had a voice and face. Building a partnership between the community and city officials, according to Little, was a major accomplishment, as well as communicating with the citizens of Ferguson because they needed information as simple as road closures and whether city hall was open for services.

E. Little crafted messages to answer multiple media queries via a general press release it distributed regularly. The "synched messages from the city of Ferguson" also facilitated better and equal dissemination of information. "We didn't prioritize to say we were going to send this to CNN and MSNBC and the local Fox station here . . . we just sent it out to everyone." Talking points for city officials also aimed to reflect clear and consistent messages. Little also launched social media for Ferguson, which had a less-than-robust Facebook presence. Twitter and Facebook became key engagement communication components, especially because large numbers of people were "sending out messages" after the second wave of unrest. Working with the mass media was still a priority, Little said, "But social media allowed the city to really engage on a grassroots level with citizens who had a Twitter account."

Creating regular media briefings sought to facilitate better media relations and message dissemination, according to Little. Journalist knew that at 1 p.m. every day they would learn about new developments from the city. These were not necessarily press conferences. Little said sometimes he also instituted 24 to 48-hour media blackouts in order to give the city more time to gather information the media were requesting and to coordinate dissemination rather than responding to one person at a time.

Like Bentele, Little paid attention to both national and local media coverage. Because so much was happening every night, they monitored media coverage to learn what they might have to address in the morning. Little also had minimal direct interaction with individual journalists. He noted that serving local media was important because they would be the ones remaining in the community after the crisis ended. During the month after the grand jury action, national and international journalists were flying in to Ferguson for two-to-three weeks and leaving, Little said. Both public relations representatives said the work was "physically exhausting."

On the journalism side, the St. Louis Post-Dispatch assigned Deere to a newly created Ferguson beat. Deere said the information situation became much better than what he called the initial communication "disaster." The reporter could not remember "any method that was really successful in getting information out there," adding attempts were made to have the mayor talk to the media after the grand jury announcement, but the mayor often appeared "defensive" and sometimes lectured reporters.

The crisis in Ferguson had escalated with the Devin James controversy; yet another controversy erupted a few months later when a person identified as a spokesperson for the police department referred to a memorial set up right after Brown's death as a "pile of trash" (DelReal, 2014, para. 3. Media reported on Christmas day that a car intentionally ran over and destroyed the memorial in the middle of Canfield Drive near the Canfield Green apartment complex. When a *Washington Post* reporter asked the Ferguson Police Department if it was investigating the incident, spokesperson Timothy Zoll referred to the makeshift memorial as trash and remarked: "I don't know that a crime has occurred" (DelReal, 2014, para. 3). After the story ran, people in Ferguson were incensed, according to Deere. To complicate matters, Zoll, who was a police officer, responded that the newspaper misquoted him. However, after a police department investigation, he admitted to making the statement. This lack of credibility is an example of why journalists often characterize public relations practitioners negatively. It also shows why media training and one assigned spokesperson for all outlets is necessary. Major news outlets such as TIME, CBS News and NBC News reported on Zoll's statements and the public's negative response to it.

On December 28, 2014, two days after Zoll's statement, the department announced via a press release that it had placed him on an unpaid suspension, and emphasized that his "negative remarks" were not a reflection of the department's feelings. Furthermore, they were "in direct contradiction to the efforts of city officials to relocate the memorial to a more secure location" (DelReal, 2014, para. 4). Despite the progress toward enhanced communication and crisis management the public relations representatives had made, on-going incidents precipitated additional lack of trust as well as perceived insensitivity. Public relations can only be effective if the client considers the wants and needs of its stakeholders and builds mutually beneficial relationship built on trust (Grunig & Hunt, 1984; Ledingham & Bruning, 1998).

Moving Forward

In June 2016, nineteen months after the crisis began, Jeff Small was still handling media relations in Ferguson on a full-time basis, a move crisis expert Gerard Braud would describe as wise. Little was still checking in with

Small every day and continuing to strategize. Deere said his interactions with Little and Small were positive. He acknowledged that communication problems are not always the fault of the public relations staff, but PR ultimately bears some responsibility. For instance, Small might have to rely on the city attorney or other officials to obtain answers to questions. That person might not provide the information to Small, but he also might not get back to Deere with any response. "I just say he's probably not getting back to me at this point and he probably doesn't have a choice, so I'll leave him alone."

Seeking to build rapport, Deere was courteous with Little and Small, even notifying them of stories the *Post-Dispatch* was working on to give them time to gather information and prepare the city to respond and react to questions or issues raised. Still, Deere sometimes does not call the public information office, choosing instead to go directly to the source of the information he is seeking. Sometimes he just calls the new city manager, De'Carlon Seewood.[9] Other times, Small facilitates the contact. Interactions between Deere and Knowles have not been as productive. "The mayor has been a big part of their PR problem," Deere said, adding the Ferguson charter indicates the mayor is the city's chief spokesperson, or according to the reporter, the official "public relations guy." Here is an example Deere provided about a conversation on September 2014. "I see him at a Ferguson Commission meeting and I say 'hey mayor, how you doing?' I asked him if he read our Sunday story." According to the reporter, the mayor, thought Deere was referring to one of his stories, and replied that he tried not to read anything the reporter wrote. Deere said until that exchange, he did not know Knowles was displeased with him or any of the stories he had written or the newspaper had run. "I wanted to ask him why, but I just brushed it off and said, 'I'm talking about another reporter's story.' The mayor then replied he 'stopped reading it after the second graph.'" Deere wondered why the mayor would "say such a rude thing to the reporter assigned to Ferguson," adding, "If he had called me up and said, 'Hey I wish you could have done this or thought about this,' I would have accepted that. I would accept it today. That's an example of a poor public relations practice" and suggests the mayor might "need a little media training." Public relations scholars would agree that creating and maintaining dialog and harmony extends beyond the practitioner, but to those who represent the organization. No amount of effort on the part of the PIO can mitigate negative exchanges or actions with journalists, especially from elected officials.

Lessons Learned

Much can be learned about crisis communication and media relations through the lens of Ferguson. According to Doorley and Garcia (2015), "The longer it takes to resolve a crisis, the harder it is and the more painful it will be for the company and its leaders" (p. 297). The public relations practitioners and journalists shared the lessons they learned, much of which aligns with what PR scholars and expert practitioners posit.

An excellent relationship and interaction between public information officers and media personnel are important at all times, but even more so during a crisis. Both entities are the vehicles through which the public and specific stakeholders obtain information that enables them to make decisions and act, when warranted. Therefore, PR practitioners for government as well as journalists must be attuned to the needs of the other and their publics. Mutual respect and trust enable development of relationships between government and citizens and between government and journalists prior to a crisis and facilitate better communication during and after the event. As a press release on President Barack Obama's "Task Force on 21st Century Policing," reported:

> Recent events in Ferguson, Missouri and around the country have highlighted the importance of strong, collaborative relationships between local police and the communities they protect. As the nation has observed, trust between law enforcement agencies and the people they protect and serve is essential to the stability of our communities, the integrity of our criminal justice system, and the safe and effective delivery of policing services.[10]

The same is true for public relations professionals and journalists.

Takeaways for PR Practitioners

Be Cognizant of Stakeholders and How Actions (or Lack of Actions) Affect Them

How publics perceive the organization is crucial to acceptance, confidence and support of the organization. If Ferguson and St. Louis officials had taken into consideration how residents would perceive the actions of the police and the city's response, officials would have involved a credible minority crisis communication firm long before E. Little Communication started representing the city ninety days after the shooting. More than three decades ago, Grunig and Hunt (1984) put forth the basic premise that organizational effectiveness occurs when the organization not only considers the wants, desires and needs of its publics, but relates to them.

Have a Crisis Communication Plan That Provides Training and Clear Duties and Guides a Coordinated Team Response

It makes sense that large cities with airports or coastal cities with weather threats have crisis plans. However, Ferguson showed that *all* municipalities need to be ready. Shootings, for example, can happen anywhere and bring small towns into the glaring limelight. The list of examples is almost endless.

Also, what good is a crisis communication plan that sits on a shelf? According to Wilcox and colleagues (2013), "Some crisis plans are thorough and comprehensive, but they are never communicated. Then, when a crisis occurs, employees either don't have a copy of the plan or how to follow its instructions" (p. 324). Employees need to practice the plan and have direct jobs assigned to them so they can get to work immediately.

Make sure the team is truly a team—assigning only one or two people to manage and communicate the crisis is insufficient. As noted, Bentele and her staff member were inundated. The team should be composed of individuals who have crisis communication experience, training and clearly delineated roles before, during and after a crisis.

Crisis communication expert Gerard Braud said cities and organizations should prepare for unforeseen crises, planning on a "clear and sunny day" because the organization doesn't have time to figure things out during cloudy crisis days.

Provide Accurate Information Quickly and Frequently

This takeaway seems simplistic, but this case shows it is worth repeating. Bentele said an optimum crisis response would have involved having "one communications team at one place giving good information throughout the day, making people available throughout the day." That would have prevented the information vacuum that rumors, speculation and misinformation created. This is consistent with other cases in this book and the recommendations crisis communication scholars suggest.

Streamline the Decision-making Process

Having witnessed how municipalities, county and state government were acting, Bentele said Ferguson was "absolutely a crisis waiting to happen." Braud advised that during a crisis no more than five people should be in the room to respond to and manage a situation. "Most organizations make the mistake of putting too many decision makers in one room." The five become a kind of concentric circle that has a team of five more in the next circle. "If you need to communicate with your team of five, you leave the room and go to the room where that five are and communicate with them."

Local Officials and Experts Should Be the Primary Voices and Faces of the City or Organization

That did not happen in Ferguson until the November 25 press conference that followed the grand jury decision. Rotate city officials for different media opportunities, however, with a caveat. In this case, even when primary voices were talking (Zoll), often what was said was not helpful to managing the situation or reputation. The primary voices and/or city officials need media training first, then crisis media training in order to represent themselves and their constituents well in the press and on camera. No training equals no talking.

Establish a Crisis Command Center

A centralized operation and location would have enabled Ferguson to serve the media and, by extension, the public with updated information early in the process. This would have cut down on the hundreds of "random" queries Bentele and Little received from multiple media that converged on the small suburb. A center was established months later when Little became the lead public relations presence. Even then, it happened serendipitously because a large parking lot was the location where dozens of media trucks parked. Media personnel were physically at that one location and city officials were able to disseminate information to media every day at the same time, according to Bentele and Little.

Utilize Social Media

Little and Bentele both agreed that utilizing social media was crucial to disseminating information and engaging citizens. Reporters Deere and Bogan, who had not used the technology before the crisis, also acknowledged its important role in communicating. Bogan said he perhaps had tweeted once before Ferguson. Deere added he "had no idea the role that Twitter was playing . . . and didn't really have a full grasp of how to be successful on social media." His newspaper wanted its reporters to tweet when something interesting happened. Still, Deere did not know how successful tweeting was because he was not familiar with social media analytics. Bogan said he had to use Twitter, which he called "a real challenge."

Do Not Ignore Local Media in Favor of Major National or International News Organizations

Recognize and understand the crucial role of all media prior to, during and after the crisis. Meeting the needs of broadcast and print international, national and local media was crucial because of the need to provide information and context. Although major national print and online media and organizations such as CNN, Fox News, MSNBC and the broadcast networks reached a broader audience, Bentele and Little noted that practitioners should ensure local journalists receive as much or more attention because of their on-going role in the community. Local media, in public parlance, are primary stakeholders. As Little offered, international and national media came, stayed a few weeks and left, but local media still remain and are invested in the community and residents.

Little and Bentele said out-of-town journalists do not have the background knowledge about the area or situation. Many did not comprehend the county organizational structure and that Ferguson was just one small entity in St. Louis County. Public relations professionals must be attuned to those circumstances and prepare background information packets that provide basic information about the organization or city to cut down on basic questions journalists ask.

Behave Ethically and Remain Calm and Professional Despite Demands

Bentele suggested that public relations peers should "stand up" for their profession and role in crisis. She said she did that when a *Washington Post* reporter asked her multiple times in succession why the city hired a PR firm. Not feeling the need to justify what she was trying to do, Bentele answered that her role was to "help manage media queries," such as the reporter's and she followed with, "how can I help you?" Engaging a PR firm in the midst of a communications crisis should not be construed as something negative, Bentele explained. "If our PRSA Code of Ethics says practitioners are to provide for a free flow of information, why do we allow ourselves to be tagged with somehow . . . sinning . . . hiding or obfuscating?"

Deere cautioned that PR people must "be honest and don't lie" because once they do, they destroy "all trust" from "any potential relationship" with reporters. His advice is in line with the PRSA Code of Ethics.[11] "If you can't be honest or tell the truth, just say 'I can't tell you.'" Throughout the crisis, Deere said, Ferguson "couldn't tell the truth," or did not provide accurate information as quickly as possible and did not keep open lines of communication. The Devin James controversy reinforced the negative perceptions journalists have of practitioners.

Build Relationships and Recognize It Is a Reciprocal Process

A rocky relationship exists at this writing between reporter Deere and Mayor Knowles, whom the Ferguson charter designates as the city's primary spokesperson. Scholars and experts argue that anyone who is the public face of an organization or who serves as a spokesperson must foster a relationship built on professionalism and mutual respect. Coombs and Holladay (2010), in writing about the role of spokespersons in organizations, argue that the individual should be "a source of clear information that constituents need" and that "he or she should not create an unflattering portrait to the organization due to incompetence" (243). Public relations scholars agree that creating and maintaining dialog and harmony extends beyond the practitioner, but to those who represent the organization. No amount of effort on the part of the PIO can mitigate negative exchanges or actions with journalists (Broussard, 1986).

Communicate Concerns

Deere, who is assigned to Ferguson now, said a more positive relationship would exist if the practitioner "politely and professionally lets the journalist know" if he or she doesn't like a story and why. "Don't get passive/aggressive or moody." According to the reporter, he has a "very good relationship" with Small and Little sixteen months after the crisis. All have worked on cultivating that relationship by considering the needs and constraints of the other.

Be Prepared for Whatever Circumstances the Crisis Presents

Practitioners should recognize that crises are different and situational and require different resources and strategies. For instance, a reporter compared what happened in Ferguson to other crises. "If a flood occurs, PR people want to get the information out, but in shootings or crimes, they are concerned about such issues as lawsuits."

Takeaways for Journalists

Work Around Unhelpful PR People

Yes, you read that correctly. In crisis, the information is too important not to obtain and disseminate. Do not "deal with a PR person who appears to have information but doesn't have a desire to be helpful and doesn't recognize that getting accurate information out to the public is important," Deere advised. It does not matter if the person is doing what his or her client wants. "Try to bypass and work around that person… At the same time, be open to having a lot of background conversation with PR people because they can be super helpful in pointing you in a direction or telling you the truth about where you can obtain information."

Be Prepared to Use Your Investigative Skills to Obtain Information

Bogan engaged in enterprise reporting and did not rely on Ferguson's official public relations people except for filing FOIA and document requests. Bogan said that as a general rule, he tries to avoid public relations people because they often do not know the answer to questions and have to go out and find it from others in the company. "In previous decades, PR people were more like handlers; they knew what was going on. They were in the same room for decisions. Nowadays, I don't see that."

Be Prepared for Any Crisis Situation, Even Dangerous Ones

As the *Post-Dispatch* reporters recalled, they were placed in potentially dangerous situations but still had to perform their professional duties. NPR reporter Elise Hu found herself right behind the police lines during one of the protests in Ferguson. When the authorities fell back, they found themselves at the nexus of the conflict. She and her colleague had to take shelter in an unlocked car as the confrontation between sides turned violent—and they were in the middle of it. All reporters must pay attention and be ready to act to prevent harm to self.

Learn to Use Social Media and Only Report Factual Information

Writing about the extent to which social media contributes to legitimacy, McCluskey (2016) noted: "Various online and social media tools have become important components of media relations practices, and journalists are turning to these tools in their daily content and decision-making routines" (McCluskey, 2016, p. 8). Henderson & Miller (2014) found that ninety-six percent of broadcast journalists who responded to a survey indicated they used their organization's Twitter account to follow city officials. Eighty-eight percent followed law enforcement on Twitter. In fact, Twitter supplemented "the traditional beat call system" and inspired news reports that ran in newscasts (Henderson & Miller, 2014, pp. 14–15). Reporters still need to double and triple check information to make sure it is factual. Just because it is on an official Twitter feed, does not mean it is right. Using social media to both gather and disseminate information is now a core reporter duty.

The Ferguson, Missouri case gives public relations practitioners many examples of what not to do, as the communication effort went from nonexistent to repeated, self-inflicted wounds. And while the pressure to report was intense and dangerous, this case is also an excellent example of the watchdog function of the press. Journalists, local and national, brought into the light a systematic pattern of wrongs and injustices. The end result of all the communication was an important one.

Notes

1. Media and other reports sometimes refer to the small community as a St. Louis suburb.
2. Each journalist and public relations practitioner interviewed for this chapter was interviewed only once, unless otherwise noted; therefore, the first citation will provide that information. Individual in-text citations will not continue throughout.
3. The U.S. Department of Justice report following the events that unfolded in Ferguson said the 39-year-old Shaw was responsible for the circumstances leading to the civil rights unrest in Ferguson. For reference, see "Investigation of the Ferguson Police Department: United States Department of Justice Civil Rights Division" (March 4, 2014). Retrieved

December 19, 2016 from https://www.justice.gov/sites/default/files/opa/press-releases/ attachments/2015/03/04/ferguson_police_department_report_1.pdf. A *New York Times* article on the findings said the report indicated Shaw was responsible for the "financially driven policies that led to widespread discrimination and questionable conduct by the police and courts" in Ferguson. Shaw resigned in March 2015. For reference, see John Eligon, "Ferguson City Manager Cited in Justice Department Report Resigns," *The New York Times*, 10 March 2015. Retrieved December 19, 2016 from https://www.nytimes. com/2015/03/11/us/ferguson-city-manager-resigns.html

4. Bentele began her career as a member of Amoco's North American crisis team, based in Chicago, and worked as a part of its hazardous materials team, where she engaged in crisis communications with first responders and worked with reporting agencies, providing guidance on conveying accurate, timely, and consistent information to the public. She later worked on major corporate crises, bankruptcies, international environmental issues and Peru, other issues.

5. For reference, see http://www.prnewsonline.com/water-cooler/2014/08/19/fergusons-hiring-of-a-pr-agency-may-need-some-pr-of-its-own/, Retrieved August 31, 2016.

6. O'Connor is listed as the director of the *Joy Reid Show* for the episode. See complete citation in the reference section of this chapter.

7. For reference, see Macnamara, J. (2014). *Journalism & PR: Unpacking "spin," stereotypes, and myths*. New York, NY: Peter Lang.

8. Toler's account of the incident appeared in a blog post for the *Riverfront Times*.

9. De'Carlon Seewood, an African-American, who was born in East St. Louis, was hired in November 2015 from his position as village manager of Richton Park, Illinois. He previously served as assistant city manager or Ferguson from 2001 to 2007. For reference, see "Ferguson, Missouri names new city manager," Reuters, http://www.reuters.com/article/ us-missouri-ferguson-idUSKCN0T726V20151118, Retrieved December 19, 2015.

10. "Fact Sheet: Strengthening Community Policing," Press Release, December 1, 2014. Retrieved December 19, 2016 from https://www.whitehouse.gov/the-press-office/2014/12/01/ fact-sheet-strengthening-community-policing

11. For reference, see Public Relations Society of America (PRSA) Member Code of Ethics, which lists honesty as one if the profession's core values. Can be retrieved at prsa.org.

References

At Last Communications. (2015). Government communication and public affairs through the eyes of John Verrico. Retrieved December 19, 2016 from http://www.atlastcommunications. com/our-observations/government-communication-and-public-affairs-through-the-eyes-of-john-verric/

Bogan, J. (2014, October 19). As low-income housing boomed, Ferguson pushed back. *St. Louis Post-Dispatch*. Retrieved from www.stltoday.com/news/local/metro

Broussard, J. C. (1986). *Establishing a public information office for the city of New Orleans* (Unpublished master's thesis). Louisiana State University. School of Journalism. Baton Rouge, Louisiana.

Byers, C. (2014, January 18). NAACP files complaint against St. Louis County police. *St. Louis Post-Dispatch*. Retrieved from http://www.stltoday.com/news/local/crime-and-courts

Capehart, J. (2015, July 16). How Eric Garner changed the national conversation on race and police. *The Washington Post*. Retrieved from https://www.washingtonpost.com/blogs/post-partisan/wp/2015/07/16/how-eric-garner-changed-the-national-conversation-on-race-and-police/?utm_term=.b384ce45ab85

Coombs, W. T. (2007). Crisis management and communications. *Institute for Public Relations*. Retrieved from http://www.instituteforpr.com/essential_knowledge/detail/crisis_managementand_communications

Coombs, W. T., & Holladay, S. (2010). *PT strategy and application: Managing influence*. New York, NY: Wiley and Blackwell.

Davies, N. (2009). *Flat earth news*. London, UK: Random House.

Deere, S. (2014, September 26). Ferguson PR man was convicted of reckless homicide: Loses contract. Retrieved from : https://www.stltoday.com/news/local/crime-and-courts/ferguson-pr-man-was-convicted-of-reckless-homicide-loses-contract/article_c5c3d517-edd8-511b-9912-566909e54a09.html

DelReal, J. A. (2014, December 26). Michael Brown memorial destroyed overnight. *The Washington Post*. Retrieved from http://www.highbeam.com/doc/1P2-37526969.html?refid=easy_hf

Doorley, J., & Garcia, F. (2015). *Reputation management: The key to successful public relations and corporate communication*. New York, NY: Routledge.

Fearn-Banks, K. (2007). *Crisis communications: A casebook approach* (3rd ed.). New York, NY: Routledge.

Fearn-Banks, K. (2017). *Crisis communications: A casebook approach* (5th ed.). New York, NY: Routledge.

Fink, S. (1986). *Crisis management: Planning for the inevitable*. New York, NY: American Management Association. Cited in Doorley, J., & Garcia, F. (2015). *Reputation management: The key to successful public relations and corporate communication*. New York, NY: Routledge.

Grunig, J. E. (1997). A situational theory of publics: Conceptual history, recent challenges and new research. In D. Moss, T. MacManus, & D. Vercic (Eds.), *Public relations research: An international perspective* (pp. 3–46). London: ITB Press.

Grunig, J. E. (2001). Two-way symmetrical public relations: Past, present, and future. In R. L. Heath (Ed.), *Handbook of public relations* (pp. 11–30). Thousand Oaks, CA: Sage.

Grunig, J. E., & Hunt, T. (1984). *Managing public relations*. New York, NY: Holt, Rinehart and Winston.

Heise, J. A. (1985). Toward closing the confidence gap: An alternative approach to communication between public and government. *Public Administration Quarterly*, 9(2), 196–217.

Henderson, K., & Miller, A. (2014). Twitter's role in the modern newsroom: Circumventing the gatekeepers and pounding the digital pavement. In B. A. Musa & J. Willis (Eds.), *From Twitter to Tahrir Square: Ethics in social and new media communication*, Vol. 1 (pp. 3–19). Santa Barbara, CA: Praeger.

Hohenberg, J. (1973). The professional journalist: A guide to the practices and principles of the news media. 3RD. ed. Holt, Rinehart, & Winston: New York: NY.

Hudson, D. (2014). President Obama creates task force on 21st century policing. *White House Blog*. Retrieved from https://www.whitehouse.gov/blog/2014/12/18/president-obama-creates-task-force-21st-century-policing

Institute for Crisis Management. (2013). Annual ICM report: News coverage of business crises during 2012. *22*(1), p. 4. Retrieved July 2, 2018 from https://crisisconsultant.com/wp-content/uploads/2014/11/2012-Crisis-Report_FINAL.pdf

Kent, M. L. (2013). Using social media dialogically: Public relations role in reviving democracy. *Public Relations Review, 39*, 337–345.

Ki, E., & Hon, L. (2009). A measure of relationship cultivation strategies. *Journal of Public Relations Research, 21*(1), 1–24.

Kohler, J. (2014, September 30). Ferguson PR consultant told city he had a college degree; now he says he doesn't. *St. Louis Post-Dispatch*. Retrieved from https://www.stltoday.com/news/local/crime-and-courts/ferguson-pr-consultant-told-city-officials-he-had-a-college/article_cc328485-3c0c-5fc6-98a0-b66b4ca1739f.html.

Ledingham, J. A. (2003). Explicating relationship management as a general theory of public relations. *Journal of Public Relations Research, 15*(2), 181–198.

Ledingham, J. A., & Bruning, S. D. (1998). Relationship management in public relations: Dimensions of an organization-public relationship. *Public Relations Review, 24*(1), 55–65.

Lee, T. (2014, October 2). Fired Ferguson rep Devin James' public relations nightmare. *MSNBC*. Retrieved from http://www.msnbc.com/msnbc/fired-ferguson-rep-devin-james-public-relations-nightmare

Liu, B. F., Horsley, J. S., & Yang K. (2012). Overcoming negative media coverage: Does government communication matter? *Journal of Public Administration Research and Theory, 22*, 597–621.

Loftin, https://www.washingtonpost.com/news/grade-point/wp/2015/09/17/mizzou-chancellor-responds-after-student-body-president-is-called-the-n-word/?utm_term=.0c71aff3a328

Lowery, W., Leonnig, C., & Berman, M. (2014, August 13). Even before Michael Brown's slaying in Ferguson, racial questions hung over police. *The Washington Post*. Retrieved from https://www.washingtonpost.com/politics/even-before-teen-michael-browns-slaying-in-mo-racial-questions-have-hung-over-police/2014/08/13/78b3c5c6-2307-11e4-86ca-6f03cbd15c1a_story.html?utm_term=.1986af95d85d

Lukaszewski, J. E. (1997). Establishing individual and corporate crisis communication standards: The principles and protocols. *Public Relations Quarterly. 42*(3). 7–14.

Macnamara, J. (2013). *Journalism & PR: Unpacking "spin," stereotypes, and myths*. New York, NY: Peter Lang Publishing.

McCluskey, L. (2016). *Examining local law enforcement public relations* (Unpublished doctoral dissertation). Louisiana State University. Manship School of Mass Communication. Baton Rouge, Louisiana.

The New York Times. (2015, August 10). What happened in Ferguson? Retrieved from https://www.nytimes.com/interactive/2014/08/13/us/ferguson-missouri-town-under-siege-after-police-shooting.html.O'Connor, M. (Director). (2014). New PR headache hits Ferguson police [Television series episode]. In Larry, E. (Executive Producer). *The Reid Report*, New York, NY: MicroSoft National Broadcasting Company.

PRSA Code of Ethics. Retrieved from https://www.prsa.org/ethics/code-of-ethics/ethics-pledge.

Sanchez, R. (2014, August 15). Michael Brown shooting, protests highlight racial divide. *CNN*. Retrieved January 27, 2017, from http://www.cnn.com/2014/08/14/justice/ferguson-missouri-police-community/

Serrano, R., & Pearce, M. (2015, June 30). Police response to Ferguson protests, in a word, failed, federal draft report says. *Los Angeles Times*. Retrieved from http://www.latimes.com/nation/la-na-ferguson-draft-report-20150630-story.html

Suchman, M. C. (1995). Managing legitimacy: Strategic and institutional approaches. *Academy of Management Review, 20*(3), 571–610.

Toler, L. (2014, September 26). Post-dispatch reporter, Ferguson PR CEO get in Twitter tussle over deadlines, clothes. *Riverfront Times*. Retrieved from: https://www.riverfronttimes.com/newsblog/2014/09/26/post-dispatch-reporter-ferguson-pr-ceo-get-in-twitter-tussle-over-deadlines-clothes.

United States Department of Justice Civil Rights Department. (2015). Investigation of the Ferguson Police Department. Retrieved December 19, 2016 from https://www.justice.gov/sites/default/files/opa/press-releases/attachments/2015/03/04/ferguson_police_department_report.pdf

Wilcox, D., Cameron, G., Reber, B., & Shin, J.-H. (2013). *Think public relations*. Boston, MA: Pearson Education.

Williams, P. (2015). Justice Department: Police response made Ferguson unrest worse. *NBC*. Retrieved from https://www.nbcnews.com/storyline/michael-brown-shooting/justice-department-police-response-made-ferguson-unrest-worse-n421116

Wilson, L. and Ogden, J. Strategic communication for public relations and marketing. 6th ed. Dubuque, Iowa: Kendall Hunt.

· 5 ·

A MOVEMENT IN THE HEARTLAND, PART II

Racial Tension at Mizzou

Jinx Coleman Broussard and Shaniece Bickham

Former University of Missouri President Tim Wolfe sat atop a red convertible with his wife as they prepared to ride in the university's 2015 homecoming parade. It was a Saturday morning in October at Mizzou, the common moniker used for the university, and students and supporters were on the parade route ready to commemorate the occasion. Alumni often brag that Mizzou was the first to host a "homecoming" back in 1911, therefore the football holiday holds special significance at the university. Parade spectators would soon learn, however, that this homecoming parade would not be like any other in recent history. Racial tensions were strained on campus, ultimately turning the event into a platform for protests.

One protest involved several students carrying a banner in the parade that read, "We Support Our Minority Students" (Serven & Reese, 2015). And while this protest piqued the attention of parade goers, it was the Concerned Student 1950 protest that brought the parade to a screeching halt.[1] Adorned in matching black shirts with a red, green and black fist graphic on the front, jeans or black bottoms and black shoes or boots, members of the organization linked arms at the front of the car carrying President Wolfe. Their human chain inevitably blocked the car from moving forward. Using bull horns, the student protesters stressed that they would "not be called n*****s" on the campus any longer. Some of the protestors even had tears streaming down their faces, as they continued to chant that it was "their duty to fight for freedom," and "to win." The protest ended with chants of "power, power, power," before police officers on duty ushered the protesters to the side of the street.

These protests were in response to several racial discrimination incidents on campus during the semester. The protests support the fact that Concerned Student 1950 and others on campus did not believe the university had responded appropriately to these incidents. The 2015 homecoming parade protest would not be the end of expressions of outrage and disappointment in the university's response, or lack thereof, to the racial discrimination issues. But it served as the beginning of the end for President Tim Wolfe's tenure at the University of Missouri.

A Semester to Remember—A Timeline of Events

The fall 2015 semester proved to be a difficult period for Mizzou faculty, staff, students and administrators. Several campus issues reached a tipping point that semester, many of which had been brewing for quite some time. To name a few, portions of graduate students' (many of whom are minorities and international students) health benefits had been axed, and the student body president, Payton Head, and at least two campus organizations, Concerned Student 1950 and the Legion of Black Collegians[2] were direct targets of racial slurs.

The First Amendment rights of students were being violated. (Izadi, 2015). These, of course, were in addition to the continued unrest and dissatisfaction with the university's response to the 2014 killing of unarmed African-American teen Michael Brown by Darren Wilson, a white police officer, in Ferguson, Missouri, that was discussed in Chapter 5 (Izadi, 2015). Several African-American students from Mizzou had even protested after a grand jury failed to indict Wilson. Ferguson, a St. Louis suburb, is less than a two-hour drive from Columbia. In 2016, the university reported that more than 9,500 students from the St. Louis area attended Mizzou. Although the university dealt with these issues simultaneously, racial conflict was the one that spread beyond the campus and garnered national and social media attention. A series of events, beginning with the shooting of Brown, heightened racial tensions on campus resulting in a crisis for Mizzou with several moving parts. Both internal and external communication strategies were needed, but with so many factors contributing to the crisis, communication among university administrators, public relations officials and journalists at times proved difficult.

Taylor (2011) asserts that effective crises communication in higher education settings require public relations practitioners to be part of the dominant coalition that typically includes core leaders who determine an organization's strategies and policies. Berger and Reber (2006) contend that the inclusion of a public relations practitioner in an organization's dominant coalition is an indication of formal authority. In addition, any crisis plan developed for an organization must include key leaders and the top public relations professionals. When this does not occur, managing a crisis becomes much more difficult (Taylor, 2011).

The described cooperation and coalition did not happen. Information sharing among top university administrators and public relations practitioners reached a stalemate during the university's handling of the racial slurs conflict on campus, according to Mary Jo Banken, executive director of the University of Missouri News Bureau. A lack of continuous communication from university higher ups affected the ability of the public relations practitioners to provide regular updates to media (Banken, personal communication, June 2016).[3] The successful relationship between public relations practitioners and journalists hinges on the effective flow of information between the two groups. This involves a high level of relationship building during times when organizations are not battling a crisis, and open communication and transparency during times when they are. Though the relationship between public relations practitioners and journalists might be viewed as a "necessary evil" at times, without the relationship, journalists otherwise might not receive some information (Sallot & Johnson, 2006). In the case of Mizzou, the public relations practitioners had already established a good rapport with journalists who regularly cover the university. Thus, transparency and open communication would not have been a problem if the public relations practitioners would have had access to the decisions being made about the crisis.

Ferguson and Columbia—So Close, Yet So Far

Racial tensions and conflict at the university did not start in 2015. It had been a little more than one year after the killing of Michael Brown in Ferguson, yet trouble was on the horizon about one hundred-twenty miles away on the campus of Mizzou. Other than proximity, Columbia and Ferguson had very little in common. Ferguson—predominantly African-American, economically depressed, and arguably despairing; Columbia—home to the state's flagship university, predominantly white, and viewed positively. U.S. Census 2010 data indicate that approximately 67 percent of Ferguson's population is African-American, and between 2011–2015, only 20.9 percent of the residents over age 25 had earned bachelor's degrees or higher. The median household income for the same period in Ferguson was $42,738. The 2015 population was 21,059. On the contrary, in Columbia, U.S. Census 2010 data show that 79 percent of the city's population is White, and between 2011–2015, 55.5 percent of the residents in the area over age 25 had earned bachelor's degrees or higher. The 2011–2015 median household income was $44,907. Columbia's 2015 population was 119,108.

Despite the differences in population and demographics between Ferguson and Columbia, the one thing the two areas had in common was the issue of race. Race was at the center of protests that followed the shooting of Michael Brown on August 9, 2014, and race was at the core of developments that led to the fall of President Wolfe on November 9, 2015.

The Issue of Race and Mizzou

While the rest of America might not have been aware of racial tension at Mizzou, the first public university west of the Mississippi River, the fall 2015 semester was not the first time these issues had taken center stage on the campus. Mizzou was founded in 1839, but African-American students were not admitted to the university until 1950. The university did not hire its first African-American faculty member, Arvarh Strickland, until 1969 (Division of Inclusion, Diversity & Equity, University of Missouri, n.d.; Eligon, 2015). Now, more than 50 years after the admission of the first African-American student, and more than 40 years after the integration of the faculty, African-American students complained about a hostile environment in which their reports of racial incidents elicited little acknowledgment or rectification (Eligon, 2015). Racist graffiti on buildings, including a Swastika drawn with feces, and being called the N-word were just some of the complaints from students (Eligon, 2015).

In recent years, Mizzou had made some attempts to address inclusiveness. The university began conducting a periodic climate study in 2001 to ascertain the culture on the campus. The study included data collection from 2002 through 2005, and again in 2009. In 2016, the study expanded to include all University of Missouri campuses and administrative offices. The most recent survey results available are from 2009. This phase of the study focused solely on Mizzou students. Approximately 12 percent, 3,522 students, of the student population responded. Key results showed that approximately 85 percent of the survey respondents believed that Mizzou became a more welcoming campus over a two-year period (Mizzou Climate Survey, 2009). Similarly, 86 percent of the respondents believed diversity should be embraced among campus administrators, faculty staff, student leaders and students. A slight minority of the respondents, 42.6 percent, had taken between one to three diversity courses (Mizzou Climate Survey, 2009).

In 2005, Mizzou appointed its first diversity officer, Roger Worthington. This was also the year that the Legion of Black Collegians requested a required diversity course (Bergen, 2010). Another attempt from the university to address inclusiveness in the form of a proposed diversity course did not materialize until 2010 (Landsbaum & Weber, 2015). Led by Worthington, a Campus Climate and Training Task Force submitted a proposal for the course to the university's Faculty Council in 2009, which also did not pass (Bergen, 2010). In spring 2010, the faculty voted down yet another proposal that had the support of the Legion of Black Collegians and the Four Front Minority Presidents Council[4] (Bergen, 2010). Shortly thereafter in 2011, Worthington resigned from his position with Mizzou. Five years later, a proposal to require students in the College of Arts and Humanities to take a three-hour course designated as "diversity intensive" passed. An article from the college stated that "the events of fall 2015 forcefully demonstrated that the concerns students first raised in 1990 have not disappeared" (Yount, 2016).

The continuous negative votes over almost a decade arguably signaled to students of color a lack of commitment on the part of the university's faculty to address racial concerns, specifically the wants and needs of an underrepresented group. Public relations scholars note excellent public relations is grounded in creating and maintaining mutually beneficial relationships between organizations and their publics, also called stakeholders (Grunig & Hunt, 1984; Grunig & Grunig, 1992). Absent those basic tenets of relationship management, crises can occur.

"To say that the communications function can make or break an institution, particularly in a time of crisis, is an understatement" (Lawson, 2007, p. 97). According to Fearn-Banks (2007), "a crisis interrupts normal business transactions and can sometimes threaten the existence of the organization" (p. 8). Mizzou's failure to address diversity and inclusion issues allowed racial tensions to rise over the years. Fearn-Banks explains that there are five stages of a crisis: prodromes, preparation/prevention, containment, recovery, and learning. The first, prodromes, are warning signs organizations must notice and heed in every effort to avoid a crisis, with the realization that some crises are inevitable. The preparation or prevention stage is where organizations plan for a possible impending crisis. Did anyone at Mizzou see this crisis coming or recognize the warning signs? And did the university pay attention to avoid the crisis?

Triggering Events

A Facebook post on September 12, 2015 from Payton Head, president of the Mizzou Student Association, detailed his experiences with being called racial slurs. For instance, he wrote that men riding on the back of a pickup truck on campus called him the N word. His post also included descriptions of some of the many stereotypes and slurs that were spewed on the Mizzou campus.

> I really just want to know why my simple existence is such a threat to society. For those of you who wonder why I'm always talking about the importance of inclusion and respect, it's because I've experienced moments like this multiple times at THIS university, making me now feel included here. (Head, Facebook post, September 12, 2015)

The post went viral, resulting in people expressing support for Head and disdain for the university's handling of the situation (Helms, 2015). R. Bowen Loftin, the university chancellor at the time, did not release an official statement from the university until September 16, 2015, along with the tweet: "Hate has no place on the Mizzou campus" (Helms, 2015). In the statement, Loftin expressed regret for not speaking out about the issue sooner.

> I regret the delay in providing a clear statement of our position to the Mizzou community, but during the intervening days MUPD interviewed affected parties, and we have been in conversation with the students involved in recent incidents to ensure that their wishes are taken into account in any public statement that we make. (Loftin Statement, cited in Syrluga, S. September 16, 2015).

Loftin also spoke out against bias incidents in his statement, while reiterating Mizzou's core values of Respect, Responsibility, Discovery and Excellence.

Angry and disappointed with the response from the university regarding Head's experience, several students coordinated a "Racism Lives Here" rally on September 24, 2015, just 12 days after Head's social media post. One week later, a second "Racism Lives Here" protest occurred in the university's student center.

The rallies did not serve as deterrents for those who wanted to engage in discriminatory actions, however. Racial slurs were again expressed on campus in early October, but this time against the Legion of Black Collegians during a homecoming rehearsal. Chancellor Loftin again released a statement acknowledging the existence of racism at Mizzou, but this time through a video message on the Office of the Chancellor's website (McDowell, 2015; Pearson, 2015). Though Loftin had responded to the evolving situation, President Wolfe still had not. This led to the homecoming parade protest led by Concerned Student 1950 on October 10.

Also in October, Concerned Student 1950 developed a list of eight demands it wanted the university and Wolfe to address. The group demanded a handwritten apology from Wolfe as well as his immediate removal as president. The list also requested that the 1969 demands from the Legion of Black Collegians be met, a curriculum that creates and enforces awareness and inclusion be developed, a 10 percent increase of African-American faculty and staff, a 10-year strategic plan for retaining marginalized students, increased funding and resources for the university's counseling center, and increased funding, resources and personnel for the university's social justice centers. Though Wolfe met with the group, he did not agree to the list (Pearson, 2015). Wolfe's lack of action illustrated a lack of adherence to Fearn-Banks' (2007) third stage: containment or when an organization works to minimize the duration and impact of the crisis. The crisis situation escalated. The president's inaction violates one of Doorley and Garcia's (2015) "ten precepts of reputation manage," that is, "know and honor your constituents" (29). In this case, the protesting students were a vocal constituent who believed their needs and concerns were not addressed.

To get the attention of the university president, on November 2, 2016, Jonathan Butler, a graduate student at Mizzou, began a hunger strike. Butler decided to refrain from eating until Wolfe either resigned or was fired (Schuppe, 2015). Students and faculty from various departments expressed support for Butler and concern about the university's leadership through official statements, walkouts and boycotts of the dining facilities (Pojmann, 2016). Even the Mizzou football team, with the support of their coaches, took a stand. The team members stated they would not practice or play until Wolfe resigned.

The Movement Goes National

This action caused a media stir as national and international news organizations descended upon the campus and placed Mizzou in the epicenter of racial strife. The expanded coverage also required the public relations practitioners at Mizzou to work with journalists whom they had not yet established a relationship. The crisis and the fact that it was not being handled smoothly were also at the forefront of news being disseminated to an audience beyond the university's local community. Coombs (2007) said long-term negative consequences can occur if a crisis is not handled properly. Mitroff and Anagnos (2001) point out that "In order for a major crisis to occur, it must exact a major toll on human lives, property, financial earnings, the reputation, and the general health and well-being of an organization" (pp. 34–35). A potential boycott by the football team posed a major threat to the school's reputation, but would have a financial impact on the school and businesses that benefit from directly or indirectly from football on a Saturday in Columbia and beyond. A forfeited game would have potentially cost the university $1 million (Tracy & Southall, 2015).

Finally, on November 9, 2015, both President Wolfe and Chancellor Loftin resigned. It is important to note, however, that Loftin's resignation was mainly because of other campus issues, while Wolfe's was a direct result of the racial tensions and his lack of response to them (Addo, personal communication, June 2016; Banken, personal communication, June 2016).

Wolfe's resignation, in particular, marked the end of Butler's hunger strike and student boycotts, but the racist acts on campus continued. For example, on November 10, an anonymous user on the social media application Yik Yak made violent threats. Additional fake social media accounts were created and used to post racial slurs, and the Black Culture Center sign was vandalized on November 12 (Pojmann, 2016). Though the resignations had occurred, the university still faced an uphill battle while dealing with the crisis.

Mizzou's School of Journalism Faces Its Own Crisis

An irony of this case is that Mizzou is home to one of the preeminent journalism and public relations schools in the nation—the highly acclaimed Missouri School of Journalism. A situation within a situation—it was also experiencing a crisis. While the university was immersed in its on-going crisis, on November 10, 2015, newspaper websites, cable and television broadcasts, and Internet stories showed Melissa Click, identified as a Mizzou faculty member in the department of communications, in a videotape trying to impede student journalist Tim Tai from documenting the protest that was occurring in a public space. Tai, who was freelancing for ESPN, cited his First Amendment rights and stood his ground, but as KCTV 5 News in Kansas City reported, Click called for "'muscle' to stop Tai (Collman, November 10, 2015, headline). Other media reported similar language.[5] The video of Click's action and exchange went viral and reflected negatively on the preeminent University of Missouri School of Journalism.

In reality, Click was not a member of the journalism school's faculty but was what is termed a courtesy appointment.[6] Such a distinction was not evident to the perhaps millions of viewers who saw the video and viewed or read the coverage in such media organizations as *The New York Times*, CNN, National Public Radio (NPR) and *The Washington Post*. As Suzette Heiman, professor and director of planning and communication for the School of Journalism, noted, ". . . it really quickly became an issue" because "people were asking how the school could hire somebody on the journalism faculty who doesn't know about rights guaranteed in the First Amendment." That, "of course, was not the case" (Heiman, personal communication, June 2016). The School of Journalism had to handle that crisis absent direction from the University. Its dean, himself a former reporter, producer and news director, observed the actions of public relations professionals, but in his capacity as head of the school, he interacted with local, national and international journalists. His perspective as well as takeaways will follow later in this chapter.

The University's Crisis Response

Even with the continued racist incidents, protests and boycotts, the university did not operate in crisis mode right away. Seeger, Sellnow, and Ulmer (2003) describe crises as unique events in the history of organizations that come as a surprise, pose a significant threat, and require immediate response. Additionally, crises interrupt the achievement of an organization's "high-priority goals" (p. 7). Crises at Mizzou could usually be defined as events that pose danger to the university, such as shootings on campus, natural disasters and cyber issues. (Banken). Mizzou's racial conflict crisis was different from other crises the university had faced, however. The school clearly did not recognize this different type of crisis; it ignored Fearn-Banks's prodromes or warning signs, and it was not prepared. To complicate matters, two top leaders from the university were involved, but a consistent message from both was nonexistent, according to Banken, executive director of the University of Missouri News Bureau. Public relations literature and practice hold that messages must address the concerns or needs of stakeholders, communicate what the organization wants them to understand and remember, and must be consistent and believable. Source credibility is essential, especially during a crisis, but the message sender should not appear overly assuring (Seeger, 2006). In this case, the university was lacking on all fronts; its decision makers and administration officials who should have been spokespersons were silent. Seeger (2006) said it is crucial to distribute accurate and useful information to restore order.

Thus, to keep the media informed to the extent possible, Banken, along with five professional staff members and three or four undergraduate and graduate students, worked to release statements about each incident as it occurred. Banken recounted for this chapter that she realized that this was not a good strategy. Excellent public relations entails being proactive and scanning the environment to identify, assess and manage issues that could potentially become a problem. Writing primarily about organizations, Doorley and Garcia (2015) say challenges should be neutralized before they become crises. "Manage the issue so that you won't have to manage a crisis" (p. 270).

Mizzou already had a crisis team, as well as a crisis communication plan that had been in place for at least 15 years (Hollingshead, personal communication; Banken, personal communication). Therefore, the school should have been poised to manage the crisis even as it unfolded. In hindsight, the team should have been called together earlier because the university was facing a reputational crisis. Banken concluded that this did not happen initially because the vice president of marketing and communications and her supervisor were focused on how to keep their jobs, while still not realizing that the university was in the middle of an actual crisis. Those actions can be characterized as short-term and personal instead of what was needed for the good of the university now and over time. It was not until the chancellor and president resigned, and the violent threats were posted through Yik Yak, that the staff and university officials entered crisis communication mode and developed strategies to deal with the situation. The vice president of marketing and communication also lost her job.

After the Yik Yak incident, a small crisis team met with the provost to develop email messages for Mizzou's internal stakeholders, which in turn were also sent to alumni, and prospective students and their parents. The media also reported on the emails, according to Banken.

One of the basic tenets of public relations is being transparent and keeping the lines of communication open among stakeholders. Building relationships and trust with media professionals is as important as harmonious relationships with such stakeholders as students—as in the case of Mizzou. Crisis communication is even more important than day-to-day two-way communication for an organization because it is the major means of mitigating negative outcomes. One goal is to communicate actions the organization is taking to address the situation and to propose actions stakeholders should take (Spence, Lachlan, & Griffin, 2007). As Fearn-Banks (2007) explains "crisis communications…is concerned with the transferring of information to significant persons (publics) to either help avoid a crisis (or negative occurrence), recover from a crisis, and maintain or enhance reputation" (p. 2).

Banken had employed these practices over the past 28 years while serving as the official liaison between the university and the media. Prior to the racial conflict crisis, Banken had always had a strong relationship with top administration that allowed her to be kept "in the loop consistently especially concerning potentially negative issues." Banken said her relationship with the administrators granted her direct access to them so that she could easily reach them when reporters had tough questions. "They [top administrators] have trusted me and have given me full information from which I have offered recommendations on what is conveyed to the press," Banken said. "They have relied on my expertise and University knowledge as well as my knowledge and experience with the press."

The fact that this was not happening during the racial conflict crisis negatively affected Mizzou's reputation. According to leading scholar Charles Fombrun (1996), reputation "is the sum of the images various constituents have of the organization" (p. 9). Doorley and Garcia (2015) take the definition further, arguing that reputation equals "the sum of images," which are based on the "critical components" of "performance," "behavior," and "communication" (p. 4). Jennifer Hollingshead, interim vice chancellor for marketing and communications, came on board in the aftermath of the crisis.[7] Also recognizing the need for consistent messaging to strengthen Mizzou's reputation, Hollingshead went to work immediately with Banken and staff members to create two communications pieces titled the "State of Mizzou." Communication was at the top of the agenda, and the goal was to recap events and to report on the progress the university had made with addressing issues of concern. The "State of Mizzou" pieces were made available to the public and media, and posted online. Work also began immediately on a "State of the University Address," which was delivered in January 2016. Key target audiences for the "State of Mizzou" pieces and public address were students, faculty, staff, alumni, donors, legislators, media and the general public in Columbia. Hollingshead said that the written communication pieces and public address were well-received.

In hindsight, Banken said, the crisis team outlined in the plan, which varies according to the crisis, should have been called together immediately. Though Hollingshead was not on the team during the time when the crisis communication plan could have been implemented, she agreed with Banken that not doing so was "a pivotal mistake" for the university (Hollingshead, personal communication). That is also the view of crisis communication expert Gerard Breaud (personal communication, October 2016), who argues that the team should prepare long before any type of unforeseen crisis occurs. He called the process planning on a "clear and sunny day," before a storm is at an organization's front door. Moreover, one must communicate before, during, and after the crisis. Prior systematic and productive planning and action are crucial because the organization does not have time or luxury to figure things out during the crisis.

The lack of a consistent message also hindered Banken's ability to provide as much information to the media as she normally would, because she simply did not have it. The University of Missouri News Bureau had spent years cultivating relationships and building trust with the media. Therefore, the media understood that if the university's public relations team was not talking to them, there was a pretty good reason. "We never say 'no comment' to media," Banken said. "Instead, the public relations practitioners are honest in conveying when they don't have the information, apologizing for not being able to provide it, and explaining why they are unable to give them what they are requesting."

The breakdown in communication between the University of Missouri News Bureau and the administrators led to a breakdown in public relations strategy. The staff fielded calls and emails from both the public and the media. Clear messages from the university were not available, but members of the media were free to come to the campus to cover the events associated with the crisis, and many of them did, Banken said. Fearn-Banks' fourth stage in crisis communication is recovery. The News Bureau's efforts to provide the most up-to-date information as possible was the first step in rebuilding the university's image and reputation.

Even with the initial breakdown in communication between the university and the media, in the end, Banken said that she does not think her relationship with the media was substantially affected. "We've worked very hard to establish relationships, you know, exactly for this reason. So when we do have these negative issue stories, reporters trust us enough to know that we are going to get the information to them," Banken said.

The Journalists' Perspective

One of the journalists with which the News Bureau staff had interacted frequently was Koran Addo of the *St. Louis Post-Dispatch*. As the higher education reporter, he covered news stories at Mizzou quite often, even though he physically worked two hours away in St. Louis. He had covered the protests in Ferguson, Missouri, in 2014, and he was poised to cover the crisis at Mizzou in 2015. The paper had provided consistent coverage of the various protests at the university, but the coverage picked up steam when the news broke about the football team's decision to refuse to practice or play until Wolfe resigned. The football team released a statement through the Legion of Black Collegians, which also tweeted a photo of the team on the night of November 9, 2015.

Addo, who was also on duty as the Saturday night reporter, immediately began to tweet players to secure interviews, called student contacts at Mizzou and reached out to the university's public relations staff and athletic department for official statements.

"A Division 1 football team saying that they're not going to play; they're not going to practice until the president of the University steps down, was a big moment," said Addo during an interview for this case study.

The *St. Louis Post-Dispatch* assigned two staff reporters, one student reporter and three photographers to cover the crisis, said Addo. Back at the newspaper, the editors; the education team, Elisa Crouch and Jessica Bock; data reporter, Walter Moskop; and other key staff people followed the crisis closely.

Addo indicated that his coverage of the crisis could be categorized as both descriptive and interpretative. In the days immediately following the resignations, his stories focused mainly on the basic facts of who, what, when and where. After three days of coverage, his stories became more analytical, and explored the underlying issues that resulted in the resignations.

Throughout the crisis, Addo said that he communicated frequently with the university's public relations officials. Though there were instances when they could not get information to him right away, Addo understood that it was not because they were stonewalling him. Was confident in that assessment because of the positive working relationships that existed with the public relations officials prior to the crisis. Even with the added requests the PR practitioners were receiving from national media, Addo said that he still feels that they did a good job of managing it all. "There was certainly some questions and some things that were requested that we did not get right away as far as specifics," Addo said, adding that sometimes information trickled out. Overall, he received the information he wanted, even though it didn't come as quickly as possible.

As the local reporter, Addo used a combination of communication methods to reach university public relations officials and to receive information. Cell phone communication proved most beneficial, but he also relied on email, social media and public records requests. Key advice that Addo would give to future journalists is to build working relationships in advance. Addo offered the following.

> If something happens on a Saturday night, you need to know that there are certain people that you can call on the weekends on their cell phones and they are going to get back to you with some information. You just need to have those relationships because you just never know when you're going to need somebody after hours when the offices are closed.

The *Columbia Missourian* also dedicated several staff members to covering the crisis. According to executive editor Tom Warhover, at various times, between three and eight reporters were assigned to the coverage, with three reporters dedicated specifically to the higher education beat. It was early in October 2015 when Warhover's newspaper made the decision to "retool" so that the paper could place more focus on the crisis as it unfolded.

Warhover described the relationship with the public relations officials at Mizzou as "on again, off again" even before the crisis. At times, it appeared as if the university's public relations team was making it difficult for reporters to get information, Warhover said. For example, some faculty members would direct reporters' requests to the News Bureau, but the News Bureau practitioners would then say that they had to speak with faculty members before following up with the journalists. Once the follow-up occurred, if journalists had additional questions, the public relations officials would again have to get back to them with the answers. Warhover said he believes that this process introduced the "potential for error." No method of communication proved more beneficial than another, Warhover said. Effective communication truly depended on the day and the person being contacted. Even with these factors, Warhover said that the *Columbian-Missourian* did receive dedicated attention from Mizzou's public relations team just by virtue of the newspaper's longevity. Warhover added that the newspaper's staff covered all press conferences associated with the crisis and published and/or addressed all press releases sent from the News Bureau.

David Kurpius had been on the job as dean of the School of Journalism less than six months when the protests began and when a smaller crisis enveloped the school. As a working journalist before earning a doctorate and joining the academy, Kurpius was involved as both the public face of the J-School and as an observer of journalists and their interaction with sources.

According to Kurpius, Tim Tai was extremely professional when confronted by the protests and Click. "He demonstrated that he understood his role as a journalist and the boundaries under which he should operate. He knew the First Amendment protected the rights of the press as well as the rights under which the protestors could operate," and he proceeded accordingly (Kurpius, personal communication, 2017).

Students in the J-School's documentary journalism program also succeeded in reporting on the protests because they used their relationships with protestors to get more insight in the protests and to film from the inside. Kurpius stressed that relationships were built on trust, not friendship. "Because of the trust, they got stuff others would not have gotten and they provided citizens with a perspective they wouldn't have gotten."

Relationships also benefited local reporter Koran Addo, according to Kurpius. Both men knew each other from when both worked in Baton Rouge years before. "He kept my cell phone number and called me," Kurpius said. "There were so many media requests, I could not get through them all." He took Addo's call.

As a former working journalist who has also taught and now leads one of the largest and preeminent journalism schools in the nation, Kurpius put himself in the shoes of journalists who interviewed him. Here is what he observed: Many journalists did not understand the issue they were covering and were unable to provide context. This was especially true for out-of-town journalists who just parachuted in to cover the protests. "I dreaded the interviews with reporters who had not done their homework. It was hard to discuss the topic with reporters who did not." The situation was even more difficult when talking with reporters who did not understand the issue of race. "Reporters who did understand the issue had much better interviews because we did not have to explain as much… I remember reporters who had experience in covering racial issues that almost made them experts," Kurpius said.

Takeaways for PR Professionals

Recognize When You Are in Crisis

Fearn-Banks' (2007) final stage of crisis communication is learning. During this stage, public relations practitioners work to determine what went wrong so that the crisis can be prevented in the future. The glaring miscalculation that would have helped Mizzou deal with the situation better was recognizing that "the definition of a crisis includes the reputational crisis" (Hollingshead, personal communication). If this would have happened, Hollingshead said that there would have been authority to activate the crisis plan to bring key players together immediately—in the middle of the night—if needed.

Strong, Informed Leadership Is Necessary in Crisis

For public relations to be done effectively in a university setting, strong leadership must be present. Recognize that public relations managers are members of the dominant coalition and are what DeSanto and Garner (2001, describe as "the coordinating force leading to the collaborative effort" (p. 546). Even if the organization's decision makers—leadership—are not involved, the communication manager should step in and serve as the boundary scanner and facilitator for the organization, identifying issues and problems that could become crises, and becoming the crucial liaison that facilitates communication between the organizations and its stakeholders during and after the crisis. This means they need to determine and respond to external threats and become the gate- and door-keeper of the organization who handles crisis communication.

These are the roles Banken and her staff aspired to. However, the leadership above her prevented her from being successful. As she stated, these leaders must know the university and the people it serves; and they must "care about the university more than their own brand or reputation," (Banken, personal communication). Without being in the dominant coalition with the leaders of the university, Banken and her staff were functioning during the crisis only as communication technicians who engaged in the technical or craftwork of public relations.

University PR Professionals Must Build and Maintain Relationships with Key Stakeholders, in This Case, African-American Student Communication Was Key

Through two-way symmetrical communication, Mizzou can engage in targeted outreach to minorities and others affected by the crisis to develop a mutually beneficial relationship (Grunig & Hunt, 1984). This involves listening to ascertain the wants, needs, issues and concerns of each public, and addressing those in the appropriate manner that benefits the stakeholder and the organization. Building relationships with the opinion leaders in the specific public can maximize trust and legitimacy and contribute to transparency. Those affected would be able to share their concerns with the university, and the university would also be able to communicate honestly and effectively in a crisis and beyond. "Establishing positive relationships and a reservoir of goodwill before an event is critical to the successful management of a crisis" (Seeger, 2006, p. 238). As DeSanto and Garner offer, relationship building is "crucial to the overall success of the institution . . ." (p. 546).

Build and Maintain Relationships with Journalists and Social Media Experts Who Cover Higher Education

Don't wait for a crisis. Consider holding quarterly to semi-annul briefings with media gatekeepers and journalists. Meet at least once a year with journalists to apprise them of significant milestones or happenings. Produce facts sheets and other data that can be circulated during briefings and crises.

Be Honest and Factual in a Timely Manner

Journalists in this case felt stone-walled, even though good relationships existed between the two sides. The radio silence from the leaders in the administration was deafening. This trickled down to silence from the public relations professionals. As we have seen elsewhere in this book, lack of information contributes to a vacuum in which rumors and misinformation can circulate and be viewed as facts. The lack of information allowed others to control the narrative and frustrated the journalists and their audiences. The void also contributed to poor relationships with journalists who are main conduits of information during a crisis. Hence, everyone in crisis must communicate consistent and truthful messages from the official source(s).

Takeaways for Journalists

Do Not Allow Public Relations Practitioners to Get Away with Not Answering Questions

Be persistent and keep asking. Journalists should call repeatedly to get answers, and when they still are not getting responses, they should find other sources to get the information. Going around public relations practitioners, however, does take courage, Warhover admitted (personal communication).

Challenge PR Professionals About the Answers They Give

If it is clear they are withholding information, dig deeper. Even with good PR-press relations, some practitioners tend to withdraw or give just the information basics in crisis. Do not allow this to happen, especially in a case that highlights an important social issue. Provide the needed context and information that will allow journalists to tell a deeper, richer story.

Establish Relationships on Your Beat…and Beyond

Addo's prior relationships with PR people in the Missouri News Bureau enabled him to communicate frequently with them and to understand they were not "stonewalling him." Kurpius suggested having a good reliable network of sources beyond official spokespersons. These individuals can be helpful contacts and even more available during a crisis. Addo gave similar advice, noting that he was able to talk to contacts in the university's athletic department and other areas, as well as students. And if you move away, don't discard contact information! You never know when you might have to reach out to a source again. That served Addo well when he contacted Kurpius during the crises at the University of Missouri.

Understand the Laws and Protocols That Govern the Profession

As Kurpius noted, Tim Tai persisted and successfully did his job because he knew what the First Amendment allowed both him and the protestors to do. If you know your rights and behave respectfully, it will help you establish trust and credibility as well as successfully do your job. "You can stand up for your rights and be respectful at the same time," Kurpius said, adding that is what Tai did. Additionally, he continued that the documentary students "had access because of relationships based on trust."

Out-of-Town Press Can Affect the Local Press

When the story finally went national, press from across the nation converged on the small town of Columbia, Missouri. As we have heard across cases, this is standard in crisis. However, Kurpius had a different take on the onslaught because many reporters in the *Columbia Missourian* are students. Kurpius said news organizations should also understand the pressures national reporters can put on local newsrooms. Many who parachute go to local news operations to "try to get shorthand on context," thus taking an additional toll on newsroom staff. Again, we encourage national press to do their homework before they come in to an area to cover a complicated story.

Recognize That It Takes an Army to Cover Crises

A newsroom must have enough boots on the ground to cover the story. However, the organizations must also have good newsroom leaders who pay attention to fairness, accuracies, redundancies or other information that could be problematic. Good editors have to organize, fact check and make the information ready for dissemination to the public.

A Special Takeaway Unique to Higher Education

Six years before those arguments, DeSanto and Garner (2001, p. 546) recommended six "hands-on" best practices for public relations in higher education settings. Internal goals must support the short and long-term institutional goals, key stakeholders for individual units as well as for the institution must be identified and prioritized, relationships with opinion leaders should be identified and established, communication must occur through one clear voice, evaluations should be on-going, and public relations should be "recognized as the coordinating force leading the collaborative effort."

Public relations practitioners in higher education should want to work for an institution that they can believe in, while also making sure that the leaders of that institution care about the institution (Banken, 2016). From there, they can build their credibility with the administrators, as well as with the media.

"Solid, mutual respect will pay off during a major reputational crisis such as what we experienced. I believe we will come back stronger than ever but we must find solid permanent leadership first. It's critical," Banken said.

Conclusion

University public relations practitioners and journalists working during the Mizzou racial conflict crisis recognized that the flow of information was not at a level that the two groups were used to. This was unusual because a pre-established, working relationship was already in place. Existing relationships between public relations practitioners and journalists usually make working together easier when crises arise. In this case, though the lack of information was frustrating at times, because the relationships were already in place, no one group felt as though the other was trying to prevent the other from doing assigned jobs.

The public relations practitioners provided information as they received it, while welcoming journalists to explore the crisis to obtain any information they needed on their own. The media dedicated teams of journalists to the crisis to ensure that they had the manpower to fully investigate and report on the issue, with or without the PR professionals. This case is unique because usually the two sides of communication (journalism and PR) are blaming each other. However, the strife at Mizzou was internal, and it manifested itself in the dysfunctional relationship between the top leaders of the entire university and the leaders of the crisis communication effort. The blame for the lack of communication in this case could be laid directly at the feet of those in charge, outside the communications team, who failed to understand or allow for a response to their constituents. Upper administration did not even know their university was in crisis. Necessary information was not given to the people in charge of communication. The journalists know this and did not put the blame on the PR professionals. This mutual understanding and respect between the public relations practitioners and journalists is unique to this case compared to the others we explore in this book.

Notes

1. Concerned Student 1950 is named after the first year African-American students were admitted to the University of Missouri.
2. The Legion of Black Collegians was founded in 1968 on the campus of the University of Missouri as an advocate and government for African-American students. The university first recognized the organization as a campus government in 1969.
3. Each journalist and public relations practitioner interviewed for this chapter was interviewed only once, unless otherwise noted; therefore, the first citation will provide the pertinent information. Individual in-text citations will not continue throughout.
4. Four Front Council collectively represents minority student groups on the campus of the University of Missouri.
5. See, for example, Folkenflik, D. (November 10, 2015). Analysis: At the University of Missouri, and unlearned free speech, NPR, Retrieved from: http://www.npr.org/2015/11/10/455532242/analysis-at-the-university-of-missouri-an-unlearned-free-speech-lesson; Huguelet, A. & Victor, D. (November 10, 2015) "I need some muscle": Missouri activists block journalist, Retrieved from https://www.nytimes.com/2015/11/10/us/university-missouri-protesters-block-journalists-press-freedom.html; University of Missouri professor Click illegally KICKS OUT, Daily Mail, November 10, 2015, Retrieved from wwwdailymaily.co.uk; Oberholtz, C. (2015, November 19). Missouri University communications professors calls for "muscles" to stop student reporter covering protest. KCTV5 News. Retrieved from http://www.kctv5.com/story/30479435/mu-communications-professor-calls-for-muscle-to-stop-student-reporter-covering-protest.
6. According to Suzette Heiman, professor and director of planning and communication for the School of Journalism, a courtesy designation can denote when a faculty member in one department or school is "working with doctoral students in research" or similar capacity, and not teaching (Heiman, personal communication, June 8, 2016).
7. Ellen de Graffenreid held the vice chancellor for marketing and communications position during the crisis. She was terminated soon after the crisis.

References

Bergen, K. (2010, March 3). Road to diversity course has bumps, hurdles. *Columbia Missourian*. Retrieved from http://munews.missouri.edu/daily-clip-packets/2010/03-03-2010.pdf

Berger, B. K., & Reber, B. H. (2006). *Gaining influence in public relations: The role of resistance in practice*. Mahwah, NJ: Lawrence Erlbaum.

Collman, A. (2015, November 10). "I need some muscle": Bizzare moment University of Missouri media professor illegally KICKS OUT journalist from covering race demonstrations. *Daily Mail*. Retrieved from https://www.dailymail.co.uk/news/article-3311950/

The-moment-University-Missouri-activists-including-media-professor-encircled-student-ESPN-photographer-tried-kick-public-protests.html

Coombs, W. T. (2007). Attribution theory as a guide for post-crisis communication research. *Public Relations Review, 33*(2), 135–139.

DeSanto, B. J., & Garner, R. B. (2001). Strength in diversity. The place of public relations in higher education institutions. In R. L. Heath & G. Vasquez (Eds.), *Handbook of Public Relations* (pp. 543–550). Thousand Oaks, CA: Sage. Doorley, J., & Garcia, F. (2015). *Reputation management: The key to successful public relations and corporate communication.* New York, NY: Routledge.

Division of Inclusion, Diversity & Equity, University of Missouri. (n.d.) Multicultural Mizzou: A brief timeline of social change and notable firsts at the University of Missouri. Retrieved from https://www.cnn.com/2015/11/09/us/missouri-protest-timeline/index.html

Eligon, J. (2015, November 11). At University of Missouri, black students see a campus riven by race. *The New York Times* Retrieved from https://www.nytimes.com/2015/11/12/us/university-of-missouri-protests.html?_r=0

Fearn-Banks, K. (2007). *Crisis communications: A casebook approach* (3rd Edition). Mahwah, NJ: Lawrence Erlbaum.

Fombrun, C. J. (1996). *Reputation: Realizing value from the corporate brain.* Boston, MA: Harvard Business School Press.

Grunig, J. E., & Grunig, L. A. (1992). Models of public relations and communication. In J. E. Grunig, D. M. Dozier, & W. P. Ehling (Eds.), *Excellence in public relations and communication management* (pp. 285–325). Hillsdale, NJ: Lawrence Erlbaum Associates.

Grunig, J. E., & Hunt, T. (1984). *Managing public relations.* New York, NY: Holt, Rinehart & Winston. Helms, N. (2015, September 17). Students, administration react to MSA president's statement about campus racism. *Columbia Missourian.* Retrieved from http://www.columbiamissourian.com/news/local/students-administration-react-to-msa-president-s-statement-about-campus/article_5619365e-5d8a-11e5-919e-7baa7afe0778.html

Izadi, E. (2015, November 9). The incidents that led to the University of Missouri president's resignation. *The Washington Post.* Retrieved from https://www.washingtonpost.com/news/grade-point/wp/2015/11/09/the-incidents-that-led-to-the-university-of-missouri-presidents-resignation/?utm_term=.edba4dec26ac

Landsbaum, C., & Weber, G. (2015, November 9). What happened at the University of Missouri? *Slate.* Retrieved from http://www.slate.com/blogs/the_slatest/2015/11/09/timeline_of_u_of_missouri_protests_and_president_resignation.html

Lawson, C. J. (2007). Crisis Communication. In E. L. Zdziarski, N. W. Dunkel, & J. M. Rollo (Eds.), *Campus crisis management: A comprehensive guide to planning, prevention, response, and recovery* (pp. 97–120). San Francisco, CA: John Wiley & Sons.

McDowell, M. (2015, October 5). MU Chancellor Loftin responds to report of racial slurs used on campus. *Columbia Missourian.* Retrieved from http://www.columbiamissourian.com/news/higher_education/mu-chancellor-loftin-responds-to-report-of-racial-slurs-used/article_38c31300-6b76-11e5-bf31-cf8f3d5cd67b.html

Mitroff, I., & Anagnos, G. (2001). *Managing crises before they happen. What every executive and manager needs to know about crisis management.* New York, NY: AMACOM.

Pearson, M. (2015, November 10). A timeline of the University of Missouri protests. CNN. Retrieved from http://www.cnn.com/2015/11/09/us/missouri-protest-timeline/

Pojmann, K. (2016, Spring). Mizzou in Fall 2015. MIZZOU looks back at a memorable semester with a chronology of major events. *MIZZOU*. Retrieved from https://mizzoumag.missouri.edu/2016/02/mizzou-in-fall-2015/

Sallot, L. M., & Johnson, E. A. (2006). Investigating relationships between journalists and public relations practitioners: Working together to set, frame and build the public agenda, 1991–2004. *Public Relations Review*, 32(2), 151–159.

Schuppe, J. (2015, November 10). Jonathan Butler: How a grad student's hunger strike toppled a university president. *NBC News*. Retrieved from http://www.nbcnews.com/news/us-news/jonathan-butler-how-grad-students-hunger-strike-toppled-university-president-n460161

Seeger, M. W. (2006). Best practices in crisis communication: An expert panel process. *Journal of Applied Communication Research*, 34(3), 232–244.

Seeger, M. W., Sellnow, T. L., & Ulmer, R. R. (2003). *Communication and organizational crisis*. Westport, CT: Greenwood Publishing Group.

Serven, R., & Reese, A. (2015, October 10). In homecoming parade, racial justice advocates take different paths. *Columbia Missourian*. Retrieved from http://www.columbiamissourian.com/news/in-homecoming-parade-racial-justice-advocates-take-different-paths/article_24c824da-6f77-11e5-958e-fb15c6375503.html

Svrluga, S. (2015). Mizzou chancellor after student-body president is called the n-word. *The Washington Post*. Retrieved from: https://www.washingtonpost.com/news/grade-point/wp/2015/09/17/mizzou-chancellor-responds-after-student-body-president-is-called-the-n-word/?utm_term=.0c71aff3a328.

Spence, P. R., Lachlan, K., & Griffin, D. (2007). Crisis communication, race and natural disasters. *Journal of Black Studies*, 37(4), 539–554.

Taylor, E. (2011). *HBCU crises and best practices in the discourse of renewal: A crisis communication case study of three institutions* (Unpublished doctoral dissertation) . Louisiana State University. School of Mass Communication. Baton Rouge, Louisiana.

Tracy, M., & Southall, A. (2015, November 8). Black football players lend heft to protests at Missouri. *The New York Times*. Retrieved from https://www.nytimes.com/2015/11/09/us/missouri-football-players-boycott-in-protest-of-university-president.html

University of Missouri Campus Climate Study. (2009). Retrieved from https://diversity.missouri.edu/climate/2009-Mizzou-Climate-Study.pdf

Yount, J. (2016, March 23). A&S faculty approve diversity course requirement. *Coas*. Retrieved from https://coas.missouri.edu/news/faculty-approve-diversity-course-requireme

· 6 ·

A DIVISIVE ISSUE

Susan G. Komen and Planned Parenthood

Andrea Miller

October is the month of pink—pink ribbons, pink race t-shirts, pink football socks and sweatbands. But it was the winter of 2012 that became a black eye for the nonprofit organization perpetuating all that pink, the Susan G. Komen organization. In the nonprofit's 30th anniversary year, a decision at the highest levels appeared to become about politics and not about a cure, a decision that many say still affects its funding intake some six years later.

The Susan G. Komen organization (Komen) was founded in 1982 by Nancy Brinker after her sister, the organization's namesake, died of breast cancer. Brinker vowed to do everything she could to find a cure. The result was a highly-respected global organization that funds breast cancer treatment, research and programs to create awareness and help for those with the disease. In its three decades, Komen has raised more than $2 billion and enlisted millions of women and men, survivors, friends and family members to raise the pink flag for the cause (ww5.Komen.org). Currently those flags fly in more than 50 countries around the world making it a truly global nonprofit. The rise to an international phenomenon had other nonprofits aspiring to mirror its efforts. Because of Komen, many causes are tied to specific colors—gold brings awareness to childhood cancer, royal blue is the color of autism awareness, teal is the color of ovarian cancer awareness. In fact, the pink cause was the gold standard of nonprofit awareness, fund-raising and goodwill. However, a controversial decision and a questionable communication response put the organization into a defensive tailspin; its fall was fast, and its climb back to the top steep and slow as it tried to get back in the pink.

The Decision and Timeline of Events

"They had everything to lose and they squandered it," *Dallas Morning News* columnist Jacquielyn Floyd[1] said. "I mean, and honestly, I'm just telling you what I truly think and some of what I wrote. But, I mean, to no political advantage, to in fact profound political disadvantage that I'm not sure they've completely recovered from" (personal communication, August 31, 2016).

On Tuesday, January 31, 2012, the Associated Press (AP) broke the story that the Komen Organization would no longer give money to Planned Parenthood; it was withdrawing some $700,000 in grants. At the time of the announcement, Planned Parenthood was under federal investigation for misusing government funds related to abortion services. Komen officials offered no reason for the cut, but later used the above as a starting point saying a new bylaw called for withholding funds from any agency under government investigation.

From the very beginning, Komen did not manage the information coming out about the decision in an effective or timely manner. However, Planned Parenthood did. Its response was immediate, calling the decision "politically motivated" (Groeger, 2012). Not only was the organization "alarmed and saddened" by the cut (Groeger, 2012), but the move also angered the public and many Komen affiliates as well (Watt, 2012).

Initially, Karen Handel, Komen's vice president of public policy, was accused of being the sole reason behind the move to defund Planned Parenthood (Bassett, 2012). This was a case of what scholars call the press using attribution of responsibility frame, which is one of the main intentional (or unintentional) frames used by the press in crisis situations. Handel was a well-known conservative and the public believed the decision was made to help her in a future election in Georgia, a traditionally solid red state (Bassett, 2012). Other reports suggested the decision was inevitable and a long-time coming. But that speculation came from competing voices no longer in the organization who blamed each other and everyone else for the decision to defund Planned Parenthood (PR deflect strategy). This latter strategy is like a blame hot potato. Instead of taking responsibility, each voice deflects blame on to someone else. Communication scholars have found that deflection is often a strategy when there is no strategy.

Handel, in a book titled *Planned Bullyhood* that came out in 2012 just months after the initial controversy, claimed Planned Parenthood was the one being political and partisan, calling the organization "a bunch of school-yard thugs" (Pesta, 2012). Handel describes months of heated discussions internally as well as with Planned Parenthood. The issue, Handel wrote, is that Komen wanted to restructure grants to phase out those that were awarded to middlemen. Planned Parenthood does not directly provide mammograms but refers women to other, local medical facilities for the service. Handel also claimed Komen was under pressure by the Catholic Church, which had reportedly instructed its parishioners to send their money elsewhere. At this point, Handel said she discovered the policy that appeared to make Planned Parenthood ineligible for receiving grants due to a congressional investigation into its practices. And that was that.

The communication between the two sides, Komen and Planned Parenthood, was there, Handel alleged, but said when the discussions were not progressing, it was Komen president Cecile Richards, who went to the media first—before Komen had issued a public statement. Handel described the results as an unprecedented assault on Komen from outside forces. While Handel laid the leak at the feet of Richards, she blamed the rest of the communication fiasco on Leslie Aun, the communications vice president at the time. When the Associated Press called asking questions, Aun, Handel claimed, did not stick to the negotiated script. Instead, she said Aun talked about the under investigation policy that made Planned Parenthood ineligible, a policy that many in the media would later determine appeared to be selectively applied. The agreed-upon script, according to Handel, was to focus the message on restructuring of grants, not the ineligible-by-investigation part. In an interview regarding her book to *The Daily Beast*, Handel said, "I don't know what she was thinking. It was only one of two things—it was either some sort of not handling the interview properly, or some sort of complicity … I don't know what her motivations for that were. I just know that she did it" (Pesta, 2012).

The Daily Beast was able to get a reaction from Aun, who like Handel, is no longer with Komen (Pesta, 2012). She claimed that not only was the message she delivered that day on point, but Handel had personally approved it (Pesta, 2012). "Before speaking with the AP reporter, I made sure to check in with Karen, letting her know that I would be using the messaging that she had OK'd and then I read it nearly verbatim to the reporter. If there were alternative messages I was supposed to deliver, they were not shared with me," Aun told *The Daily Beast* (Pesta, 2012).

Andrea Rader, a spokeswoman for Komen, had repeatedly declined to clarify the events or comment on the matter further to other news outlets and to this author, who reached out multiple times in spring of 2016. When reached by phone, Rader told this author that the event was in the past and that Komen Dallas was moving on. Even with time, continued stonewalling and absence of transparency can further contribute to a lack of understanding and legitimacy as well as continued poor relationships with the press.

Whoever or whatever was behind the decision, the communication effort to explain the decision was slow and inadequate. This created an information vacuum that allowed rumors and misinformation to flourish. The nonprofit waited for twenty-four hours before providing a statement via press release. Notably, while press releases are staples of PR and media relations, they often fail to answer all the questions or address issues that would be better explained via press conferences / briefings, and even via social media. It was another 12 hours, 36 total before Komen addressed the swift and growing criticism online. Komen was excoriated. The damage was done.

Kivi Leroux Miller runs a company called Nonprofit Marketing Guide with the mission to train communications directors at nonprofits on how to do their jobs. She started her 20-plus year career as a communications consultant before she started a mentoring/coaching program for communications directors who work specifically at nonprofits. She has also written two books considered the bibles on how to do the job.

"They [Komen] blew it from every direction. What they did here was just a nightmare all the way around," Miller said. "I would say the biggest thing is that they didn't communicate for more than 24 hours."

Planned Parenthood and constituency criticism filled the void.

In the next days, Brinker starred in a YouTube video, appeared on major news programs, and Komen offered two additional press releases to address criticisms (Watt, 2012). In these messages, Brinker repeatedly tried to emphasize Komen as a leader in fundraising for breast cancer research and services. Taking a page from Benoit's image restoration (1997), this step involves denial that the organization did anything wrong. Watt (2012) argues that Brinker's use of transcendence, a form of evasion of responsibility, backfired because, "by appealing to a larger moral code the rhetor may alienate that portion of the audience that does not share the rhetor's values" (p. 71). A message option within the theory of image restoration, transcendence is a technique to reduce the "offensiveness" of the action by placing the act in a more favorable context (Benoit, 1997). Brinker did this by attempting to emphasize the overall good works of the organization over the current misstep. "This attempt at image maintenance prevented her from repairing the rift Komen's decision created with supporters of the larger women's health movement" (Watt, 2012, p. 70).

Additionally, many believed Brinker made the situation worse in her MSNBC interview with Andrea Mitchell. Comments like Komen was getting favorable responses from "people who have bothered to read the material, who have bothered to understand the issues" did not translate well on camera and to her publics. Her words were perceived as insults, implying that "those who were opposed to the decision did not have a sophisticated understanding of the situation" (Watt, 2012, p. 73). After that, recommendations were made for Brinker, the founder and face of Komen, to keep a lower profile and distance herself from the controversy (Bruell, 2012).

"Regardless of how you feel about abortion, I don't think they had any sense for the implications of what they were doing by cutting off Planned Parenthood and trying to say it was for this reason or that reason. And that was part of the problem is they changed their excuse for it about five times in that many days. So, you know, again, it sort of went to the whole credibility issue," Miller said.

Crises for nonprofits are indeed different than for-profit crises because peoples' values and beliefs are involved. Economic loss can be greater for nonprofits who rely on the goodwill giving of others based on those shared and aligned values. Nonprofits are not selling a product, in the case of Komen, they are selling care for others—as long as the care aligns with the donor's values.

Nonprofit crisis expert Miller said, nonprofits are dependent upon goodwill more than the business sector, adding, "if you're buying tennis shoes or pizza or whatever, you're really looking at the product." Hence, if a company does something customers don't like, such as use child labor, she said, people may overlook that. "They just want to buy the iPhone. They want to buy the tennis shoes." In Miller's view,

> It doesn't really work that way in the nonprofit world, because nonprofits are really doing things that are very value-based. Nonprofits exist to change the world in some way that the business world isn't changing it, or government or individuals can't change it… People have to believe and trust that the organization is really doing

what it says it was going to do in a way that the donors and supporters and volunteers believe.

The publics of Komen and Planned Parenthood overlap—those who support abortion often work races side by side with anti-abortion supporters. Komen brought the sides together in an apolitical context where there is a common goal and a common value. Both nonprofits are leaders in reproductive care and staunch advocates for women's health. After the decision, Komen supporters were left in the middle, confused, conflicted and disappointed. Survivors felt betrayed. Pro-choice advocates who were at first pleased with the decision, became angry at the reversal. Both groups served many of the same women and trust was violated.

Crisis communication expert and researcher Dr. Timothy Coombs from Texas A&M University said that if an organization is involved in social issues, tracking where stakeholders stand on issues is key (personal communication, September 29, 2016). "If you're going to make a change, you need to know how people are going to react, and I think that's a mistake they made. They assumed because one side wasn't saying anything, that only one side was talking, that it was fine to switch courses," Coombs said.

Floyd believes Komen should not have waded into the political waters in the first place.

"I think that there was not enough thought given" into the situation, which involved "political feelings" and "sort of trying to crowd out Planned Parenthood and defining Planned Parenthood as an enemy. That was a mistake for that group." For emphasis, she added, "that was a disastrous decision on their part" because of the extent to which the many constituencies overlapped.

Miller said "When you have a crisis that violates that trust, I think it could be really catastrophic, in a way that is different than someone that's just selling tennis shoes." Miller continued that Komen had rebranded itself overnight from a breast cancer charity to a pro-life breast cancer charity.

"Grant-making decisions are not about politics," a Komen spokeswoman told CBS News in a much panned interview and response over the outrage following the announcement (Floyd, 2012). But many, including the press, were not so sure. Simply put, Floyd said it became a political event and it depended on your beliefs as to which side you were on. Other tragedies, like natural disasters, are shared tragedies where everyone feels similar in spite of individual values or political beliefs.

Miller said "If you're going to dive into something that's a red hot political issue, you've got to be really clear about what you're doing, and they were not. I don't think they acknowledged that they were diving into the issue in the first place and then... they were really vague... about the Why?... And as a result, I think it really changed the way people feel about them."

Tom Benning, a *Dallas Morning News* reporter whose mother and mother-in-law both have had breast cancer, was one of the reporters covering the controversy.

"If I would have had to imagine what their [Komen's] big takeaway was, it would be, stay out of these issues, because there's just a no-win for them," he said. "I mean you're going to alienate a portion of your supporters no matter what you do, once you start getting involved in that kind of a thing."

Dallas Morning News columnist Floyd agreed. She wrote a scathing column likening the controversy to a change in fashion—from the pink race t-shirt to the pink burqa—chastising the "respected-bordering-on-sanctified" organization for giving in to pressure from outside forces and wading in to the political waters of abortion.

"Young women everywhere went ballistic... I think they [Komen] were a canary in a coal mine—at finding out just how profound social media can now shape public opinion. . . and solidify it on the spot in a way that didn't happen five . . . or ten years before that, certainly," Floyd said. "I won't call it naiveté, I mean since I don't really know the inner-workings. I think there was a failure to anticipate the introduction of a political component into what had been kind of an apolitical system."

In February 2012 in her DMN column she continued:

> The nation's largest breast-cancer charity voluntarily donned the theocratic burqa of anti-abortion ideology Tuesday with its decision to defund Planned Parenthood, the nation's largest provider of reproductive health services... They got bullied into shrinking away from Planned Parenthood by an organized lobbying effort that wants to make the oldest nonprofit reproductive health organization in our nation too radioactive to touch.

Media's Role and the New News Cycle

Again, whoever or whatever was behind the decision, the media did not take kindly to suddenly being ignored. Years of goodwill stories and covering races, was met with dead air. Media coverage plays a significant role in organizations communicating with publics during a crisis. An organization's crisis communication messages should provide consistent and accurate messaging to the media in order manage stakeholder reactions (Vielhaber & Waltman, 2008). However, in this case, the organization's messaging was either nonexistent or inadequate. The outcomes were both media and public anger at the communication response. The media's primary role during a crisis is to provide information to stakeholders and publics and an organization's crisis communication should explain responsibility, expansiveness and implications from the crisis (Austin & Jin, 2015; Seeger, Sellnow, & Ulmer, 2003). Komen did not live up to its side of this bargain, and the media was limited because either no one would talk to them or the answers were conflicting or superficial.

This author talked to Kivi Leroux Miller, a nonprofit crisis expert about the case, informing her that Komen representatives were not quite ready yet to talk to me almost four years later. Miller said that has been the problem all along. Fearn-Banks (2012) recognizes the final stage of crisis communication is learning—or a postmortem dissection of the communication and strategies in order to determine what went right and what went wrong. Not participating in this stage and failure to learn and share the lessons might hinder the organization from being prepared for future crisis. Again, because Komen representatives would not talk to us, there is no way of knowing if there was full participation in the learning phase.

"Which is not a surprise. They didn't want to talk about it then either," Miller said.

Rene Syler, a media personality who has had a preventative double mastectomy due to breast cancer history in her family, has a personal relationship with Komen Dallas and Nancy Brinker. Syler worked in television in Dallas and New York (among other places) before she became a "mommy blogger" and runs the blog and trademark "GEM" or "Good Enough Mother." She said she was surprised at the silence from Komen at the beginning. And when it released a press release finally on Friday afternoon, then went radio silent again for another 48 hours. In the meantime, Komen woke up Saturday to an avalanche of social media responses.

Syler said that once the social media machine gets going, there is no way to get ahead of it. Social media has shortened the news cycle—you must respond right away on all platforms, especially on Twitter. Memes will be out in minutes that create pithy, visual meaning for the event (see Blue Bell chapter).

Social media now must be highly integrated into an organization's crisis communication strategy, however, these platforms bring different implications to the messaging (Coombs, 2014). The fact that social media is more interactive, is primarily used by a younger audience, and allows for information to spread quickly requires additional considerations (Schultz, Utz, & Göritz, 2011). The news cycle is shorter and the criticisms will be continuous. A monitoring of social media (social listening) 24-7 is necessary and without negotiation. Proper use and monitoring of social media during a crisis allows an organization to influence messaging provided to its publics and by its publics.

Nonprofit crisis expert Miller, on her blog stressed the need to shorten the news cycle.

> Nature and the news media abhor a vacuum—the story will be told, with or without you. Ignoring a crisis is one of the best ways to ensure that it will drag out even longer. Take the Komen story. The first news cycle was about the backlash against their decision to stop funding Planned Parenthood. But it didn't end there. The second news cycle was about how Komen failed to respond to the first cycle. Even after the apology and reversal, the story continued on into a third cycle of "lessons learned from the Komen debacle." Now we simply refer to the "Komen story" and most people know what we are talking about. (Miller & Spivey, 2012)

DMN columnist Floyd who wrote the scathing pink burqa column said, "You're going to get what you get if you refuse to talk to me," Floyd said. "I think that was an early case of social media, a failure to anticipate the weight of social media and how rapidly that speeded up the whole cycle of response and, and oh, and criticism."

Miller continued: "One of my biggest criticisms of Komen at the height of the controversy was their complete silence on social media for almost 24 hours (longer on Twitter), followed by official statements only."

So, what should Komen have done? In Miller's opinion, Komen could have "simply posted" messages such as "We are listening. We hear you. We are talking internally about our next steps and will get back to you soon." That "would have been infinitely better than the nothing, followed by [the] official-speak, that we got" (Miller, 2012a).

Other Nonprofit Crises

Komen is not the first to wade into political waters (either intentionally or unintentionally). So how did it come to pass that Komen appeared so unprepared for the crisis? Especially in light of multiple nonprofits facing scrutiny from CEO pay to mismanagement of donations. There was even a prodromal situation where Target pulled funding from Planned Parenthood. An uproar followed and the decision was reversed as well.

Like Planned Parenthood, the American Red Cross is a nonprofit that seems to be in a perpetual state of crisis. In 1990, the Red Cross faced the first in a series of domestic crises, all different, all damaging. Its executive director and bookkeeper of the Hudson County Chapter (New Jersey) of the American Red Cross embezzled millions of dollars from donations and federal grants (Sisco, Collins, & Zoch, 2010). The Red Cross is not only the nation's largest private relief agency, but a global leader in blood donations as well (Sisco et al., 2010). In 1998, it was revealed that the American Red Cross failed to adequately screen blood donations before distribution, which resulted in the organization being blamed for thousands of people contracting life-threatening diseases (Sisco et al., 2010). This crisis resulted in sweeping policy change and reorganization of the system by the Food and Drug Administration (Sisco et al., 2010). After Hurricane Katrina hit the Gulf Coast in 2005, the organization sent in relief efforts to help with recovery; however, two other international Red Cross organizations stated that the American Red Cross was ignorant, arrogant and not prepared to help with recovery (Salmon, 2006). Furthermore, the American Red Cross was accused of treating minorities insensitively and neglecting the areas where minorities lived (Salmon, 2006). Late in 2012, after Hurricane Sandy claimed more than 100 lives in ten states, elected officials told people not to donate to the Red Cross to help with recovery efforts accusing the Red Cross of a slow response (Associated Press, 2012). In the summer of 2016, the floods in Baton Rouge created another flood of criticism for the Red Cross as it was accused of not accepting donations (leaving them on the street outside a shelter) and throwing away food donations. Citizens in the affected areas took to social media to once again discourage contributions to the organization.

The point of this list is to argue that Komen had both prodromes and other nonprofit crises to prime the organization to prepare. However, no one expected Komen would have a crisis of its own, not even Komen. Both sides—journalists and PR professionals—wondered if Komen had a crisis communication plan in place. It is difficult to determine this, but again, because of the fumbling at the beginning, our communications experts were doubtful.

Miller argued a crisis plan that outlines how you will interact with the press is necessary.

She wrote on her blog "the actual substance of the crisis is less important than whether you are ready to respond quickly and competently to it" (Miller, 2012b)

Miller continued, "There was just an arrogance within the leadership of the organization that they were really untouchable. They were, you know, too big to fail," Miller said. "...even if it was going to be bad press for a few days, they'd get through it. I really think they under-estimated how the trust with women across America... had been slowly eroding."

Planned Parenthood Strikes Back

While Komen was not accustomed to this level of controversy, for Planned Parenthood, this crisis was another day at the office. Some would say that Planned Parenthood was an easy target because it appears perpetually attacked and in crisis mode. Yet when you add up its constituents, many of whom overlap with Komen, and couple that with its social media response machine, the target became formidable.

Planned Parenthood Federation of America is one of the nation's leading reproductive health care providers, operating some 700 health centers across the United States (Planned Parenthood, 2014). In 2014 alone, the organization served some 2.7 million patients, all of which are from underserved populations (Planned Parenthood, 2014). Those services included sex education in schools, birth control and emergency contraception, sexually transmitted disease testing, cancer screenings and breast exams, vaccinations, research, and other preventative health services for both men and women (Planned Parenthood, 2014). Fifty-nine percent of Planned Parenthood's funding comes from private donations, non-government health services revenue, and other sources such as nonprofits like Komen (Kurtzleben, 2015). A nonprofit itself, it provided more than 10 million types of services to its patients in 2014 only 3 percent of which were abortion services (Planned Parenthood, 2014).

Planned Parenthood has continually been subjected to attempts to restrict its efforts, policies and governmental funding, not to mention clinic and doctor attacks, by anti-abortion constituencies (https://www.plannedparenthood.org). Crisis communication mode has become second nature to this organization coupled with its legal efforts to protect its mission, reputation and services (https://www.plannedparenthood.org).

In February 2012, it was reported that grants to Planned Parenthood from Komen paid for an estimated 170,000 breast cancer screenings over the five previous years. None of the grant money went toward abortions (Floyd, 2012). Despite what appeared to be a successful partnership in helping underserved women, the grants were discontinued. Planned Parenthood faced intense public scrutiny and once again entered crisis mode because of the Komen organization's actions (Hensley, 2012). Again, because Komen would not talk or was not sure how to respond, Planned Parenthood and its social media machine owned that narrative for the first days of the crisis. Planned Parenthood received three million dollars in donations in the first three days of the controversy before the decision was reversed within the week (Skene, 2014).

Consequences

The outcomes were not as favorable for Komen as it continued to insist the public had misinterpreted its actions as politically-based when they were not. Another area of confusion for the public was the allegation that Komen reinstated the funding due to the public outrage. Komen never addressed this issue outright, and instead media speculation skyrocketed in the wake of a continued lack of information and access to those with the answers (Watt, 2012). By the time Komen reinstated the funding less than a week later, the charity's reputation was already damaged (Bruell, 2012). According to Doorley and Garcia (2007), "a crisis is not necessarily a catastrophic event, but rather an event that, left to usual business processes and velocities, causes significant reputational, operational, or financial harm." The efforts began to fix the harm to finances and reputation. There were two statements reflecting regret and misunderstanding. There were new board members added.

In an attempt to restore brand reputation, Komen launched a new fall ad campaign that clearly focused on how it helps underserved women. The PR efforts focused not on the controversy, rebuilding or regaining trust, but serving minorities and those with low socioeconomic status—the perceived targets of the Planned Parenthood grant debacle. This promotion was designed to reaffirm that funding from Komen was being used for outreach programs, advocacy and research. The campaign also included human interest stories from people who benefitted from these services. Komen wanted the public to know that pulling funding would hurt its ultimate goal of providing services for women diagnosed with breast cancer, as well as hinder research for finding a cure. This approach reflects the image restoration strategy of bolstering, which again, calls attention to the good works of the organization. Amazingly, the campaign exceeded the funding for previous campaigns (Bruell, 2012).

However, the ad campaign did not completely repair the damage the controversy caused. As Nancy Brinker announced she would step down as CEO, its signature race attendance that so many local affiliates count on for fundraising across the nation plummeted. At the height, there were 138 races with 1.7 million participants around the world (Hiltzik, 2014). In the year following the crisis, more than a dozen had to be cancelled and at big city races, attendance was down in the thousands, dropping from 1 percent to 35 percent in some areas (Bruell, 2012).

When you add it all up in that first year—contributions, sponsorships and entry fees, the losses were substantial—more than $77 million, or 22 percent of the organization's income in the fiscal year ending March 31, 2013, compared with the previous year (Hiltzik, 2014). Overall the numbers are $270 million compared to $348 million in the year before the scandal (Hiltzik, 2014). The decision, which many call a blunder, ended up damaging the core mission of the organization. In response, Dr. Judy Salerno of the nonprofit Institute of Medicine in Washington was announced as Komen's new CEO in June 2013.

Also in 2013, Komen partnered with bloggers who were favorable to them to help with the social media response, #Komenblogsummit. Media personality Rene Syler was one of the invited bloggers. She said they still talked about the crisis, and she felt it had left a significant mark. While she feels they are still dealing with this, at this summer event, she said, there was a revitalized feeling around them.

The communication problems were not just with their external constituencies, but also with the network of affiliates—its internal, grassroots-level employees. The trust was broken now between the parent organization and its affiliates. Miller believed the organization lost touch with its "ground game." Journalist Benning agreed. "There was always kind of this disconnect too between there and the local affiliates," he said. "I remember talking to some of them and they seemed to be confused by what was happening. So I think there was, even setting aside the communication, like, hourly to the public, I think there was some sense of a lack of communication between levels of the organization."

Benning said that the Komen organization does admirable work and had built up years and years of goodwill with the press, the medical community, politicians and even major corporations. But he said, the nonprofit lost sight of the people on the ground and the political nuances of the landscape in which it operated. Benning said "I think they totally just under-estimated, as impossible as this sounds, but underestimated just how much of a third rail the abortion issue is. I don't think they realized the whole scope of what this all meant."

Recovery Takes Its Time

Despite the radio silence at the beginning, as the crisis unfolded, a contact at Komen did give the *Dallas Morning News* a heads-up and the first communication regarding the reversal, when it decided it would not block the grants to Planned Parenthood. Reporter Tom Benning, who was the recipient of the call, believes it was not his relationship with Komen that allowed him this access, but the *Dallas Morning News'* reputation that he believes caused the Komen representative to give him the first look at the reversal.

A June 2016 Digital News Report from the Reuters Institute for the Study of Journalism at Oxford contained some interesting news about legacy media brands. The study surveyed 50,000 online users in 26 countries. The study found that while digital-only news brands are gaining traction, traditional brands remain valued (Newman, Fletcher, Levy, & Neilsen, 2017). The solid news brand of the *Dallas Morning News* and the local aspect appeared to have been a good target and partner for Komen's reversal message.

Benning also conceded he was in the right place at the right time and that his paper had three reporters on the story. The policy revision was posted on the *Dallas Morning News* website a few minutes before it was posted on Komen's website.

"I remember when I called her back, like a day or two later, she said something like, 'Yeah I was glad you were able to get that, you know, our hometown newspaper,'" Benning said. "If these other outlets had been kind of driving the coverage nationally, maybe it was kind of a sense of 'Let's get back to [you know] our base, or like our core, you know, where this all started kind of a thing.'"

Because of that connection, *Dallas Morning News* bosses let him know that this was "his" story now and he was tasked with trying to interview Nancy Brinker. This task turned out to be a more than a year-long pursuit.

Benning remembered that Brinker struggled during an interview with MSNBC's Andrea Mitchell, offering that "the interview was kind of panned."

An open letter to Sally Quinn that the *Washington Post* published still did not sufficiently address "all these unresolved questions, like 'Why did this happen? Who was responsible?'" Benning said.

More than a year later, Benning was in Africa covering the George W. Bush Institute's African First Ladies Summit. Komen and the Institute were partners in the fight against cervical and breast cancer in Africa. Nancy Brinker was no longer CEO, but was transitioning into her new role as chairwoman of global strategy and was also at the event. After some staff convincing, and although the organization was still "being buffeted by the waves," Brinker sat down for an unfettered conversation with Benning.

"Certainly, her aides mentioned repeatedly their concern at that point was like, 'Every time we bring this up, then it starts the cycle all over again.' But my kind of response to that was, 'Well, there's still unanswered questions.'"

In his July 3, 2013 *Dallas Morning News* article, Benning said Brinker again apologized for the mishap with Planned Parenthood and admitted "mistakes were made."

In the article, he quoted Brinker as saying "You have to go through stuff every once in a while." And that the leadership "got to take a deep look at our organization and fix some of the things that weren't working right" (Benning, 2013). She also told Benning that although donations and race attendance were down, that the organization was "way beyond it" and the result was improved leadership and communication (Benning, 2013).

Benning said, "She was very forthcoming, almost like eager to talk and try and get her story out about what happened. And, which was counter to… this whole shut down mentality that happened, in particular in the media aftermath of it." Benning said she also admitted 'we should've explained our message better.'"

Benning acknowledged that Brinker is the face of the brand and her followers needed that closure, even though it was a long-time coming. When selling a product, people have choices, forget and go on to another brand. When groups are intertwined with community service and values, people do not forget—it is more personal.

In October 2015, some three years after the controversy, a letter from CEO Judy Salerno was published in *The Sacramento Bee* touting Komen's accomplishments. She said Komen had helped reduce breast cancer death rates by 34 percent since 1991. Its staggering $889 million research investment is the largest of any nonprofit and second only to the U.S. government. Annually, Komen and its affiliates help 30,000 people pay for treatment, insurance and daily expenses.

In a book of crisis communication cases, this is a case of nonexistent, limited, insulting, inconsistent and way-too-late communication. A case where one party's supporters in the disagreement controlled the narrative. This left the other side—the hundreds of thousands of Komen stakeholders—affiliates, survivors and all the women it serve confused and wondering what happened.

"I think they really thought they were untouchable and just sitting up on the throne way up there, and just listening to their little inner circle," Miller said.

Takeaways for PR Professionals

The authors preface these takeaways with the fact that nonprofit public relations is different than for-profit public relations. PR professionals need to remember that publics feel a passion for and commitment to the core mission of the nonprofit organization. This is not akin to the use of a product that can be changed by visiting a store shelf full of alternative brands. Nonprofits cannot send their publics a coupon for $1 off. This is tied to value systems. Because of that, emotional responses should be expected after every decision, and the crisis communication must account for that verve.

Internal Communication Is Key

Large companies, even nonprofits, need to listen to the people on the front lines and in the grassroots. Miller said all entities need "to be really good at listening at all levels," noting that they "train communications directors . . . to be the ears for their organizations" and that includes listening to social media. Most important, however, is "really paying attention to your frontline staff… if you're doing social work, it's the social workers, it's the people that are actually taking appointments of clients. For an organization like Komen… they have *all* of these regional affiliates, with all of these staff people that are running all of these races. And those people felt very disconnected from the headquarters office," Miller said.

External Communication Is Key

Organizations must respond, now and continuously. Radio silence is unacceptable.

"Generally speaking… you can't not respond, that there has to be some kind of response and fairly quickly. Even if it's something like, 'We hear you. We understand that you're unhappy about this, but we're working on it.' And you have to repeat that, pretty much, hourly, honestly, I think is the expectation these days," Miller said.

Remember Your Publics in Your Communication

Values and trust are a unique part of nonprofit loyalty. Do not insult your constituents and do not alienate your publics. "Be very cautious about trying to rationalize what happened. That too can drag out a crisis much longer than need be," Miller said on her website.

Acknowledge the Emotion of Your Stakeholders and in Some Situations, You Must Agree to Disagree

Good leaders put themselves in the place of their stakeholders, to empathize with their publics. Komen did not acknowledge the emotion of the decision or how its constituents would feel. Crisis communication expert Timothy Coombs says when you get drawn into social issues, people are decided and they are split. "You're never going to have a good choice. Someone's always going to be angry, and I think they just throw into the trap someone who they thought could please both sides, and you can't. When you have a social issue, you have to make your stand and then defend your ground."

The News Cycle Is Shortened, and PR Professionals Must Shorten the Cycle

"It was such a crisis and it was very difficult to know what to say, especially when you had this obvious tsunami of negative reaction coming in that, my impression, had not been very well anticipated… They kind of asked for it. You know, that there was, and I think, I don't know that I articulated this at the time, but I think there was a real failure to anticipate the depth of response that they were going to get to that. And there was a real inadequacy to handle that response when it came in," journalist Floyd said.

Social Media Can Capture and Control the Narrative— Manage It!

PR professional Miller wrote on her website "Don't do anything to drag out the news cycle, starting with ignoring the crisis." From the beginning, don't let others seize and own YOUR narrative (as opposed to the Blue Bell crisis). Know when and how to respond on social media to individual and group stakeholders.

Have a Crisis Plan in Place That Outlines How You Will Interact with the Press and Social Media, with Consistent Messages

"I think the track record is there that as much transparency as possible is always better. Answering questions sooner rather than later is always better, you know, ending the number of news cycles that you have to talk about this is always better," Benning said. The conflicting messages when a response finally did come, also helped feed the negative response Komen was already receiving.

Takeaways for Journalists

Cultivate Relationships

That effort will reward you, especially in crisis. But no matter the relationship, ask the hard questions. "When we had and probably any news organization had contact with Komen, it was in the context of how much money they're raising or how successful this race had been or getting the word out about this giant walk they would do in Dallas, kind of a thing. So for them to suddenly shift to crisis.... it certainly was different than what they'd been used to at Komen," Benning said.

Be Persistent, Everyone Has a Time to Talk

The long-awaited interviews will come at unexpected times and in unexpected places, like Africa. "And there she was [Nancy Brinker]. I was like, 'Oh my gosh,'" Benning said. "I immediately started reaching out to her people there and it was really kind of, sort of a strange. I mean, the whole thing was kind of surreal. We've been, I tried so many times to talk to her and then here we are, in Tanzania, you know, here's my shot."

Takeaways for Both Sides

Support Your Local Media

Even though Komen is a global company, it had worked closely in the past with the local/statewide media. After a perception of getting burned by national media, Komen reached out to a local source it felt it could trust as the decision was reversed (seen also in other cases). The same outlet was rewarded with a coveted Nancy Brinker interview a year later. Again, as is the case across all of the featured cases, local media is an important ally in crisis. Treat it as such. And for local media, appreciate and honor that respect and role with accurate and transparent coverage.

No Organization, Not Even a Beloved Nonprofit Is Immune from Scrutiny

Be ready to face controversy. Be ready to answer and ask the tough questions. "We definitely picked up on the notion that this is not what they were used to," Benning said. "They had built up such a sterling reputation that the extent that they got coverage, it was always going to be positive, I mean, who's against the fight for breast cancer?"

The answer is, no one. But the organization appeared to move away from that mission and would not communicate its new position—the "why" behind the decision that every side wanted to know. Less than a week later came a reversal of the decision, but the damage was already done. And everyone continued to ask, what happened? Please note, because the authors could not talk to the public relations side, there is little criticism of the press' coverage of the crisis—other than a few perceived softball television interviews for Brinker and the idea that just because an organization seems untouchable, does not mean they should be covered differently or handled with kid gloves. Yes, Komen does admirable work for women across the globe. But, everyone stumbles. Just ask the Red Cross.

Note

1. Each journalist and public relations practitioner cited in this chapter was interviewed only once, unless otherwise noted; therefore, the first citation will provide that information. Individual in-text citations will not continue throughout.

References

Associated Press. (2012, November 6). Red Cross deals with criticism against storm response: agency receives harsh reactions to its handling of major disasters. *Watertown Daily Times (NY)*.

Austin, L., & Jin, Y. (2015). Approaching ethical crisis communication with accuracy and sensitivity: Exploring common ground and gaps between journalism and public relations. *Public Relations Journal, 9*(1), 2.

Bassett, L. (2012, February 7). Karen Handel, Susan G. Komen VP, breaks her silence. *The Huffington Post*. Retrieved December 22, 2013, from http://www.huffingtonpost.com/2012/02/07/karen-handel-susan-g-Komen_n_1260608.html

Benning, T. (2013, July 3). Susan G. Komen founder shifts focus to increasing international efforts. *Dallas Morning News*. Retrieved from https://www.dallasnews.com/news/news/2013/07/03/susan-g.-komen-founder-shifts-focus-to-increasing-international-efforts

Benoit, W. L. (1997). Image repair discourse and crisis communication. *Public Relations Review, 23*(2), 177–186.

Bruell, A. (2012). Komen bows campaign in bid to restore blemished brand. *Advertising Age, 83*(31), 1–20.

Coombs, W. T. (2014). *Ongoing crisis communication: Planning, managing, and responding*. London: Sage.

Doorley, J., & Garcia, H. (2007). *Reputation management: The key to successful public relations and corporate communication*. New York, NY: Routledge.

Fearn-Banks, K. (2012). *Crisis communications: A casebook approach*. New York, NY: Routledge.

Floyd, J. (2012, February 2). Komen for the Cure's new fashion statement: The pink burqa. *Dallas Morning News*. Retrieved from http://www.dallasnews.com/news/columnists/jacquielynn-floyd/20120201-Komen-for-the-cures-new-fashion-statement-the-pink-burqa1.ece

Groeger, L. (2012, February 9). Komen's contortions: A timeline of the charity's shifting story on Planned Parenthood. *ProPublica*. Retrieved from https://www.propublica.org/article/komens-contortions-a-timeline-of-the-charitys-shifting-story-on-planned-par

Hensley, S. (2012, February 7). In reversal, Komen to continue funding Planned Parenthood. *NPR*. Retrieved January 24, 2016, from http://www.npr.org/sections/health-shots/2012/02/03/146344674/in-reversal-Komen-reinstates-funding-for-planned-parenthood

Hiltzik, M. (2014, January 8). Susan G. Komen organization discovers the price of playing politics. *Los Angeles Times*. Retrieved from https://www.latimes.com/business/hiltzik/la-fi-mh-susan-g-komen-20140108-story.html

Kurtzleben, D. (2015, August 5). Fact check: How does Planned Parenthood spend that government money? *NPR*. Retrieved December 5, 2015, from http://www.npr.org/sections/itsallpolitics/2015/08/05/429641062/fact-check-how-does-planned-parenthood-spend-that-government-money

Miller, K. L. (2012a, February 7). What Komen should do next to rebuild trust. Retrieved from http://www.nonprofitmarketingguide.com/blog/2012/02/07/what-komen-should-do-next-to-rebuild-trust/

Miller, K. L. (2012b, February 21). Nonprofit crisis communications 101: Shorten the news cycle. Retrieved from http://www.nonprofitmarketingguide.com/resources/media-relations/nonprofit-crisis-communications-101-shorten-the-news-cycle/

Miller, K. L., & Spivey, S. (2012, February 21). Guest post: What integrated marketing means to me. Retrieved from http://www.nonprofitmarketingguide.com/blog/2012/02/21/guest-post-what-integrated-marketing-means-to-me/

Newman, N., Fletcher, R., Levy, D. A., & Neilsen, R. K. (2017). *Digital News Report 2016*. Oxford, UK: University of Oxford, Reuters Institute for the Study of Journalism. Retrieved from http://www.digitalnewsreport.org/

Pesta, A. (2012, September 12). Former Komen official Karen Handel attacks Planned Parenthood in new book, calls it a "schoolyard thugs". *The Daily Beast*. Retrieved from https://www.thedailybeast.com/former-komen-official-karen-handel-attacks-planned-parenthood-in-new-book-calls-it-a-schoolyard-thug

Planned Parenthood. (2013–2014). Planned Parenthood annual report 2013–2014. *Issuu*. Retrieved from http://issuu.com/actionfund/docs/annual_report_final_proof_12.16.14_/0

Salerno, J. (2015, October 10). Another view: Komen invests millions in research, community programs. *Sacramento Bee*. Retrieved from http://www.sacbee.com/opinion/california-forum/article38729718.html#storylink=cpy

Salmon, J. L. (2006, April 5). Red Cross Katrina efforts criticized. *Cincinnati Post*.

Schultz, F., Utz, S., & Göritz, A. (2011). Is the medium the message? Perceptions of and reactions to crisis communication via twitter, blogs and traditional media. *Public Relations Review*, 37(1), 20–27.

Seeger, M. W., Sellnow, T. L., & Ulmer, R. R. (2003). *Communication and organizational crisis*. Westport, CT: Greenwood Publishing.

Sisco, H. F., Collins, E. L., & Zoch, L. M. (2010). Through the looking glass: A decade of Red Cross crisis response and situational crisis communication theory. *Public Relations Review*, 36(1), 21–27. doi:10.1016/j.pubrev.2009.08.018

Skene, K. (2014, March 21). A PR case study: Susan G. Komen and Planned Parenthood news generation. Retrieved from http://www.newsgeneration.com/2014/03/21/pr-case-study-susan-g-komen-and-planned-parenthood/

Vielhaber, M. E., & Waltman, J. L. (2008). Changing uses of technology crisis communication responses in a faculty strike. *Journal of Business Communication*, *45*(3), 308–330.

Watt, S. (2012). A postfeminist apologia: Susan G. Komen for the Cure's evolving response to the Planned Parenthood controversy. *Journal of Contemporary Rhetoric*, *2*(3–4), 65–79.

A NATIONAL DAY OF MOURNING

Sandy Hook Elementary

Andrea Miller

"In the newsroom, you're not used to people sobbing. But, you know, it's like in that Tom Hanks baseball movie, where he tells the women's team, 'There is no crying in baseball.' You know, we all have a sense, 'There is no crying in journalism'" (Clark, personal communication, September 29, 2016).

The event that the *Newtown Bee*'s retired editor Curtiss Clark[1] referred to was the Sandy Hook Elementary School shooting; the event that had many people shedding tears across the nation and the world. Born and raised in Connecticut, Clark spent 43 years in what he calls community journalism before he retired in 2015. He had never covered a story like this.

How the Day Unfolded

Less than two weeks before Christmas, on December 12, 2012, the small town of Newtown, Connecticut became the latest in a pages long list of American school shootings. A 20-year old gunman with a history of mental illness killed his mother in the home they shared, then traveled to Sandy Hook Elementary. After shooting his way into the school, he killed 20 children, four teachers, the school's principal and the school psychologist before he killed himself as police arrived. The children, all first graders, were ages 6 to 7.

Janet Robinson, the superintendent of Sandy Hook Schools at the time, had also been a part of the community for a very long time.

"For me, Newtown was going home," Robinson said. "It was right next to the town that I'd lived since '79, raised my kids… I was excited to go to Newtown. I was there a total of five and a half years. And you know, we did a lot of great work there and Sandy Hook" (personal communication, June 20, 2016).

Robinson had worked as a school psychologist as well as a professional developer in education for almost 40 years. At the beginning of the interview, Robinson told me that she had recruited and hired Dawn Hochsprung, who was in another district, to be the principle of Sandy Hook elementary. She said Hochsprung stepped right in and was a very strong leader. Hochsprung was one of the 26 who died in the school that day. Robinson said of all the years and experiences she had working in and around schools, she had never received any crisis training. But she also said, nothing could have prepared her for the enormity of that day.

"There's no logistical crisis team for something, something really as big as Sandy Hook," Robinson said. While there was a team of authorities working together, much of the communications efforts fell on her, the school district's leader.

Robinson said she was in the central office standing outside her office talking to another elementary principal when her flustered secretary said a bus driver had called and said there had been a shooting at Sandy Hook. Robinson said she thought it was likely something going on in the surrounding neighborhood and asked the secretary to call the school.

> So, she [secretary] tried calling the school. No answer, no answer. So, she came back out looking *very* worried. She says, "I can't get an answer and that's just not good." So… that's what I first heard, so went in my office and I called the police department and the phone rang and rang and rang and rang. Finally, very, very harried, I guess, desk sergeant, or somebody picked it up, and I… identified myself, and I said, "We have a rumor, a report, that there's been a shooting at Sandy Hook. Is that true?" And he says, "Yes ma'am, it is." And I said, "At the school?" because I couldn't believe it. And he said, "Yes and I can't talk to you. The phones are ringing off the hook." And that was it, you know. That's all I got. So I knew the person who was our emergency communications center director. I called her and I said, "This is what I'm being told, what do you know about this?" And she said, "Superintendent, you need to sit down."

Robinson said the first order of business was communicating with the parents. She immediately sent an email blast to all of the parents in the community through a school messenger system. She said it read that there was an unsubstantiated report that there had been a shooting at Sandy Hook Elementary School. The message continued that the school district would keep parents informed of what evolved. Robinson asked her secretary to call all schools and neighboring school districts. She had heard there were two shooters. "Everybody went in lockdown."

The information about two shooters was an early rumor that turned out to be false. But in the beginning, Robinson said she had little information and information gathering was hampered. So she got in her car and drove down the two-lane winding county road that led to the school. She recalls "so many vehicles" and "so much chaos." "I even drove on the wrong side of the road just to get as close as I could. And then I finally just ran my car down an embankment and just went by foot the rest of the way," Robinson said.

She arrived at a firehouse that sat at the end of the driveway that led to Sandy Hook Elementary, which was a kindergarten to fourth grade-only school. There she saw SWAT members with rifles running to the school. She was also bombarded with questions from the teachers who were there with their children, trying to keep them calm. She did not have answers to question such as "do you know anything about Dawn?"

She said the teachers put cartoons on a widescreen TV, which started to calm the children down. Robinson still did not know the extent of what happened. After what seemed like hours, the chief of police pulled her aside.

"'This is really bad, Janet.' I said, 'Well, how bad?' And he said, 'Maybe 30 people.' And as soon as he said 30 I said, 'Mike that is… that means kids.' And he says, 'Yeah, yeah. This is… this is about kids.' See, up to that point, I was doing my own mental denial that this, that any kids could've been hurt…" Robinson continued.

> So many frantic parents were running up with, you know, phones in their ears, shouting, and… so we released kids to their parents, and we had just like, just… a piece of paper, each teacher had the parents sign the kid out, so we could have some track of kids. The police wanted to talk to them, we said, "We know how to get these kids, you can talk to them later." And then that was when we saw that we had parents with no kids.

The state police and the town's First Selectman, Pat Llodra, decided to hold a press conference at Treadwell Park, near the school. At the beginning of the crisis, no one was appointed as press secretary or official spokesperson, according to Bill Hart, Newtown Public School District Board of Education member at the time. He said there was some behind-the-scenes politics and groups were hesitant to take on the communication. But, he said there were questions as to who was in charge—the city? Or the board of education? While many people did interviews, including himself, Hart said eventually Llodra "asserted herself as the prime communicator" (personal communication, September 29, 2016).

Robinson said she was in the middle of processing everything during the first press conference, but by this time, the national press had already arrived and rumors were flying. Robinson believes that they could have given out information earlier to stop the flow of incorrect information—such as two shooters.

"I mean they did the press conference in probably what was as timely a fashion as they could," Robinson said. But she believed they could have released more information earlier in order to stop rumors such as that the shooter was let in to the building. "I wish we could have had at least some of that information out there before it just became so pervasive," Robinson said.

Robinson also said multiple investigating agencies working on the tragic event did not communicate with her well or early. That hampered her ability to do a better job communicating with parents, which was always at the forefront of her decision making.

"As they went along… they were discovering what happened and the fact there was just the one shooter and so forth. I just wish they'd been straight up with me. Just tell me [what they knew] and then let me deal with it," Robinson said.

Also inside the firehouse that day was *Newtown Bee* Associate Editor John Voket. Born less than twenty miles away in Waterbury, Voket on that day had covered the city for nine years in newspaper and radio. He was the only local media member allowed in the firehouse, which turned into the staging area for authorities as well as a gathering place for parents picking up and waiting for their children after the shooting. He had developed a respectful working relationship with First Selectman Llodra and State Police who had already communicated with others that it was okay that Voket was there.

> That's when the reporter switch went off. I was like, I just have to try to observe to the best of my ability without being invasive, but I also have to be the representative of the newspaper here who's invested in the community. I have to take care the information that I end up having to relay is sensitive and accurate and not sensational…. So, the first selectmen confirmed how many were dead. I said I'm going to be here to help if I can in terms of getting accurate communication out. If you need me to leave, I will leave. If you want me to stay, I'll stay. She said no, we want you to stay (Miller & Reynolds, 2014, p. 62).

Voket said that he had "clearance" to be there because of his local connections.

> When you have Senator Blumenthal, Senator Murphy, Governor Malloy, First Selectman Llodra, State Police Lieutenant Vance and me standing around in a circle all hugging each other crying. I guess everyone assumed I was, it was okay for me to be there. So, at one point, Vance took me aside and was like "it's okay for you to be here, but I can't account for any of my guys if they see a camera or a microphone or get any idea that you are a journalist, they are going to throw you out and ask questions later and you probably won't be able to get back in." So, I didn't have a notebook, I only took a few pictures with Shannon's camera and my phone and that was it. At that point I went in auto pilot trying to use observational skills to try and remember everything I could. (Voket, personal communication, April 8, 2013)

The day was Friday, and Fridays at the *Newtown Bee* are usually more relaxed than other work days. The paper is a weekly that publishes on Friday, so there was more banter going on the morning of December 14—especially since the staff had just won a Christmas office party radio contest. Then the police scanner traffic began, carrying news of something that sounded like a shooting at Sandy Hook elementary.

Clark, the longtime *Bee* editor said "The local ambulance crews were being asked to stage away from the elementary school in Sandy Hook. And when ambulances stage away from a site, it means that the site poses some danger to the EMTs and the police are called in to settle things down, and they call in EMTs. Now that little bit of information looked pretty bad, first of all, you have EMTs ready to administer help to people who are hurt at the elementary school, that's not good news. The police are there, trying to calm the situation, so that suggests something even more sinister."

Even before Voket arrived at the firehouse, Clark sent reporter and photographer Shannon Hicks, who is also a volunteer fire fighter, to see what was happening at the school, which is literally right down the road from the *Bee's* office, less than two miles away. (Hicks was first on the scene and took the iconic photos of the day including the picture of the female FBI agent leading students out of the school). Clark said it didn't take long before they realized something really bad was happening there.

"So it went from a relaxed, somewhat-festive morning at, at the newspaper office into full-blown, way in over our heads crisis that we had to face and, and start reporting on," Clark said.

The *Bee's* website crashed five times that day, overwhelmed by the volume of visitors. Clark said usual weekly traffic consisting of tens of thousands of visits, quickly turned to hundreds of thousands of visits in minutes. The global information search begun and so did the almost instinctive attempts to seek information (anxiety reduction theory) from those closest to the news event—local news sources (Miller & Reynolds, 2014).

"At precisely the moment when you need all the talents and tools at your disposal, it's like you're stripped of them completely," Clark said.

He continued that "miraculously" the site came back a few times during that first day and with the help of some local IT volunteers, they began to get their local reporting out to the community.

Dealing with the Media Attention

While the cruel facts of the case trickled in, the press came in like a tsunami. The town, the local press and the school district were overwhelmed, just like the *Bee*'s website.

"We were so bombarded," Robinson said. "I think it was like, something like 1,800 emails came into my email immediately. Our [school district's] website crashed… the phones were ringing off the hook. I waited twenty minutes, trying to get a free line, just to make an outside call."

At some point, Robinson called on a local friend who works in public relations. She said her friend coached her on what to expect.

"I was thrust into the media world, which is something that was new to me," Robinson said. "We are educators. We don't do media that well. We're not exactly prepared for it. There's no playbook for this. So having someone who can screen what's important, which is what I asked Kelly Donnelly [State Department of Education, hired in November, weeks before the shooting] to do, tell me when it's important, and that we need to do it… that I need to talk to someone. But I can't talk to all these people, so we set up a couple things that we could do to get some information out."

Robinson said that she did not have a good relationship with the *Newtown Bee*, calling the paper "political." But she agreed that when the national and international press come to town, the local press gets overshadowed.

"Anderson Cooper's there, so you got all these people that are coming in and frankly, I think it's hard for the local press to even get in the door unless you have that previous relationship," Robinson said. "I thought some of the press was very respectful and tried to get it right, tell the right story. I felt there were others that were just overly aggressive and just wanted to get it out first. And, and didn't check their data, didn't check the facts," Robinson said.

Clark said when the national press descended, conversations had to happen about their mission to serve the local community.

"A producer from Brian Williams, he had this news, magazine thing, wanted to interview me in my office and I told everybody, 'Let's keep our eye on the ball here, we have our own work to do. We can't be Sherpas for a lot of people on this story, because we have deadlines to meet ourselves.' We can't spend a lot of time serving an audience that isn't the one that we really have to dedicate ourselves to," Clark said.

While Clark and Robinson had deep roots in Newtown, Rick Kaufman, who was in charge of communications for Jefferson County Schools in Colorado, had been on the job only two weeks when tragedy struck Columbine High School in Littleton. When I talked to him in May 2016, it had been 17 years in April since the event. On April 20, 1999, less than a month before graduation, two students killed 12 of their classmates and one teacher in a gun and bomb attack at Columbine High School. Then less than an hour after the rampage began, the shooters killed themselves in the school's library.

"We had a person, like an air traffic controller, trying to manage the thousand media calls a day that we were dealing with, there were 750 media outlets, across the world, at the coverage of the Columbine tragedy," Kaufman said (personal communication, May 5, 2016).

He said he had little experience with the local press because he had just arrived, however, his team tried to favor the local press. Denver, at the time, had two daily newspapers.

"There's an old saying in school PR, 'you take care of the in-house before you take care of the out-house.' We were focusing on trying to treat everyone as equal as possible, but there's no doubt that we favored the local media because of the connections and ties they had with us," Kaufman said.

In Newtown, the local media also took issue that the needs of the local press were often put on the back burner during the Sandy Hook crisis. They said it took away much of their power to control the story and often what they believed their community needed in terms of locally-relevant information.

But the issues with the national press went beyond access. *Newtown Bee* reporter Kendra Bobowick, whose nephew attended Sandy Hook elementary (at school that day and returned home safely), said the aggressive national press made everyone in the Newtown community angry. Her access to longtime sources dwindled and community leaders, whom she had known for a long time, no longer returned phone calls.

"We're just another person with a camera. We weren't a neighbor, we weren't from here, we were just a part of the press and treated as such and shuffled around and controlled," said Bobowick (personal communication, April 8, 2013). "And to have people in the community who don't necessarily know me either looking at me with disgust a day or two later because there I was to tape or videotape and broadcast their hometown horror. I became a part of that crowd instead of their neighbor. And that's awful. I was embarrassed to have a camera, and downtown Sandy Hook became a really ugly place to be."

The reporters felt the need to protect victims and their community by adjusting what would be standard journalistic norms and routines in a school shooting. "Norms and routines" is a well-studied mass communication theory that explains a predictable process or daily routine of news coverage. But this day, was far from normal. The *Bee* made the editorial decision that it would not interview families of victims. The paper did not publish pictures of the victims unless the photos were given to them by family members or the funeral homes. Clark also said there is no place in crisis journalism for aggressive, hurtful questions targeted at victims' families.

"Be mindful that there are wounded people, with special needs, who you should not intrude upon, should not antagonize. You don't need to make their lives more complicated at a time when nothing in their life makes sense, especially if it's to ask a question like, 'How do you feel? Do you think you will ever get over this? What would your message to the killer's father be?' Stuff like that is not what they need at that point. So just be a human being," Clark said.

The superintendent also went in to protection mode. Robinson, along with Hart felt the intrusiveness and aggressiveness of the media would interfere with the healing process. She offered the press accessibility, within limits. Her limits also included interviews with victims' families and Sandy Hook employees.

"We put a security guard in the front of our central office, because there were just people sneaking in. Media was all over us. They were bothering the families and they were going to my teachers' houses at home," Robinson said. "So we kind of tried to set limits as best we could. So that 'here's the press conference, but don't bother these people. Leave them alone.' I said, 'I don't care if I have to talk to them, but I don't want my people bothered.'"

Similarly, Kaufman said protecting families from the press was one of the best decisions his district made after the Columbine shooting.

"We made mistakes," Kaufman said. "We weren't perfect in all of this. But if there was one thing that I'd point to, and I still hear from a survivor of the Columbine shooting, a student, when she sent me a letter that said, 'Thank you for protecting us from the media.' Because they were inundated, every place they went, media was there with a camera, or a microphone, or a pen and paper, to ask them how they were feeling. And they got tired of expressing how they were feeling," Kaufman said.

Consequences

Columbine's Kaufman began his career as a journalist, but it is when he started working in a school district and studying to be a paramedic that he became interested in emergency management.

"It [Sandy Hook] really took your breath away," Kaufman said. "That is perhaps why the school district was so paralyzed in some respects to respond not to mention, they probably didn't have experience and they probably didn't have someone that could take the lead of that and that was part of what we did at Columbine. We had to separate ourselves from the traumatic experiences we were dealing with and what we were seeing and hearing and smelling for that matter, day in and day out, with the responsibility to help that community heal."

He said he has been involved in almost every school shooting incident since Columbine with counseling, consulting and offering expertise to give these schools resources and information about what they are going to need to do through the stages of the crises. He also helped develop the first mock crisis drill in the mid-90s, involving an active shooter, which at that time, wasn't even known as an "active shooter." Kaufman said within 30 minutes of the Sandy Hook elementary shooting, a regional director from a national school association called him and asked him to send some information on what Newtown schools could expect in the first 24–48 hours in dealing with a tragedy of this magnitude.

"I did... send information of what to expect moving forward, when it comes to funerals or memorial services, what do you do with all of the donations, what does a command center look like in terms of a communications and volunteers and all of these kinds of things that were obviously very new to schools that haven't been through this or may not have access or exposure to it through training," Kaufman said. "What to expect, ways to take the lead in informing your community through this, because the ultimate goal, under it is really, truly, 'How do we heal? And how do we return to normalcy?'"

In the aftermath of Sandy Hook, Robinson said she was not prepared for the thousands and thousands of cards and gifts; someone even sent a truckload of teddy bears. A townsperson donated a huge warehouse to house everything. Volunteers spent hours sorting through the gifts that completely filled the space. She said they gathered gifts together in packets and gave them to the parents of the children.

"Whatever was left at the end, they did a disposal, and put it into, ground it into the ground and I think it's probably part of the ground at [the new] Sandy Hook School," Robinson said.

Hart said this tragedy was different because it was not what he called a "physical crisis." In natural disasters, for example, victims need clothes, household items, food and water. But he said, the Sandy Hook community did not need any of that. He said it was instead an emotional crisis, and while the outreach from people across the globe was appreciated, it became just another aspect for them to manage. Hart also said it became clear to him that the donations were not about the victims, but more about outside individuals wanting to do something to make themselves feel better. "But this wasn't about stuff," Hart said. "This was about [clears throat] 26 funerals."

As discussed, interviews revealed the instinct was to protect first—protect the victims' families, the students, teachers, parents and the community. School officials involved in Columbine and Sandy Hook said although these tragedies had put their small schools on the international map, the first instincts to protect their own were the best instincts. Kaufman said you cannot worry about the state of Connecticut or the world. First and foremost, he said, take care of you and yours—because the tragedy will affect so many locally.

"I always use the analogy, it's like a calm pond," Kaufman said. "If you throw a rock into that calm pond, where that rock hits, that's the event, that's the crisis and all those concentric circles that go out are how the waves impact others. Really tightly around the crisis point, and then it began to spread out. And the further they spread out, the less and less impact of it. It still touched every public school person and probably every parent in the country, because we all felt it in various different ways."

As is the case this researcher has found over and over again in crises, the timing of events does not necessarily favor those involved in the communication process. For example, Rick Kaufman had been on the job two weeks when armed students attacked Columbine. For Janet Robinson, she was days away from announcing to the school board that she was taking the same position at the Stratford School District, less than 25 miles from Newtown.

"I accepted and then it was due to be announced the following Monday at their board meeting," she said. "And that was the next day, next morning, Sandy Hook occurred."

Robinson remained in Sandy Hook for the remainder of the school year.

A Different Communication Response

Restorative narrative is a fairly new area of communication scholarly attention that advocates for a different strategy in approaching the information-gathering and communication processes. Essentially, restorative narrative [and Clark] advocates for a change in the way reporters think about a crisis story. The goal of the approach is to help aid in recovery and facilitate community resilience. The approach goes further than the standard story by evoking hope. In an article on the website of an organization called Images & Voices of Hope (ivoh), Tenore (2014) calls the storytelling genre "strength-based." The non-profit organization ivoh was founded by media workers on the east coast in 1999 to advocate for restorative narrative and a media that can create positive change in the world, one community (like Sandy Hook) at a time. Tenore (2014) said restorative narrative stories must have certain characteristics, among them, stories that capture hard truths. These narratives do not ignore the difficult situation that people or a community are in or have been through. And in order to foster hope, the narratives do not focus on what is or was broken, but on what is being rebuilt now. Therefore, the approach focuses on the recovery stage. Another characteristic directly related to the strengths of local journalism include writing stories consistently and continuously because recovery takes time. Local journalists who live in the community, argues ivoh, are best-equipped to tell these stories because they are part of and committed to the community. Secondly, these stories are authentic which means they are true to a person's or a community's experiences, which again takes time to understand and give context.

Clark, who considers himself a community and restorative journalist, put it this way:

> Look your audience in the eye and be the best you can, see what they need from you, rather than just thinking about what you're going to deliver to them. Just having that

be the only thing in the calculation, something that springs out of your own mind. Your reporting should come from the audience. It should be inspired by your audience. It shouldn't just come out of, you know, a lot of people sitting around a table, brainstorming story ideas that are cut off from what the audience really needs from you. You've got to make some good faith effort to go look, listen to people, and then start your reporting.

The journalistic storytelling movement that began on the east coast has spread with academics doing research all the way on the west coast. University of Oregon assistant professor Nicole Dahmen applied restorative narrative to visuals. Dahmen (2016) found the technique can function as "exemplars of resilience and hope, both for the individuals at the center of the trauma and for larger communities" (p. 97). At the same time, these stories should "not provide a sense of false security or well-being" (p. 97).

In the case of Sandy Hook, press and press releases in the months and years after the shooting clearly addressed security concerns—what the district was doing (some of which Robinson told me they did not publicize) such as armed guards at every school. The information helped reassure the community and focused on what was being done now in the long recovery stage of the crisis.

This approach also fulfills the specific mission of a local press, which is to link the public with specific information to help them make decisions, as well as foster a sense of community. These specific local media roles are called linkage and social utility (Perez-Lugo, 2004). Hart explained that they only gave the local media certain types of information, because they needed that information to reach the school community and the local community at-large, for example, the time of a counseling session. In their public relations response, the school district created a password protected website just for Sandy Hook parents that also provided specific information. "It basically had, just information they might need. You know, access to counseling, what's going on at the school. We provided that as a channel to people. But we deliberately hid it from the outside world, because we, there were trolls all over the place." The information was kept from the national press with a wider audience because they were afraid that outsiders, like conspiracy theorists, would show up at counseling sessions, invade the privacy of victims and damage the recovery efforts. To the national press they would convey broader information, such as services being offered to make sure citizens felt safe and cared for.

In the months after Sandy Hook, the need for security went beyond Newtown, Kaufman said. "As I talked to hundreds of my colleagues across the country, they experienced the same thing. Elementary school parents were taking their kids out of school, they were calling schools, 'Are you prepared? Are you ready? What would you do if this happens?' They wanted those reassurances of safety."

Another issue to consider, Dahmen said, is that this approach to storytelling can often violate a basic tenet of journalism which is reporting just the facts. Dahmen (2016) said the approach "has the potential to take on the role of 'advocate,' which, in turn, places the story and storyteller outside the scope of objective and balanced reporting" (p. 103).

Lingering political issues that accompany a mass shooting can make reporting in this method tricky for journalists. In the Susan G. Komen case, many said politics created the crisis in the very beginning, while at Sandy Hook, the politics came after. For example, gun access questions always follow any mass shooting. Ironically, one of the nation's largest pro-gun trade associations, the National Shooting Sports Foundation, is headquartered in Newtown, only about three miles away from the elementary school. But Clark said the town is not monolithic in its beliefs on this issue or other issues.

The other larger recovery issue that came out of Sandy Hook was mental health care. The shooter had a history of mental health tests and unexecuted proposed treatments. Additionally, Robinson said she was not prepared for the onslaught of mental health resources her school employees and the community would need after the event. Prior to the event, she said she didn't know the mental health specialists in the community or how to vet them. But she said finding a center that addressed trauma and offers counseling was important information to communicate to the community.

Clark said that "The thinking's more aligned on getting mental health services to people who need them. And streamlining the state's delivery of those services and support of those services. So, those issues are not just another issue in Newtown. They're of key interest to people. But like every other place, there are a range of opinions on them, and I think, especially on the gun issue, some of the organizations that grew up in, in response to the tragedy, hoping to address gun violence, mental health issues, keep those issues on the front burner... but it's like any other, smaller community. There are people on all sides of these issues."

Finding these universal issues is another part of restorative journalism that "awaken the sense of human connection" (Tenore, 2016). At this point, it goes beyond a school shooting and is more relatable to everyone.

Clark explained the approach and its necessity this way:

> We were discussing how we saw as a priority to come up with narratives that would redeem the sense of community that had been under assault, both by the tragedy itself and the response, the world's response to it. And a group of journalists and j-school people started kind of a genre of reporting called, "restorative narrative..." and I don't think it's just putting out positive news, reporting in a Pollyanna kind of way that makes people feel good. It's offering solutions to people who have lots of questions, and I think people are now thinking seriously about trauma and the responsible response to trauma by journalists, rather than just raising awareness, and reporting all, reporting what happened and who did it, but introducing other stories that are in response to that that bring it all into context, bring some measure of understanding to people who are trying to figure out what the hell happened and why am I so confused about this event?

Perhaps this type of journalism/communication is similar to civic journalism and falls under the social responsibility of the press theory that media has an important role to play in an informed and engaged democracy (Dahmen, 2016; Siebert, Peterson, & Schramm, 1963). Overall, the local journalists we interviewed said that because you live next door, people in the community trust you and the result is more context, depth and sensitive reporting. The community connection, for the most part, makes for better journalism they said, especially in crisis.

"I think the crisis kind of validated the kind of journalist I always was, but never had the opportunity to ever prove I was because I never had a situation like this," Voket said (Miller & Reynolds, 2014).

Conclusion

On Saturday, the day after the shooting, Clark asked his team to put together a special print edition for the first time in its 135-year history. The *Bee*'s special edition was free—and the staff said it received positive community feedback and Clark said it eventually won a number of regional awards. The *Bee* prints in black and white only. On its website, however, users can still find the December 17, 2012 special edition—digital and in full color in the special editions section (Miller & Reynolds, 2014).

No public memorial has been built yet for the victims. Clark said that will take a few more years to complete. The old school was torn down and a new one was built on the same property, but not in the same spot. The new school opened its doors in August 2016.

Robinson remains the superintendent at Stratford Public Schools in Connecticut.

"It was the most unlikely place that you would anticipate a shooting," Robinson said. "Educators, you know, these are peaceful people.… And it was just, it was such a contrast to the violence with such… a nurturing, caring place. It was a wonderful school."

Takeaways for PR Professionals

Your Stakeholders, Your Parents Come First! They Are Your First Priority

Mass shootings are delicate situations because while information gathering is important, communicators do not want to do more harm to the victims and the victims' families. In this case, PR professionals and journalists we interviewed had these special constituencies in mind. Procedures may need to be altered to protect the victims' families and the community from aggressive media and outside forces. Unfortunately, trolls with conspiracy theories are now a population that communication professionals need to be aware of and sometimes address.

Have a Crisis Plan in Place and Practice It

When Kaufman started working with school districts after Columbine almost two decades ago, he said only about 50 percent had crisis plans. Today, it is an absolute must. A plan must be coupled with training for all involved.

"The key to schools being prepared is having a plan, and then within that plan, training and drilling, so that you create the cultural condition to know what to do when the real world situation occurs," Kaufman advised.

Communicate, Fast and Often, and in Different Ways Depending on Your Audience

From the very beginning of the crisis, Kaufman instructs communication professionals to monitor the message, take control of the message, guide the message and engage your stakeholders and your community. However, messages to parents of victims are going to be different than messages to other school district parents. The process of recovery often depends on and begins with a successful communication response. And in cases such as mass shootings, make sure the messages are empathetic as well as instructive.

"We know that crisis communication—communication in general—is really the foundation of any crisis planning and management recovery effort. Everything you look at in a crisis, communications touch, from the onset throughout the entire recovery process. Lack of it, creates a whole lot of problems… and really puts the organization in jeopardy of surviving and with surviving, how quickly they can recover," Kaufman said.

Take Control of the Onslaught of the Press with a Spokesperson or Team to Deal with the Press and Weed Through the Requests/Questions

The requests can overwhelm an already overwhelmed staff. As with Columbine, set up a phone number or numbers to directly take interview requests and answer media questions. If one person is the designated spokesperson, no one else should talk to the media. If there is a team of spokespeople, make sure the efforts are coordinated (develop a tight circle of trust). Understand that all individual media requests cannot be honored. Frequent press conferences must be held to accommodate the rest and at convenient times that recognize the news cycle. Additionally, these authors suggest that you make sure local media is satisfied—you are going to need them even more in the community recovery stage when the national media has packed up and left.

As a side note, you may also need a phone bank of volunteers to answer questions from the community. However, these volunteers must have a consistent message/information, be trained, and know where to go when faced with a question they cannot answer.

"There needed to be someone who was talking, you know, on the phone and dealing with it, because it's, it's nonstop. And because this was children and it was such an awful tragedy, this continued," Robinson said.

Recognize That Social Media Has Changed News Cycles

Take control of the communication first—even if you know very little. Kaufman said in part because of Columbine and so many other school tragedies, school districts recognize the importance of having communications staff members and in some cases, communications departments, which wasn't the case as recent as a decade ago. And that change has to do with the rapid and rabid news cycle brought about by social media that services anxious people who want immediate answers.

They [social media outlets] provide great value, but they also create some issues and those communications experts that are not embracing and understanding that will find themselves sort of behind the eight ball… The lack of information and a short decision time you have to make in these kinds of incidents creates a lot of uncertainty. Our public, our stakeholders are motivated to reduce that uncertainty, because what they're looking for is information. So, when we used to talk about response in the first 24 hours has a direct link to the likelihood of success in managing a crisis, it really has been shortened so much more dramatically to what I consider, sort of the golden hour, and the golden hour comes from my world, as a paramedic student, in responding to a crisis as quickly as you can get a person to medical care, in that first hour, the better chance they have of survival. (Rick Kaufman, personal communication, May 2016)

Communication Now Includes Engagement

Set up a command center (can include the phone bank too) to monitor all the media coverage (environmental scanning, social monitoring/listening) and respond when necessary (when there are myths that need to be debunked or untruths that need to be called out). If a pattern of common questions or issues appears, make sure these are addressed in all communication efforts. If helpful information comes from a community member, verify it, then share it as well. Give people something to do to help with their own sense of self-efficacy.

"I think the other thing is that social media, the technology today has really forced all organizations to look at communications from a two-way dialogue perspective, it's no longer about sharing information and getting information out," Kaufman said. He continued that it is really about an expectation of engagement. "Stakeholders want to be engaged, they expect to be a source of information during a crisis. In other words, they want that information, so that they can also share it. No one wants to give out… most people don't want to give out false information. So, you have to have a system for listening and a system for responding and the organization must be a part of this conversation."

Control the Interviews/Press Conferences

Create these interactions on your terms—location, setting, time, time allotted, etc. If you don't have an answer to a question, tell them so and promise to get back to them. Make sure you get back to them with a simple phone call or follow-up email.

"You know, to just keep calling and bugging, I can set limits and say, 'I'll be happy to talk to all of you at one o'clock, we'll do a press conference and take your questions at that time.' Rather than just being pulled, because you're dealing with so many other things. You resent the intrusion of the media, because you have so much you have to do," Robinson said.

Takeaways for Journalists

Advocate for Local Press Accessibility—Local Matters!

This is a constant theme across crisis case studies. Local journalists are part of the community and know the needs of the community. Relay this value to all authorities involved in the crisis—before, during and after a crisis.

Know Your Audience and Their Needs

Again, this is where local shines. Local media know the audience and have eyes and ears in the community to help give context, identify needs and then fulfill those information needs.

"Remember who you're writing for, and also, you don't want to soften your reporting just because it'll make people feel good. When things are going bad, there's a tendency to want to report good news. You really have to, what people want is information. They want the knowledge they require to get through this," Clark said.

Don't Sugarcoat or Not Ask the Hard Questions

Mass shootings bring to the forefront difficult societal issues such as mental health and gun violence. In the wake of these tragedies, these issues need to be explored. However, continue to remember your audience and community needs.

"They just don't need feel good stories. They want stories that will help them put their lives back together in a way, where they heal to the point where good feelings can emerge again, now, going forward, and facing life after something like this. So, don't pander," Clark said.

Be Respectful of People's Space and Time

Robinson said she resented the intrusion of the media because she had so much to do.

"There's so many other things that someone in leadership has to deal with at that time. (Pause) I was going to twenty-six different services. And... sometimes, it was a matter of their timing. Just be respectful of timing, too," Robinson said.

Takeaways for Both

Be Respectful of People's Emotions—This Was an "Emotional" Crisis as Opposed to a "Physical Crisis"

"Understand the emotions of the time. Even though you want a story, just be very respectful, as someone's just lost a child," Robinson said. "They've got to be respectful. If they're going to put microphones in the face of my teachers, then... we're not going to talk to them."

Finally, Kaufman points to what he called the 5 Cs of crisis communication that are applicable to both PR professionals and journalists:

"You need to have concern, show simple human emotions. Clarity, be really clear with your messages. Control, you have to take charge. Confidence, you can't be complacent, but you also can't be overly aggressive. Competence, you need to do your job well, with the resources you have. You know, as I always say, we're always communicating. It's a matter of whether we're doing it well or poorly."

Emotions were especially raw in this case because of the number of child victims, which increased the necessity of getting the communication right. The event touched every person across the nation. And while getting information out in such cases is important, professionals must be cognizant that the people they are talking to are having the worst day of their lives.

Note

1. Each journalist and public relations practitioner interviewed for this chapter was interviewed only once, unless otherwise noted; therefore, the first citation will provide that information. Individual in-text citations will not continue throughout.

References

Dahmen, N. (2016). Images of resilience: The case for visual restorative narratives. *Visual Communication Quarterly, 23*(2), 93–107.

Miller, A., & Reynolds, A. (Eds.). (2014). *News evolution or revolution: The future of print journalism in the digital age.* New York, NY: Peter Lang.

Perez-Lugo, M. (2004). Media uses in disaster situations: A new focus on the impact phase. *Sociological Inquiry, 74*(2), 210–225.

Siebert, F. S., Peterson, T., & Schramm, W. (1963). *Four theories of the press.* Chicago, IL: University of Illinois Press.

Tenore, M. J. (2014, July 20). Restorative narratives: Defining a new strength-based storytelling genre. *ivoh*. Retrieved from http://ivoh.org/restorativenarrative/

CONCLUSION

Andrea Miller and Jinx Coleman Broussard

"Information is as important as food and water in a crisis. Air first, then information, food and water," Centers for Disease Control Barbara Reynolds said.

This book set out to show communication professionals' perspectives from both sides of that information using recent crisis cases that are now in the learning stage. These cases provide an opportunity in hindsight to dissect what went wrong and what went well and to bring to light the unique communication nuances of each event. With such exploration, both sides have the opportunity to better understand the other side's response and coverage. Just as knowledge is power for the individuals going through crisis, the same can be said for those disseminating the information: they must be familiar with how each other professionally operates in order to successfully do their jobs and reach their goals in often challenging circumstances.

An overarching finding is that crisis experience is a must. Entities such as Komen and Blue Bell that had not experienced crisis before stumbled. The city of Ferguson stumbled badly not once, but twice in the early days and weeks of the crisis. First, it hired a white firm (Common Ground Public Relations) and then hired an African-American man who had a criminal record and whose credentials as a public relations practitioner were questionable (Devin James Public Relations). Although the city of New Orleans had experienced crisis before, its communication director had not. And even individuals who had faced crisis before stumbled. Each crisis creates a different set of communication challenges where expertise and preparedness are a must. Recall that crises also came at inopportune times for many of those involved in these cases. Rick Kaufman from Columbine had been on the job for a few months as had Missouri School of Journalism Dean David Kurpius, Texas Health's CEO Barkley Berdan not even a month, and Sandy Hook's Janet Robinson was days away from tenuring her resignation as superintendent. While these four were seasoned communicators, they had less crisis experience. From the other side, all of the journalists we spoke to were well-seasoned and had developed breaking news and crisis reporting skills. Nonetheless, with crises striking at anytime, anywhere, young journalists and PR professionals must be trained to cover and manage crisis in all of its iterations before they step in to their first newsroom or boardroom. Have a plan that includes crisis training. Consistent training means employees will develop learned responses to different and difficult issues. In turn, all employers should have crisis plans in place and know where each employee fits into that plan.

In contemporary society, different types of crises are now becoming more prevalent due to new challenges that arise by operating globally and in politically-charged environments. For example, leading crisis communication scholar Dr. Timothy Coombs from Texas A&M University, who has literally written the books on PR crisis response, said that in the past, more often than not, corporations would only face operational crises, such as on-site accidents. But, he said that many companies are now being drawn into social issues. "It's going to be about your values and ethics. Going back to who you are as a company and where do you stand on this. You're going to have to take some heat for it, but you gotta figure out in advance who you want to be."

In the Sandy Hook case, former Newtown Bee Editor Curtiss Clark discussed an approach called narrative journalism that seriously considers trauma and the "responsible response" to trauma by journalists. A type of journalism similar to civic journalism or social responsibility reporting, it allows for more context, depth and sensitive reporting—a type of reporting that will help to heal and recover. Another type of journalism that can bleed over into social issues and surfaces in times of crisis is advocacy reporting, where news organizations pick a side and advocate for their community in crisis. These could be seen as "anti-sensationalistic" approaches—or just the opposite of one of the main journalistic mistakes we found in crisis, coverage that was overhyped and hyperbolic.

Organizations must not only identify prodromes and challenges they may face operationally, but also socially. What does the company stand for? How do its values align with the needs of its publics/community? How will what it values meet with opposition? How do public relations practitioners facilitate the flow of information that will help the organization's stakeholders make good decisions? Journalists must do the same. If a crisis hits the community, where do we stand as a news organization in terms of how are we willing to use our words and our platform to help our community heal? "What recent research is showing is people are beginning to respect that," Coombs said. "They're respecting companies that are willing to take a stand and speak to their values, even if they don't like them, they'll respect the company for taking that position."

The cases presented, although very, very different, each contain additional constants in terms of journalistic coverage and strategic communication. We highlighted those, but the real purpose of this book is to give new insights in to crisis communication based on practitioners' experiences from both the public relations side and the journalistic side. Again, each crisis is different and offers unique lessons for working communication professionals.

Findings That Lead to Best Practices

Be Prepared—Create a Picture of Those You Serve and the Issues They May Face

No organization is immune to scrutiny; therefore, this major finding is no surprise—be ready! Preparation for a crisis takes many forms. First, we cannot reiterate enough the necessity of training journalists in covering crisis. Crisis events and visuals can be shocking and scary. Prepare reporters with the tools to handle this on-the-job stress before and after crisis. Make sure public relations practitioners are trained in crisis *and* PR. As we saw in Ferguson, a new hire who does not know how to handle the basics of PR will not serve the organization well. That was even more evident with that hire's ethical shortcomings/lapses. And in a crisis, such a lack of experience can be especially disastrous. Secondly, before crisis, identify your organizational crisis risks and the risks that can threaten your community. What are some operational crises that are affecting your industry? Identifying possible crises for a community's largest employers is a good exercise for journalists. Before crisis hits (if it does), background information and experts can be prepped. Other questions include what personnel issues are potentially explosive? Journalistic outlets can also fall in to crisis with one unacceptable tweet from a reporter. Thirdly, monitor social issues that may affect your company, non-profit or municipality. Yes, identify social issues! Be ready for all categories of crisis. And if your company is planning a big change, i.e., adjusting the structure of funding, do some testing. Focus groups are not just for products, but social issues as well. They can not only tell you what people think about your products, but what they think about the social issue in which you are involved or that might move over in to your lane. Keep in touch with your stakeholders to know where they stand or where they have shifted. We do not live in a static world. We create products and services for people who change over time. For example, the thermometer for gay marriage is different now than it was a decade ago. Read press accounts of how your constituents are feeling. If you are a government or quasi-government entity, do a quality of life survey or town hall meeting to identify issues before they become problems and then a crisis. Create a complete picture of those you serve. Then update that picture every few years. For journalists, information can come from consumer surveys or focus groups as well. Consider your audiences with every story you write. Know their wants and needs and address them. If you develop a rapport with your audience, trust comes from relationships and trust is important in crisis. Finally, for both sides, do not lose sight of your goals and your constituencies—you should be worried about how people *feel* about your company, non-profit or news outlet. PR people and journalists should be able to constantly scan the environment and counsel their organizations on how to address people's feelings and their information needs. In other words, we should serve as facilitators and not just information brokers.

"I think that bureaucracies often are intimidated by the emotion and the degree that people feel a crisis. And they shouldn't, they should just recognize that this emotion is real, whether it's based on a real threat or not and then respond to it in an open way," Reynolds said.

Create Small Information Circles with Staff Who Will Work Nonstop

While crisis experience is a must, so is a crisis plan that includes a tight, trusted circle of individuals who are all on the same page. We heard over and over across crises that some people internally were not briefed or were not privy to some information that was necessary for them to do their jobs. We also heard that too many people were involved in the information process and therefore, the message did not remain on point. As Gerard Braud said, keep your circle small. It keeps your message tight. A small circle also allows you to be nimble in terms of getting the information out. We also heard over and over again that wrong information or conflicting information in the beginning was released to journalists. This hurts the PR credibility and the credibility of the organization and only raises more questions from journalists who are trying to communicate accurate information. A confusing communication response will likely result in a negative journalistic response. Small information circles are helpful to journalists as well. With one spokesperson, the entity is able to take control of the onslaught of the press as the remaining team weeds through the hundreds, if not thousands of requests you will receive. Journalists appreciate this because it allows for one-stop shopping for information. If multiple agencies must communicate—hold joint pressers—and if necessary, provide the experts (disease epidemiologists, counselors with school shooting experience, food safety researchers) who can give the stories expert information and context. Such experts should already be part of the journalists' communication circle. And again, know your audience and their needs before a crisis. Critics of Komen say the organization lost touch with the people they were serving, and that the inner circle became too insulated. Therefore, widen the circle before crisis, tighten after.

"…having everyone know there's a centralized distribution center of information. And then if you have someone who's running the operations in terms of the communications, not necessarily the crisis itself, but the communication, they have a direct line and they're involved in the running of the crisis, but they're always the ones people refer to and they're always sort of the primary contact," PR Institute's Tina McCorkindale said.

The above should be written in to the crisis plan. For journalists, the plan should consist of who is going to cover what, on what platform, along with contact information for all of the experts and authorities who may be involved. With the trend moving to smaller and smaller news staffs, this helps delineate the tasks. Cultivate sources beforehand and share sources during with other reporters.

Another important edict of the plan should be to make sure team members understand they are essential employees and are expected to remain with the organization and work crisis communication throughout the event. Releasing a press release Friday afternoon and expecting to have the weekend off is unacceptable. For Hurricane Katrina, much of the city of New Orleans' staff left, leaving only two people on duty in the city. For a disaster this large in scope, two people does not a successful crisis team make. When crisis hits, journalists know it is all hands on deck. However, it is important that everyone in the newsroom be aware they will be working nonstop when crisis hits. Then, it is up to managers to make sure people are rotated on and off shifts to ensure employees are rested for optimal health, reporting and successful communication.

Social Media Is a Game Changer—Control the Narrative and Engage

Each small information circle must include at least one person (at least) adept at social media because quickness and nimbleness in this arena are a must. We use arena appropriately here because often if there is a fight, it is held on social media. The news cycle has been shortened because of technology and PR professionals in crisis recognize the need to help shorten that cycle for the benefit of their organizations. Communication now includes engagement. Set up a command center to monitor all the media coverage, including social media, and respond to myths that need to be debunked or untruths that need to be called out. Refute strategically—know what to say, what information to disseminate—provide new and breaking information and correct bad information (advice for journalists as well). However, it will be impossible and unhelpful to respond to everyone. Additionally, do not rely solely on social media. It must be used in conjunction with other media, including "legacy" media. Public information officers we talked to said radio was a lifeline in Hurricanes Katrina and Sandy when information infrastructures were decimated.

Social media interaction has also become a mainstay in the norms and routines of journalists, with newsrooms now expecting their employees to not only populate the website with stories, but post pictures to Instagram, live Tweet or Facebook live events, and respond to commenters. Digital is the first line of reporting in crises. We found some reporters were not quite sure how to effectively use it. Many felt it took time away from other endeavors, but still realized its value. The reporters for the St. Louis Post-Dispatch, for example, were unsure how to use Twitter initially, but were required to tweet and retweet. However, most reporters are learning to embrace its advantages. In the summer of 2016 police ambush in Dallas, a Morning News reporter covering the protest went live on Facebook immediately after the shots rang out. Later that same summer, in the Baton Rouge Great Flood, reporters also took to Facebook live to show, by boat, flooded neighborhoods in real time. Social media now allows for this immediate, on-ground engagement that is now necessary and expected in crisis.

The Digital News Report (DNR) from the Reuters Institute for the Study of Journalism at the University of Oxford is released every year. The research, based on a survey of more than 74,000 online news users in 37 countries, has been tracking global media use for almost a decade. In 2018, the DNR found that 45 percent of those surveyed in the United States use social media for news each week for both discovery and consumption (Newman, 2018). Sixty-five percent prefer to get to news through a side door, rather than going directly to a news website or app. More than half (53 percent) prefer to access news through search engines, social media or news aggregators (Newman, 2018). Additionally, 44 percent of those surveyed trust *overall* media, while a majority, 51 percent trust the media *they* use (Newman, 2018). Looking at brand trust, the DNR found that TV brands (or digital brands with a TV heritage) score best, followed by "upmarket" newspaper brands. Despite the varied offerings, most of the news consumed by audiences still originates from newspaper groups, broadcasters or digital brands. Social media communication matters, but so do the legacy outlets and brands. The top five most trusted outlets in the United States according to the DNR are quite varied: (1) local television news, (2) *The Wall Street Journal*, (3) ABC News, (4) CBS News and (5) NPR (Newman, 2018). Crisis coverage and strategic communication crisis response means professionals must know how to tell their stories and get their messages out across all platforms. They must do it all—and do it all well in order to reach audiences and stakeholders where they consume and trust news and information.

Social media is also the place where communicators lose control of the narrative. If a company or a news outlet does not respond to or cover a story, the Twitterverse will take over and do it for them. Words come first, then the memes (Blue Bell). A delay in response of a few hours will bring out public opposition, questions and rumors (Komen & Ferguson). The public often has little ethical training and no mercy. They can manipulate the narrative so much so that it takes time to right that course. Journalists must recognize conspiracy theories, fake news and pictures and refute harmful false claims and rumors. Stay ahead of your audience and your stakeholders with the necessary verified information and again, monitor what is out there and be strategic and skillful in refutation.

Know When to Use Communication Types

In consultation with the above section, we also learned that there were specific ways that communicators used (or did not use to their detriment) different types of communication. Because information changes so quickly, social media should be used first and strategically to get facts out quickly. Have canned social media posts ready to go. Also have canned press releases ready to go that contain background and more context to allow journalists to expand on the story. For example, PR people need strategies to deal with and assist national and international media. East Baton Rouge Sheriff's Office Communications Director Casey Rayborn Hicks, who worked communication during the Baton Rouge flood and police ambush within weeks of each other, suggested preparing background material about the city/organization—along with statistics, photographs, etc.—and making those available to out-of-town journalists and others who want/need the brochure/packet. This may sound basic, but not always followed in the cases we discussed. Pressers give context prior to crisis and in the beginning stages direct your stakeholders to what they can do, for example, propose evacuation routes, a list of supplies, or strategies to protect against contracting an illness. This kind of information is always a staple and sought out by journalists in crisis, so have it ready to go. As stated above, in the beginning of a crisis, pressers are just not as useful because the situation is changing and developing. Later, pressers will again be key in crisis recovery with even more detailed social utility and linkage information. We also learned from PR professionals to move away from talking points in press releases and concentrate on facts. Both sides, the PR professionals and the journalists said they do not trust national PR folks who speak in talking points. Additionally, PR people should be proactive even when the communication infrastructure is lacking. For example, reporter Christopher Drew said that instead of ignoring the media, New Orleans PIO Sally Forman (or her deputy) should have walked to the Sheraton Hotel where numerous journalists were and were known to be housed. Again, if the main spokesperson is not available, the press will find other sources (sometimes not as informed) who will talk to them. Drew also suggested that during crisis, PR people should find a way to contact the national desks of major news organizations to learn what reporters are in town to cover the story and how to contact them. In other words, do not wait for the journalists to find you. Find them.

Manage the Press Avalanche

Crises bring hundreds of press to your community's doorstep and thousands of requests for interviews. It can be emotional and paralyzing when faced with such an overwhelming response. Therefore, do not let the emotions of the moment control your coverage or response. For PR, fight the instinct to shut down access to information. For journalists, fight the instinct to sensationalize. Throughout the book we have given tips on how to manage this onslaught that will arrive with *every* crisis. Some of these suggestions include timely and joint press conferences, additional information handouts/pressers (journalists, ask for this), one spokesperson and possibly even a phone bank. However, sometimes members of the press remain aggressive. If you feel like you can't win, be creative. We suggest shifting strategies and setting guidelines for reporter interactions as was done in Baton Rouge, Columbine, Sandy Hook and Ebola. However, don't forget to serve your local reporters—the importance of such will be discussed in the next section. The local press should also be aware that the broader community will likely lump them in with the national press, which according to our cases, has tended to be more aggressive. Again, this is where existing relationships with PR professionals and the community will hopefully help maintain information flow and trust.

Stand Up for Local Media

In our cases, the excellence of local media was discussed time after time. The 2018 DNR confirmed our findings as local television news is the most trusted outlet in the United States. PR professionals told us when comparing local to national, they believed the local news was more fair and accurate. The *Newtown Bee* served the community by what its reporters and editors called being respectful and human. "If you are the local journalist and you are invested in your community in your heart, that doesn't matter who says they reported it first because you reported it best because you know best how to report it," *Newtown Bee* Associate Editor John Voket said (Miller, 2014). The local press and the community have a symbiotic relationship. And that relationship, needs to be taken to another level during crisis. Voket said that he is an advocate for preferential treatment of the local press by local authorities during times of crisis. He advocates for the local media outlets to have frank, personal meetings with local authorities and community leaders before a tragedy strikes to build up rapport and an understanding about how the chain of information is going to be handled in crisis. "It can't be CBS News, it can't be CNN, it can't be Anderson Cooper… they don't know the community, they don't have the embeddedness," Voket said (Miller, 2014). "There has to be a voice of real truth, and that really should be the paper that is the trusted communications source and organization that may form the most in-depth historical record of what could be the worst incident to ever hit a community" (Miller, 2014). When crisis events bring parachute journalist to town, journalists and PR professionals need to stand up for local media. In many cases, PR professionals told us they were "burned" by national media coverage and therefore they said they had to circle back to local media to help set the record straight. Cultivate the relationships before crisis hits and capitalize on that existing trust and connection that local journalists have with the community during crisis. The end result is better information and better journalism and better working relationships for what could be a long recovery period. Seeking to cultivate relationships with local media, Ceeon Quiett, who became communications director for the city of New Orleans six months after Katrina, worked with FEMA to prepare *FEMA for Dummies* and distributed it via meetings to local news directors, publishers and other key personnel. The book explained key aspects of FEMA such as how federal money flowed, and other information reporters would need to understand to accurately write about the recovery stage. And as the first anniversary of Katrina, Quiett involved the media in her planning process, even obtaining contact information on which journalists would remain in the city and alternate ways of locating and communicating with them. "It worked really well," Quiett recalled, noting that the city's communication for the first hurricane to hit a year after Katrina even received a grade of "A" from CNN's Anderson Cooper.

Embrace Communication from and with Audiences/Stakeholders

Because of social media, the audience and stakeholders can be brand ambassadors and solid sources of information. Journalists have learned to use their readers and viewers for content and for story ideas (crowd-sourcing). Journalists use social media to aggregate pictures and videos of crisis events, as well as to find sources for stories of survival and recovery. For example, after a bad storm rolls through an area, journalists monitor Facebook for pictures of damage in neighborhoods. Once verified, it allows for the sharing of information quickly and helps newsrooms decide where to send their journalistic resources.

In both journalism and public relations, take advantage of any goodwill that has been established with the public before the crisis. Your stakeholders will be your best allies, your staunchest defenders, your best brand ambassadors. However, for journalists, again, you must still verify the information provided by the audience. And for PR, do not hide behind customers' goodwill. Positive branding by your stakeholders does not give an excuse to withhold information or not interact with the press as we saw in the Blue Bell case. Blue Bell fans were rabid and can be credited for keeping the attention on the brand positive via social media through dozens and dozens of fan-created memes. While this case was unique, it helps to know where your constituencies stand and how they engage with the brand.

Reynolds said, "All social media does for us is allow us to know more quickly what people are thinking so we can respond to it. In the past, it was this big black hole that we didn't hear or we might hear it from our friends and family, maybe. But we wouldn't know. So I love social media as a way to understand how people are responding to your messages. And having a true feedback loop so people know you're hearing them, I mean it's easier now than it ever was."

Give Audiences/Stakeholders a Plan of Action

In the spirit of reducing anxiety, public relations professionals and journalists need to give their publics information in crisis that provides action. Give them something to do. People need to feel a sense of self-efficacy about the situation. Provide a list of supplies they need for a hurricane, a phone number in which to call their senator, or an alternative low-cost women's clinic option. "It's easier to respond to a crisis if people give you the space to respond and they give it to you because they feel that they are participating in the response and not being told to just be a spectator," Reynolds said. As all involved in the Sandy Hook case said, give them a constructive outlet for their grief. Sending teddy bears and "stuff," they said, was not necessarily helpful and became more work for those involved in the crisis.

Communication May Be Necessary in Other Languages/ Cultural Contexts/Forms

Ebola was a public health event that began in an international community. Planned Parenthood's website says a large portion of the women they serve are immigrants who are often low income, uninsured and may not speak English.

Preparing messages in other languages and being cognizant of cultural context (is the message offensive to some?) may be necessary depending on the crisis and your constituencies. Additionally, make sure all digital materials are ADA compliant.

Understand the "Other" Side

A goal of this book was to give both sides an in-depth look at what the other side does—their structure, pressures and duties. Knowledge about what the other sides does was at times, limited. For example, some journalists told us they did not interact with PR professionals during crisis, but in fact, they had. The police public information officer, for example, is a PR professional and was not recognized as such. Additionally, WAFB-TV chief investigative reporter Kiran Chawla, speaking to a crisis communication class at Louisiana State University in February 2017, said that public relations people often think she is rude or bullying when working on deadline. The norms and routines of television journalism dictate story assignments in the morning, with a complete story due to air at 4, 5 or 6 p.m. on that same day. So when a reporter asks for an interview in the morning and no one returns the call until the next day, the source can often belittle the reporter for making a last-minute request. But in fact, if the PR professional was aware of how TV journalism operates and its deadlines, he or she would see the reporter was just doing their job on deadline—not blind-siding or rushing a story.

But the problems between the two sides are not just misunderstanding structure. Both need to also understand the goals of each side and their roles in the communication process. It is a symbiotic relationship based on information sharing. The first time a PR professional contacts a journalist should not be in a time of crisis. Conversely, the first time a journalist contacts a PR person should not be in a time of crisis. The relationships need to be built before a challenging event strikes. In the case studies, some journalists complained that communication staff did not answer emails, phone calls or return calls. The tendency during a crisis is to shut down information and protect. This urge must be quashed. However, if a relationship between the two sides exists, perhaps the phone call will be returned. Being accessible is invaluable and necessary in information exchange. Bob Mann from Governor Blanco's administration during Hurricane Katrina said do not view journalists as the enemy. On the flip side, do not view the PR professional as the enemy. Interviewees told us to try and empathize with the other side of the profession and know that often, both sides are going through crisis together. The jobs at this point are not easy or fun and can affect each professional on a personal level. All sides told us to be civil, if not kind to each other, not antagonistic.

They also stressed taking care of yourself in crisis. Self-care is an area where good crisis leadership is necessary. As talked about previously, communicators must be placed on a schedule that does not leave out eating, sleeping and down time. These professionals are committed, and it often takes an order from a superior to tell them to go home and recharge. According to Russell, you must take care of yourself and try to relax. "You've got to eat, and you've got to drink water, and you've got to try to sleep. It's hard when something like this is going on, but if you're sick and not feeling well you can't even do your job," Russell said.

Many journalists resent parachute reporters coming in from out of town with little background information. EBR Sheriff's Communication Director Hicks suggested putting together contextual packets of information for national reporters. PR professionals and journalists suggested to the national press to arrive already prepared—do your own research which will go a long way in terms of trust and credibility with the local people and press. They also suggest coming in with an open mind and not an automatic negative frame based on what little is known about the situation or area. For example, the local press felt many in the national press came in with preconceived, sweeping generalizations about Louisiana when they covered the flood in 2016. In Ebola, a local journalist said that the national press came in with a negative, narrative-pushing frame. The national press serves a different audience, but should still come in to a situation with an open mind, resisting generalizations, stereotypes and hyperbole.

Finally, both sides also had thoughts about the victims in these crises. They all said you must keep the victims and their families at the forefront and empathize with them. Reporters said you need to feel what they feel or your stories will not do them justice. Public relations professionals were especially cognizant of this and even adjusted their press procedures in order to protect survivors. They did not want the press to re-victimize the victims. Facilitating the interactions between survivors, their families and the press was one way to avoid this.

Journalism as Protector

All of the journalists we interviewed understood their duties in whatever type of crisis they faced—organizational or disaster. They took their jobs very seriously and were frustrated when other communicators, public relations professionals, hindered their job of accurate information transmission. Frustrated journalists should not be a goal of public relations. Often that can translate into "workarounds" or information from other less-informed sources. A frustrated journalist will not likely give your company the benefit of the doubt. Journalists see the profession as honorable, and believe information transmission is important for the greater good and should be free and open.

On a personal note, Sandy Hook is truly different than the other cases presented. One of the authors visited Sandy Hook in April 2013, less than four months after the tragedy. The emotions were very raw and on the surface. The reporters were very kind to let the author, a former journalist, in and tell their stories. Three and a half years later, again, they were kind and accommodating, but somewhat hesitant. Former *Newtown Bee* Editor Curtiss Clark said he had said "way too much" about Sandy Hook over the years and didn't want to be the "talking head" on the event. But what we saw in his staff and the school district was a deep, deep understanding of and caring for the community. They worked to protect the families even going as far as not publishing any pictures of victims that were not given to them by the families or the funeral homes. His staff was often lumped in with the national, and all would say more aggressive, journalists. One journalist said she was embarrassed to carry a camera in the aftermath of the crisis. They were unfairly thrust into a situation that was unprecedented and they were determined to do their best. They protected their community as best they could. Again, case by case, what that protection looks like is situational. Protecting people in Sandy Hook was different from protecting people in the Ebola case where the public's right to know, they said, often outweighed the privacy of an individual.

Journalists need to recognize the effects of trauma on their profession. The Dart Center for Journalism & Trauma at the Columbia School of Journalism is a leader in helping to provide support and resources for journalists who have experienced trauma and for years have advocated the care of journalists. Trauma effects are cumulative and a lifetime of covering crisis can be rewarding, but it can also take its toll. Many new reporters are put on the overnight beat where their first week on the job could have them covering a deadly accident or shooting. Trauma begins there and by the end of 10 or 20 years in journalism, they will have numerous stories of crisis to recount. Every journalist remembers seeing their first dead body. News outlets and we argue businesses as well, must offer emotional support and counseling for those immersed in a crisis situation once, or over and over again.

Public Relations as Protector

In the cases like Sandy Hook and Hurricane Katrina, the public relations professionals were also doing their best to protect and assist their constituencies. They put the victims and the victims' families first. Mann's staff provided such protection by having Governor Blanco use an alternate entrance as she arrived for work because it would take upward of thirty minutes for her to wade through the crush of media every morning. Additionally, former superintendent Robinson said she had to increase that circle of protection.

"We put a security guard in the front of our central office, because there were just people sneaking in. Media was all over us," Robinson said. "They were bothering the families and they were going to my teachers' houses at home... they've got to be respectful. If they're going to put microphones in the face of my teachers, then we're not going to talk to them. So we kind of tried to set limits as best we could. So that 'here's the press conference, but don't bother these people. Leave them alone.'"

Especially in cases of public health and natural disasters, the information must be free-flowing for constituencies to make good decisions. But often interviewing victims or frightened citizens for their personal stories is not fulfilling that mission and is not conducive to necessary information flow. Many PR professionals sought to disrupt that flow in order to protect their communities from additional trauma.

The Authors' Access

Again, as stated in the introduction, this protection spilled over and in writing this book we met with the unexpected challenge of some individuals refusing to talk to us or not returning our calls and email requests. This was a challenge on both sides of the cases—but mostly with public relations professionals. Again, journalists too did not get back to us, but from that perspective, we had more people to choose from. The number of PR professionals involved in a few of the cases (Blue Bell, Komen) was very small and so once they refused, we were unable to get their sides of the stories. However, we were able to interview nationally-recognized and respected PR experts and communication scholars who were able to do forensic evaluations of the crisis communication responses.

Major Mistakes

Tips are helpful, but we wanted to reiterate missteps as well. From our findings, one of the major mistakes was radio silence. If the reporters or stakeholders do not receive the information they need from you, the PR professional, they will get it from someone else and often that is from uninformed social media posts. On the other side of no information was one of the major journalistic mistakes which was that there was too much information that was sensationalized. We heard this repeatedly that the press was aggressive and favored hyperbole. Keep emotions in check and focus on accurate coverage. Another big mistake was getting behind in the social media cycle—for PR and journalism. To control the narrative, do not delay or others will own the narrative. As we said in the book's introduction and in so many of our cases, journalists and PR professionals were playing catch-up because they were already behind in getting accurate information to the public. With an endless number of outside influencers with no ethical training, who can reach large numbers of people instantly, it just makes sense for the insiders, those "in-the-know" with the accurate information, to work together and get as much information out as quickly as possible. If the narrative gets ahead of you, that narrative will likely be negative. Both PR professionals and local journalists also suggested avoiding the negative framing of stories especially at the national level.

Reynolds of the CDC also identifies five mistakes that *everyone* should avoid in public relations (also affects journalists) that we also identified in our findings. She said it is easy for bad communication or a lack there of to kill your operational success. First, as we found, there is not a bureaucracy out there that does not make the mistake of releasing information late. Be ready. Reynolds said secondly, the former includes countering rumors quickly and as necessary. Third, (as we found) make sure that information is not incorrect and not mixed—one voice, one story. Fourth, she said, again as we found, go find the journalists. Do not be paternalistic and expect them to wait until you are ready to talk or they will get information elsewhere. And finally, avoid public power struggles and confusion (we were also told about internal disagreements and even screaming matches). Journalists may highlight the conflict and it will add to negative framing. She says duke it out behind the scenes, not on camera.

Future of Crisis Communication

Journalism and Fake News

In light of fake news and conspiracy theorists who propagate fake news, Sandy Hook continues to be a case different from the rest. The victims in this case face people who believe the shooting at Sandy Hook was a hoax. Web pages and social media feeds are dedicated to this and families of victims have been threatened. Even with the saturation of coverage of this tragic event, there are still people who believe it never happened. This minority harasses the victims' families and perpetuates the shooting as a hoax. For these people, it does not matter where the information originates from or who gives out the information. In February 2017, the board of education for the town of Newtown took the unprecedented step of voting in support of a letter to President Donald Trump asking him to denounce people who believe the Sandy Hook tragedy never occurred. Another example is President Trump aid Kellyanne Conway's 2017 citing of a mythical shooting crisis—the Bowling Green Massacre. She rebuked the media for not covering a fictional shooting. It appears some want to create crisis that is not there in order to devalue journalism, journalism that is always present and dutiful during crisis.

But for the majority, these examples reinforce the importance of the credible brand in journalism. After the 2016 presidential election, *New York Times* subscriptions soared tenfold, adding 132,000, after Trump's win (Belvedere & Newberg, 2016). In 2018, the Digital New Report confirmed that last year's significant increase in subscriptions in the United States (the so-called Trump Bump) was maintained (Newman, 2018). People recognize the credible brands in journalism and trust the press institution more than individual reporters (Newman, 2018). The brands with history and legacy remain credible. The findings also show that while traditional news brands remain valued, digital brands are not far behind. This also reinforces the importance of media literacy so audiences recognize a credible news outlet, something that is often difficult to distinguish in a social media feed.

Public Relations and Fake News

In public relations as well, as we saw with Blue Bell, the brand matters in crisis. In a *Forbes* November 2016 article, author Robert Wynne addressed "Public Relations in a Post-Factual Fake News World." He said it is no longer just crackpot conspiracy theories, but basic facts in the realm of science and math that are being questioned or put forth as false information. The debate includes questions over whether social media outlets have a duty to prevent misinformation from spreading to the growing number of Americans who get their news from social media. Again, the DNR global survey puts the number of those discovering and consuming news via social media at 45 percent.

In terms of crisis communication, Wynne (2016) gave some excellent tips to combat fake news for the public relations professional. If your company falls victim to a fake news story, Wynne (2016) said, make sure all of your stakeholders, including friends and family, know that the story is not true. Second, he stressed that PR professionals continue cultivating relationships with legitimate news outlets that care about accuracy, integrity and transparency. He also suggested blocking or ignoring social media trolls. Working professionals do not have the time to respond to all commenters, all of whose minds you will not change (Wynne, 2016). And finally, he made the excellent point that micro-targeting will be essential, with a different message for everyone. Creating sustained, multiple messages for different groups, issues and products and applying the technique in crisis is what future communication will look like.

So how can this be accomplished? According to the DNR survey, smartphones and tablets now account for more news users than the desktop, with more than half of those surveyed saying they use a smartphone to access news each week. The CDC's Reynolds said the future is tailored crisis information, micro-targeted to each smart phone with specific information about what the receiver needs to do in his or her current location. Both PR professionals and journalists will need to be able to take advantage of this technology. If the two sides work together to make their communication more helpful and effective, the result may be credibility, a positive response, or in the very least appreciation of their efforts in times where everyone is looking for comfort in information.

"It's natural, we all respond to threats in different ways. And it's hard to predict how people will or won't [respond]," Reynolds said. "I would encourage response people to put the resources needed up front in the planning and preparedness and response to a crisis, and not think of communication as an 'Oh yeah, we also need to do that' but as a vital part of the response." Braud called it planning on a "clear and sunny day," before the crisis cloud is at the front door. Reynolds continued that "The right person at the right time with the right message can save lives, and gosh, we should try to do that."

References

Belvedere, M. J., & Newberg, M. (2016, November 29). New York Times subscription growth soars tenfold, 132,000, after Trump's win. *CNBC*. Retrieved from http://www.cnbc.com/2016/11/29/new-york-times-subscriptions-soar-tenfold-after-donald-trump-wins-presidency.html.

Miller, A. (2014). The importance of local news in tragedy-The Gulf Coast's dual disasters and beyond. In A. Miller & A. Reynolds (Eds.), *News evolution or revolution? The future of print journalism in the digital age* (pp. 51–66). New York, NY: Peter Lang. Newman, N. (2018). Overview and key findings of the 2018 report. *Digital News Report 2018*. Oxford, UK: University of Oxford, Reuters Institute for the Study of Journalism. Retrieved from http://www.digitalnewsreport.org/survey/2018/overview-key-findings-2018/

Wynne, R. (2016, November 14). Public Relations in a post-factual fake news world. *Forbes*. Retrieved from http://www.forbes.com/sites/robertwynne/2016/11/14/public-relations-in-a-post-factual-world/#298838c24825

CONTRIBUTOR BIOGRAPHY

Shaniece Bickham is an assistant professor of mass communication at Nicholls State University in Thibodaux, Louisiana, where she teaches news writing and media history. Bickham earned her doctorate from the University of Southern Mississippi and has published work examining censorship and influences on student media content. She also has several years of professional experience in journalism, media relations and community affairs. Bickham has received formal leadership training through the Scripps Howard Leadership Academy (2008) and the Scott Hawkins Leadership Academy (2014–2016).

INDEX

O

Obama, President Barack, 72, 104
off-the- record informational meetings, 67
Ogden, J., 107
One Fund Boston, 1
organizational crises, 6–7, 13

P

Parent, Charles, 47
persistence, 99–100, 150
Pham, Nina, 23, 32
Pierre, Monica, 50–51, 64, 76
PIOs. *See* public information officers (PIOs)
Planned Bullyhood (Handel), 159
Planned Parenthood
    Komen Organization and. *See* Komen Or-
        ganization/Planned Parenthood crisis
        overview of, 167–68
police, community relationships and, 121
    See also Michael Brown shooting
politics, crises and, 162–63, 191
Pompper, D., 74
Porjes, Susan, 95, 97
Porter, Dr. Lance, 87, 92–94, 96–97
preconceptions, 41–42
press briefings
    Baton Rouge Great Flood and, 70
    during crises, 78
    during Hurricane Katrina, 56, 60
    Michael Brown shooting and, 117–18
    PR professionals managing, 195–96
    value of, 206–7
Preston, Richard, 21
prevention/preparation phase of crises, 9,
    106, 138
proactivity, 76, 81–82, 106
prodromes, to crises, 106, 138, 165–67
protectors
    journalists as, 212–13
    PR professionals as, 213

public information officers (PIOs), 48–49,
    54, 61–63
    See also public relations (PR) profession-
        als
public relations, 104–10, 137
public relations (PR) professionals
    accurate information by, 36–37, 122,
        149–50, 214
    brand loyalty and, 98
    choice of spokesperson, 125, 194
    communication response, 193–94
    controlling interviews/press conferences,
        195–96
    crisis command center for, 123, 195
    crisis definition/response, 3–4, 6–8
    crisis plan for, 98, 122, 174, 193, 209
    crisis stages for, 9–10
    cultivating relationships, 78, 120, 121,
        125, 149, 210–11
    employing spin, 64
    external communication for, 173
    fake news and, 215–16
    in higher education settings, 151–52
    history of, 7
    honesty by, 37, 125, 149–50
    internal communication for, 172
    joint briefings and, 37, 78, 203
    joint information center for, 77–78
    lack of ethics in, 110–11
    leader preparation, 76–77
    locate/contact reporters, 78–79, 206
    managing press, 207
    managing social media, 174, 204–5
    positive visuals by, 38
    proactive PR/crisis management, 76
    as protectors, 213
    recognizing crisis situation, 148
    sensitivity to stakeholders, 121–22, 137,
        173, 193, 197
    shortening news cycle, 173–74
    social media and, 123–24, 194–95
    strategies during Hurricane Katrina,
        55–56
    streamlining decision-making, 123

W

Warhover, Tom, 146–47
The Washington Post, 53, 107, 119
Watt, S., 160
Weiss, Jeffrey, 27
Wilcox, D., 106, 122
Williams, Brian, 185
Wilson, Officer Darren, 104–5, 107, 116
Witt, James L., 76
Wolfe, President Tim, 133–34, 139, 140
Worthington, Roger, 137
WWL-TV's website, 5
Wynne, Robert, 215–16

Y

Yasmin, Dr. Seema, 31

Z

Zimmerman, George, 104
Zoll, Timothy, 105–6, 119

CPSIA information can be obtained
at www.ICGtesting.com
Printed in the USA
LVHW081702230222
711837LV00011B/1434

9 781433 163524